Cuba: Russian Roulette of the World

THE CUBAN LIGHTNING

CUBA: RUSSIAN ROULETTE OF THE WORLD

By Dr. Julio Antonio del Marmol

© Copyright 2010, 2012 Dr. Julio Antonio del Marmol.
All rights reserved. No part of this publication may be reproduced, stored in a retrieval system, or transmitted, in any form or by any means, electronic, mechanical, photocopying, recording, or otherwise, without the written prior permission of the author.

ISBN: 978-1-68588-003-3 (sc)
ISBN: 978-1-68588-005-7 (hc)
ISBN: 978-1-68588-004-0 (e)

Because of the dynamic nature of the Internet, any web addresses or links contained in this book may have changed since publication and may no longer be valid.

Cuban Lightning Publications, Int rev. 12/07/2012
www.cuban-lightning.com

Introduction

The most amazing stories are not works of fiction; they are the stories of real men and women who have lived extraordinary lives. One of these men is Dr. Julio Antonio del Marmol. As a young boy, he never dreamed he would become a spy and a freedom fighter, but that is where his fate took him.

Becoming a part of the Castro government at the age of twelve, he quickly learned the true nature of Fidel Castro. He used his position of trust in the government to embark on his own covert resistance to the new communist regime. What information he could not directly use he had transmitted to U.S. intelligence at the Guantanamo Bay Navy Base. After receiving his doctorate in genetics, Dr. del Marmol worked directly for Castro in the prime minister's office. Exposed by the public release of classified information that could only have come from his office, he was forced to flee his home country of Cuba to the small town of Montauk, New York, in the United States, where he was trained in espionage by the best agents in the elite intelligence services. He has traveled all around the world, fighting to stop plans of terror and tyranny. He has survived and documented fifty-six attempts on his life.

The drive for patriotism and duty is in Dr. del Marmol's blood. His great grandfather, Major General Donato Del Marmol Tamayo, fought at great personal cost for Cuba's freedom from the Spanish. The general freed his slaves, declared his opposition to the occupiers, and headquartered himself in the jungle to fight for the independence of his island. He is recorded in history as a great patriot, and his great grandson shares his tenacity and strength.

This is the story of Julio Antonio's childhood in Cuba, his relationship with Castro and Che Guevara, and his eventual death-defying escape from the island. It is only one of the many incredible stories of Dr. del Marmol's life.

The author, Dr. Julio Antonio del Marmol, is an international bestseller with his original Spanish language 1976 publication of *Cuba, Russian Roulette of America* by Orbe Publication in Hollywood. Prestigious European academic publisher Lambert Academic Publishing selected this work for English translation for universities in 2010, and it was used in political science and other courses.

FROM THE AUTHOR

Something of apparent little importance was happening in a small Caribbean island on the morning of December 31, 1958. Soon after, however, it shook world opinion and caused the exodus of almost a million of its inhabitants. This small island took the world to the verge of a nuclear disaster and World War III. The name of the island is Cuba. The event was the downfall of General Fulgencio Batista's regime, overcome by the revolutionary Commander Fidel Castro. Castro's men carried out a bloody terrorist plan that brought panic to the island.

Promising welfare and prosperity for the Cuban people, Castro became the man of the day: benefactor of the humble and helpless. Such was the mass fanaticism that many intelligent and well-educated individuals joined the Revolution. Castro was even depicted by a certain artist as the Resurrected Christ. Yet it wasn't precisely Christ who had been resurrected in Cuba.

My father had been one of the countless followers and supporters of the Revolution. So openly had he cooperated with Castro that on several occasions Batista's police searched his business premises. He, too, had been deceived by Castro's promises to put an end to corruption and injustice as well to give all Cuban citizens a better life regardless of their race or religion.

As a child, I remembered my home being visited by a multitude of people opposed to the government. An inside hatch in our old piano concealed proclamations urging people to fight, as well as tacks and clamps to be spread in the streets at the right moment, blocking traffic and provoking chaos. The first stage of citizen terrorism had begun. My father had, in my eyes, been the epitome of honesty, integrity, courage, and honor. I am truly proud of him. For a man of his caliber, his mistake with regard to the revolution remained an open wound which caused him regret all of his life.

The news of Batista's defeat brought joy to my home. This happiness, shared by so many, would soon turn sour for us all. But in the early days, I was as happy as the rest. My father called me "his little man." Every weekend, when school closed, he would take me to his work, not for the little help I could provide, but to make me feel grown up and responsible.

"You'll have to take care of all this when you're a man," he'd say.

His trust greatly pleased me. Every day, I tried to be better, to continue the effort to be worthy of his trust.

My mother was the only one who did not join the general joy of the victorious revolution. In her opinion, Fidel Castro was nothing but a gangster who had secured his diploma as a doctor in civil law at gunpoint, intimidating university professors. Her refusal to help the Revolution was always punctuated by the same phrase: "Soon we shall be governed by hoodlums."

With the typical enthusiasm of a 12-year-old boy I wrote Castro, asking permission to form a Military Youth Brigade, organizing youngsters with revolutionary ideas and serving as another military organization for the revolution. Apparently, my letter was convincing. Probably intrigued by my thoughts at such a tender age, he agreed to my petition. At my home in the city of Pinar del Rio I received a communiqué requesting my presence for an interview at Rius Rivera, the Provincial Military Camp. Naturally, they had thoroughly investigated my nearest relatives and, upon verifying my father's participation in the revolution, I was appointed Commander-in-Chief of the Juvenile Commandos of the Rebel Army, the military corps I created. Castro personally handed me my appointment and a .38-caliber gun.

This is how the Little Commander was born!

INTRODUCTION

Cuba: Russian Roulette of America was been a Spanish-language bestseller when it was originally published by Orbe Publication in 1976. This book was released five years after I escaped Cuba by swimming for several hours to the U.S. Naval Reservation at Guantanamo Bay. I took an enormous risk leaving my entire family behind on the island. I took an even bigger risk publishing my story, but I have a strong commitment to the people I left behind in Cuba to denounce to the world the false image the communist regime in Cuba has presented to the entire world. Considering the possible threat to my family's security, I tried to narrate the story in a way that would not affect my loved ones at that time. I tried, to the best of his ability, to camouflage the details and important successes in my life of espionage while still inside my native country.

Now that many years have passed, I am able to go back and add many details and tell many parts of the story heretofore untold. This includes greater detail now of my story as a spy in Cuba, starting at the beginning as I put together the most complete and important facts of my life. While only twelve years old, I attained the highest military rank in the Rebel Army in Cuba, and I became the Commander-in-Chief of the Juvenile Commandos that Fidel Castro used to prepare for the future of the island. Within a year, at the age of thirteen, I had witness enough of Castro's depredations that I converted myself into a spy, accepting the opportunity to work covertly against the regime. Over the next ten years, I became the most dangerous spy hunted by the Cuban intelligence, taking information from the highest military commands in the government itself and the Prime Minister's office from right under their noses. Undetected, I bore this responsibility on my shoulders, without even being able to share this with my closest friends, who were also fighting the regime. This silence was one of the things that kept me alive and undetected for so long—this incredibly sophisticated spy they called "The Lightning."

I revealed the most important movements of Castro's troops around the world, and took the first pictures of the Soviet nuclear missiles when they first arrived in Cuba, precipitating the now-famous October Crisis, which put the world on the precipice of World War III. These missiles were ultimately revealed as long-range intercontinental missiles and also allowed the establishment of bases for Soviet nuclear submarines.

Today, no matter what has been told to the rest of the world, these missiles are still active on the island and are one of the greatest dangers to the American continents and the entire world. This is the only and most powerful reason that no U.S. president, whether Republican or Democrat, has ever initiated a confrontation or even tried to stop the Cuban Marxist regime openly. For over fifty years, the United States has continued to allow the Cuban communist government to send terrorists and military troops all over the world to create chaos, revolution, and destruction in free and democratic nations. They hide with impunity behind these nuclear weapons.

Freedom Is in Our Blood

With freedom one has the greatest treasure anyone can ever dream to grasp

Without freedom comes the emptiness of the eternal black void

With freedom one sees the path to peace and the way to walk through life

Without freedom there is sadness, frustration, and guilt heavier than a millstone

With freedom one's heart is light and the sun dawns on our soul

Without freedom the sun's light is covered and darkness never ends

This is why one should fight for freedom

Freedom for one's self and others

Fight, until the very last drop of blood
For that blood flows with freedom
Down to our very souls
As precious as the gift of life itself

Dr. J. Anthony D' Marmol

DEDICATION

For Esteban Zenen Hernandez Chirino
April 17, 1936-October 30, 2012

I want to dedicate this book to the memory my brother-in-law, Esteban Zenen Hernandez Chirino. I considered Zenen my blood brother all my life, for his high standards, and his valor, integrity, love, and generosity, not only for his family but also for his friends. He was a great-hearted man, caring for all who crossed his path. This love and generosity was brought out most by his spiritual mentor, Pastor Vasquez (as Zenen called him) of the Baptist church in Pinar del Rio. Zenen never abandoned those principles, even though he had to carefully conceal them from the revolution due to his official position in the Revolutionary Army as a high-ranking staff officer. No matter how he was able to conceal them from the public view, I saw with my own eyes Zenen put his Bible under his pillow when he came home to rest from a long day of duties to the socialist revolution—usually when they demanded him to persecute his brethren in the Baptist church, and he needed to seek the guidance of God, so that he could help them without compromising his position. Those who didn't know him never knew the real brother Zenen, the one who put everything at risk for his ideals of God and a free Cuba, his life, his family, and his official position. He was a revolutionary and a Christian, but never a communist.

I can now reveal that in this book he is known as Canen. I can say that openly, since he is a free man after living so long in tyranny. No one can harm him any longer. Many of his ordeals inside the armed forces in Cuba have been edited for obvious reasons. Since he has passed away, I intend to bring to the eyes of the public his deeds in future publications.

Zenen, I don't weep for your death, even though as I write this a few tears emerge, because your ideals, like mine, are linked together and will live forever in the hearts of everyone who knew you. For those who did not, I will make it an honor and a privilege for them to come to know you with my pen as I describe you for the great man, father, brother, and leader that you were. You leave in our hearts the most beautiful memories a man can offer in his life: your undeniable generosity, valor, and love that many people did not know because you knew how to hide it very well. And like all great gentlemen, you take them with you in silence all the way to your death, without incriminating your associates in the cause to free our beautiful Cuba. Bravo!

For the love of our God you will take with you His blessing. Rest in peace, brother Zenen, my brother-in-law and brother in cause, in heart, and in feelings; our Lord will receive you in glory. A thousand trumpets will be blown by angels on white horses as you enter the gates of heaven. Bless you as the great and dignified man you grew to be; you leave behind you the greatest example for future generations. God bless you.

Your brother,
Julio Antonio del Marmol

"Words were created to expose the truth, not to hide it."
José Martí

This story is based on true events. Names, places, times, and other details have been changed to protect the innocent.

CHAPTER I: ABUSE OF POWER: THE DEATH OF DEMOCRACY

"Freedom means love and respect for ourselves and equally to others; that we love them enough to live free without enforcing our own beliefs upon others." – Dr. Julio Antonio Del Marmol

La Habana, Cuba 1942

My father, Leonardo del Marmol, was born to a family with six siblings. All of his brothers and sisters completed university and were professionals. One brother was a doctor, one was a professor at Havana University, and the other was an attorney. His sisters were teachers in high schools and elementary schools. He was the only one who told his father he did not want to go to University. He wanted to be a businessman and did not want to waste more time in school.

My grandfather, Donato del Marmol, did not want to contradict him because he knew that would only incite him more, and so he said, "I have a cousin in Pinar del Rio in Puerto Esperanza who has a grocery store. You can work for him and learn how to conduct your future business."

My father was very surprised at my grandfather's attitude, as he had always been so adamant that his children go to university and learn a professional career. He felt that it was the only way to secure their future, and he had told them repeatedly that was the only way he could die in peace. My father was overwhelmed by his reaction. He was so happy to be allowed to have his own way with no resistance that he hugged his father and thanked him for supporting his decision. Little did he realize how clever a man my grandfather was and that he already had conceived a plan that would make his son's life miserable in Puerto Esperanza, causing him to return home right away and continue in university.

As soon as my father left the room, my grandfather picked up the phone and called his cousin in Puerto Esperanza. He told him, "I am sending my son Leonardo on the bus tomorrow to your house. I will pay whatever expenses he incurs there. Let him stay with you so you can keep an eye on him, but under no circumstances give him work in your store! Tell all your business friends that the only work that can be arranged for him will be loading and unloading the pineapple ships and the other merchandise ships in the port. That way, he will not be able to find work anywhere else. I want to teach him a lesson he will never forget and make him understand that with no education, he will only be able to find this kind of work. Please, do not tell him of our conversation. This is extremely important for his well-being and for his future. I want him to come back as soon as possible and continue his education!"

My grandfather did not realize that you cannot kill a lion with a water balloon. My father had a spirit like a lion, and when he arrived in Puerto Esperanza, my uncle told him he could not give him a job because he could not afford to pay another salary. My father was really disappointed, as he had thought his father had already pre-arranged a job for him. His uncle said he was welcome to hang around and learn the business, but with no pay. For a while, he did that, but he started to feel uncomfortable, like a parasite, as he did not know his father was paying his cousin to feed and house him. He started looking for a job.

The only job he found was the one my grandfather wanted him to find, which was extremely hard labor to which Leonardo was unused. Even though the coworkers laughed at him because of his skinny physical appearance and because they knew he was from affluent family and never did manual labor in his life, he earned their respect; in spite of bleeding arms and hands, he persevered and worked with them shoulder to shoulder.

When asked to do extra work, such as unloading a ship in the middle of the night, he never said, "I cannot," but always said okay and did his best. He was determined to make a little money in spite of everything to start his dream. After a while, even though he paid his uncle a small amount for his keep, his uncle sent the money back to my grandfather, keeping the secret between them. My father was still able to save enough money to start a little grocery store business on the other side of town from where his uncle had a store. He thanked his uncle for his support and moved into his little business, sleeping on a folding bed.

Little by little, his business grew. He allowed the fishermen to buy groceries on credit and pay him when they sold their merchandise. If they were unable to pay the whole bill and they stopped coming to his store, my father would go looking for them and offered to divide the bill by two, three, or even four payments. He told them not to worry, that if one were a decent man, he would pay his bill even if he just paid a nickel a week. In this way, he convinced his customers to come back and patronize his store.

Word of this got to his uncle, who burst out laughing. He was sure my father would fail and, in a few months, would be back working at the docks. My grandfather called his cousin periodically and they would say goodbye laughingly, convinced that in a few more months he would fall on his ass.

My father was taking a big chance, but because of his honesty, his good will, and his faith in others, his business flourished and the fishermen spread the word of his trust in them, and eventually his business expanded. It became a general store where you could buy nearly everything—clothing, fishing equipment, and hardware.

Time went by quickly, and my father became very successful and very well respected. I remember my father repeatedly saying, "I am the most honest businessman in this town and, ironically, the biggest thief as well. Because of my honesty with my customers, they come back to me and I wind up stealing business from all the other stores."

One of the times when my grandfather called, about a year and a half later, to check on my father's progress, he was astonished to hear from his cousin what had happened. He decided to travel from the capital, Havana, to Puerto Esperanza to see for himself exactly what was happening. What he was hearing was unbelievable to him, but when he arrived, he was stunned to find it was actually true. My father was already starting to build a house and had been paying on the land where the store was located.

Then my grandfather unexpectedly suggested my father should relocate his business to a slightly larger town, Guane. My father was very happy and proud that his father was pleased with his success and told him he had been thinking along the same lines because he did not want to hurt his uncle's feelings and be in direct competition with him as his own business grew. My father gave him so many groceries, wine, and clothing for the rest of the family that he had to hire two men to help carry the boxes to the train. Ironically, my father was the only one of his siblings who did not finish university, and still he helped them all financially to finish their educations and later became the wealthiest one of the whole family.

Whenever his brothers and sisters graduated, my father always traveled to be there and gave them gifts. He also was the one who helped them to acquire offices and make sure that whatever they needed in the way of furniture and other necessities was paid for so they could practice their professions with no worries. He met my mother, a very striking young lady, when her family came into one of his stores to buy clothing. From the first minute he saw that gorgeous, tall Spanish/Italian woman with long, beautiful hair, fair skin, and eyes the color of honey, he fell in love. Not too long after that, he married her, and she was not only lovely but was a hard worker like him, and much more. She was also very talented and dedicated to his business. She worked late into the night. All this only increased his success, thanks to her. He eventually hired more women to help her do these special things, and also to help her with household chores.

Julio's parents, "Mima and Papi"

May 21, 1947
Small town of Guane, Province of Pinar del Rio

My father had by now built a plantation house on the outskirts of town by the river. A hurricane was raging this particular night, and my mother was in bed, screaming with a very difficult labor. She had already lost a lot of blood. The black midwife, Majito, was sitting at the end of the bed. She told my father, "This is not good. She has lost a lot of blood." My father was standing on the other side of the bed, dressed in an impeccable white suit. He rushed from his business as soon as he was told that my mother was in labor. Majito continued, to my mother, "Come on, my lady...push hard, please! Push hard, we're almost there. I can see his head."

My mother was exhausted and pale from all the blood lost, her flawless beauty still reflected in her stunning eyes, even through her perspiration. She gave a last strain, and her final push.

"Yeah!" Majito exclaimed, full of joy. "Yes. Fair skin, pure like a coconut. Red hair like a fighter. He is going to be a blessing for this family." She wrapped the baby in white linen, turned to my mother, and said, "Good job, my lady. Beautiful baby. I will be right back. I will take him, because he must be protected."

My father scowled in anger and reached out his hand to Majito. "No," he said as he tried to take the baby away from her. "No. I don't believe in that voodoo garbage. Don't take my son to do that."

Majito's face grew sad, and obediently started to hand the baby to him. My mother, compassionate and lovely (even though she didn't believe in these things, either), said, "Take him. If you believe in that, it won't hurt him. I know you mean well. Bless him in your own way." My father looked at my mother as if he were about to deny this again, but she looked at him so appealingly, and he halted. "Please, Leonardo," she said, "let her do this. It won't hurt him, and she's been taking care of all our babies." Her look of appeal was so moving, and his concern of her loss of blood worked on him that he finally relented. My mother said to Majito, "Go on, take him, protect him. But get back quickly."

Majito's face lit up like the sun, and she held the newborn child closely as she scurried out. She had been preparing for this ritual for weeks. She went out into the courtyard, ran through the partially covered hallways, fighting her way through the hurricane winds which were still blowing wildly. She ducked into a doorway and inside. She descended some stairs into the servants' quarters, and went into her small room. In the room were a small bed and a strangely decorated altar. Another black lady was there, cleaning the altar. Majito said, "Camilla, come here quickly." Camilla ran to Majito's side. "Quickly," Majito continued, "help me."

Together, the two women unwrapped the baby and placed him on a small table surrounded with candles. Camilla asked, "Leonardo let you take the baby?"

Majito replied, "Shh! Let us do this quickly. I'll explain to you later."

She opened a glass jar, and the two women rubbed the baby with different oils and lotion. At the same time, Majito chanted something in an African dialect. She took three bottles of blood from the altar, each of a different shade of red. Camilla watched closely, fascinated. Majito took the first bottle and poured some of the blood onto her fingers.

In a very deep voice, Majito intoned, "Yemaya! Blood of the bull! Give strength and power to the little creature I bring to you now." She dabbed some of the blood on the baby's forehead, chest, and legs. After that, she took a second bottle and poured more on her fingers. "Chango! Blood of the fox, give intelligence to this newborn." She once more dabbed the blood on the baby's forehead, chest and legs. She reached for the third bottle, poured more blood. "Elegua! Blood of the peacock, enlighten, cleanse, and give beauty to the soul of this baby."

She took a mouthful of rum from a bottle, held it for a moment, and then blew it out over the baby and the candles. The flames ignited the rum and erupted in a flash of fire. She did this three times. In the meantime, the baby had fallen asleep and lay there quietly.

She then took a colorful rooster from a cage and quickly beheaded the bird with a small hatchet. She went over to a small fireplace and let most of the blood from the rooster drip into the fire. She then turned to the baby and dripped blood in the sign of the cross on the baby's chest. The warm blood made him awaken, and he started to smile. Majito looked at Camilla, and said, "Look, Camilla—he is smiling, like he knows we're trying to protect him! What a beautiful boy." She looked up and prayed, "God, let the blood from this rooster protect him for the rest of his life."

Majito, midwife, nanny, friend, and maternal confidant

The two women washed the baby and wrapped him clean white linens. Majito quickly left her quarters to rush him back to the house. She entered the room, where my mother received her with a big smile, while my father looked relieved at the return of the baby. Majito said, "My lady, he is protected now forever."

My mother held her hand, looked into her eyes, and said, "Thank you, Majito."

My father came over, took the baby, and held him up. "We shall name him Julio Antonio Donato del Marmol. Julio Antonio, for the son of my great grandfather, killed by the Spanish soldiers in the War of Independence. Donato for his great grandfather, the Major General, del Marmol because he is my son. The pride of our family goes with him."

Yes, this baby was I.

My mother smiled with pride and watched Leonardo with the baby in his hands. That, according to Majito and my mother, is how I was born.

By about 10:00 the next morning, the hurricane had blown past, bringing a beautiful, sunny day in its wake. In the street not too far away, a car with large loudspeakers on top drove by blaring a political message with music. The lyrics for the music sang "Ae ae, Ae La Chambelona!" The message followed: "Vote for Noriega! Vote for Noriega for Alcalde and you will have new roads and new schools for your children."

A small crowd of people with political signs followed the car, cheering, "Arriba Noriega!"

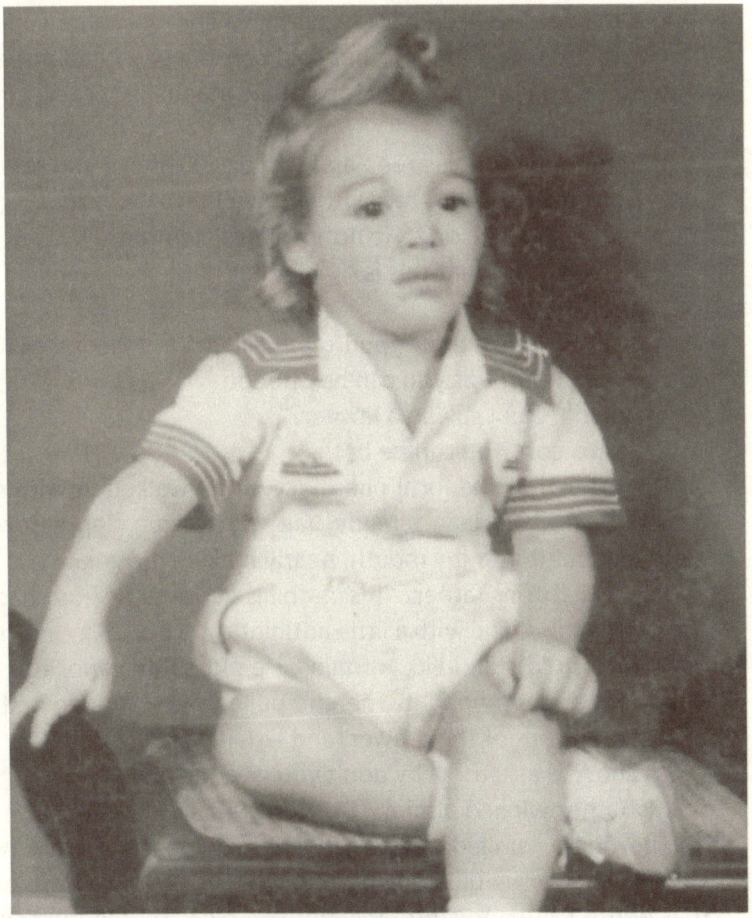

Julio Antonio at five years old

One sunny day five years later, my mother was sitting with me in her lap on the porch in a rocking chair. I had just been sick, and we were watching another political parade going by in the street. I had been crying, and my mother was trying to cheer me up. My father said to her, "Why are you watching this? All politicians are dirty."

"Don't listen to him, Julio Antonio," my mother said to me, "just watch the happy parade."

"You have to come with me," Papi said to me. "We have to go to the doctor for a checkup." He looked at my mother as he picked me up. "We'll be back in a little while."

"It will be okay," my mother said consolingly. I had already learned that a visit to the doctor's office meant shots and other unpleasant things.

Dad put me into his green and white 1951 Buick and said to me, "Don't worry about it." On the drive there I was looking at my father's Masonic ring. He noticed my attention.

"Do you know what this is?"

I shook my head no.

"It is from a group of good men called the Masons. When you grow up, perhaps you can be one too."

I replied, "Can I still be a lawyer?"

"Yes, my son. You can be both."

We arrived at the local pharmacy, and I walked in with my father. Doctor Noriega already had the tongue depressor in hand and put it into my mouth, nearly making me gag.

He said to my father, "It's nothing serious. He just has a throat infection, and with a little antibiotic, he'll be okay in a few days. Now hold still, Julio Antonio." He put some vapor rub on my throat and wrapped it. Then he pulled out a syringe with a blue stopper out of the drawer, and I made a face.

"A shot?" I asked. "Why don't you give me a pill?"

My father winked at him. "Dr. Noriega?"

The doctor smiled. "Ah, yes. Well, you see, we have two kinds of shots. The blue one here is for boys. Now we have one that doesn't hurt. It is for girls and it is pink. Should I get that one?"

I hesitated for a moment, looking from one man to the other. Finally, I shook my head in resignation, pulled down my pants and bent over. "No, the blue one is okay." The last word came out more as a grunt as I felt the pinch from the needle going into my rear.

Guane, Pinar del Rio, Cuba 1951

Through much hard work, my father, with the help of my mother, already owned several businesses in the little town of Guane—except for the funeral home. The only reason he did not own a funeral home, he said, was because he did not want to be happy when someone died. It meant to him that his business would be lucrative thanks to someone else's misery.

By the time I was four years old, I had two sisters, an older brother, and a brother three years younger than me. We always got up before my father, even though he got up very early to go to his business.

One beautiful sunny day, my father woke up, happy with his family and his business success. He said good morning to my mother and got ready to go to work. After shaving and getting dressed in a beautiful white linen suit with a very refined black and white silk tie, he went to the safe in the house for the cash he would need for that day. He took his gun, a .38 caliber revolver, from the safe and put it into his briefcase before leaving the house, said goodbye to his children, and went to the only bank in town, Banco Continental Cubano, to get smaller bills for the day. Everything went well at the bank. He was well-known and was greeted happily by everyone. He left the bank and headed for his clothing store, which was the first stop he made every day, in order to give the cashier the change she would need for that day. He parked his car in the parking lot and walked slowly towards the store. As he approached the store, he saw through the front display windows there was someone holding a gun pointed at the cashier and the manager. The person holding the gun had his back to the window and so did not see my father approaching. The glass door made no noise as my father entered and quietly approached the intruder.

He put his pistol against the neck of the man and said commandingly, "Drop the gun, or you die right here and right now!" The would-be robber tried to move his head to see who was holding the gun to his head. Out of the corner of his eye, he saw a huge, black revolver, and his eyes bulged out in terror. My father shoved the revolver harder into the man's neck and repeated, "Drop your gun!"

The holdup man placed the gun on top of the glass counter and raised his arms in surrender. The manager, El Moro, and the other employees rushed to bind the man with a rope. One of them called the police immediately. In a few moments, the police arrived, arrested the man, and took him away.

My father's friends and other business acquaintances all came right away to congratulate him, as this thief was well-known in the little town of Guane. Father continued to make his rounds to his other businesses: a Shell gas station, a furniture store, and a commercial truck rental shop.

As he was getting out of his car, he was surprised to look across the street and see the same man who had just been arrested that very morning. The man smiled cynically and gave him a look of arrogant contempt.

Father immediately felt his heartbeat accelerate as the blood rushed to his ears and face. He reached into his briefcase, but before he could pull the gun out, the thief began to walk faster, finally breaking into a run, until he reached a corner and turned. Father was frustrated and stood there, looking at the corner where the man disappeared, feeling anger and disappointment. He put his gun back into his briefcase, went into his business, gave them the money they would need for the day, and then immediately went to the police station.

He demanded to talk to the chief of police to know what happened, why a thief caught red-handed had been released. The chief of police was an arrogant, drunken, lazy bum and thoroughly corrupt. He did not like my father because he was one of the few business owners who did not kiss his ass. It was customary in those times when a high-ranking police official came into a store to purchase groceries, clothing, or other goods that the owner of the business never charged them for fear of retaliation. My father was a rebel, and he did not have the fear that the others had. He believed this only magnified the corruption which already existed, and he felt it was bad enough already. The police chief did not want to help my father, but he had no alternative. He called the two policemen who had made the arrest that morning to find out what had happened. My father questioned the pair and found out there was no record of the arrest, no paperwork, no trace whatsoever. Moreover, the thief had never even been brought to the police station.

When the two policemen came into the office, they also acted very arrogantly. One said, "We had no reason to hold him. The gun he had was a toy, and he's mentally incompetent, so we let him go."

"Shouldn't a judge decide that?" my father asked. "Besides, I saw the gun! It was no toy. I held it in my hand!"

The chief leaned back in his chair and said, "Well, there is nothing I can do. We have no proof."

Father was angered and extremely frustrated. He could not contain himself any longer and felt they were just making fun of him. He banged his fist on the desk of the chief, locked eyes with the policemen, and declared, "Money! That is what this is all about! How much did that thief pay you guys? You know that makes you accomplices to the crime!"

The two policemen looked down at the ground and said nothing, but the chief said, "Be careful, you are treading on dangerous ground. You cannot go around accusing police officers of corruption unless you have conclusive proof. Other people in the past have done that, and they wound up with their mouths full of ants in the gutter of a dark street."

Father looked the chief in the eyes and said, "I am going to get to the bottom of this, even if I have to talk to the president of this country. You cannot get away with this corruption and immorality!"

He stormed out of the station and went directly to one of his best friends, a man named Emilio, a district judge and a brother in the Masonic lodge to which my father belonged. When my father arrived at his office, there were several people there, waiting to see the judge. However, when the secretary told Emilio that Leonardo del Marmol was there, he told her to send him in immediately.

After they hugged and greeted each other, Emilio offered my father a well-known Cuban beer called Hatuey. My father sat down on a comfortable sofa and explained to Emilio what had happened that morning. He asked what could be done legally and to whom he should speak in order to put a stop to the corruption that was obviously eating Cuban society like a cancer and making decent and honest people lose hope in the current political establishment.

Emilio reclined in his chair and sat with a sad expression on his face. "Leonardo, let it go. You have a family. You do not need this in your life. You do not want to make the law enforcement institutions your enemy. They are too strong and too corrupt!"

Father scratched his head. He could not believe what he heard from his friend and brother Mason. "You tell me there is nothing we can do about this?"

"My friend and brother, Leonardo, there is a lot we can do, but there is very little we can accomplish. In the end, they have all the power, and they will win. Don't risk your family's future doing this."

They said their farewells, and my father left the office an extremely disappointed man. He went directly to his own office and telephoned another personal friend, Francisco, who was the Senator of Pinar del Rio.

Francisco talked to him very cordially and seemed to be in agreement with him. He promised to send him all the official forms to make his complaint. However, he added, "Are you sure you want to do this? It could lead to a great deal of harassment and problems for you and your family."

My father replied with conviction, "Yes, I want to put a stop once and for all to this shit wave and politics that are destroying our roots that our ancestors died for."

Shortly after my father filed the papers accusing the police of corruption, he began to experience problems with his businesses. He received great response from his friend, Francisco, and a huge investigation began of the police department. Some of the police officers were indicted but never went to trial. Just when everything seemed to be going well, Francisco was killed in a car bombing in front of his house. He started his car, and it blew up right in front of his family. After Francisco died, the investigations came to a sudden halt. None of the indictments were executed, and none of the police officers that were involved were disciplined or dismissed.

Father began to find himself being harassed by the police and other law enforcement agencies. Instead of help from them, he found his businesses to be at risk. The police demanded a monthly mafia-like quota in order to protect his businesses. He refused, and the first retaliation took place when the clothing store where the thief had originally been apprehended mysteriously burned down. The burning of several more of his businesses followed. My father traveled to the capitol in Havana, and went all the way to the President of Cuba with his complaints. He received no help.

One day, he met an up-and-coming political figure named Eduardo Chibás who was running against the established president. He also gave radio broadcasts, railing against the corruption and gangsterism that was rampant in the government. In the office of Chibás was another man, who was helping the political candidate. This man had even more severe and radical ideas as to how to restructure the political system in Cuba. This man's name was Fidel Castro Ruz, and he told my father his ideas to make a free and more democratic Cuba, with equal opportunity for all and with no distinction of race or religion. He convinced my father that he had a plan for the good of all the people of Cuba. He felt the only way to eradicate completely the political corruption was the same way our ancestors had done in order to free Cuba from the Spanish Crown's colonial authority: revolution. My father fell wholeheartedly for his ideas. He asked him what he needed, and the response was the common need for all ventures: money.

"Don't worry," my father assured him, "you will have the money you need." He told Castro everything that had been going on with his businesses, how they had released the thief that had been caught red-handed robbing his store, how his businesses had subsequently been burned because he had refused to pay the quota, how he had reported these offenses all the way up to the president, and how nothing had been done about it.

Fidel pulled out a little notebook and asked my father what the names of the corrupt police were who had been harassing him. He wrote the names down in his little notebook, and also wrote down the name of the chief of police who was protecting them, who had threatened to kill my father if he continued to create problems for them. He patted my father on the shoulder and said, "Don't worry about it anymore. We will take care of this problem for you. You are one of us now. Go in peace."

A few days later, the police chief and the two officers who had been harassing my father were shot down and killed by persons passing in a car as they were exiting the station. The whole town was in shock, because nothing like that had ever happened in Guane. All the people in the town attributed the assassinations to the urban guerillas who had been growing stronger and had been threatening law enforcement agencies to stop their corrupt practices or face the consequences. My father knew for a fact that Fidel was the one directly involved in those killings and was disturbed by the knowledge. He did not approve of violence, but at the same time was glad that his troubles were over, and so did not ask any questions.

My father came to be the chief financier for the Fidel Castro movement, the 26th of July, on the occidental side of the island. This side was comprised of Pinar del Rio, La Havana, and Matanzas.

Pinar del Rio, Cuba, 1958

On a beautiful weekend seven years later, when I was eleven years old, I traveled in my father's Buick from our house in Pinar del Rio. My father had moved the family in order for my older brothers and sisters to attend high school. This left our house in the little town of Guane empty, but my father would stay there when he was taking care of his business.

I did not want to leave Guane, but I had no choice. I was happy when my father took me with him on the weekends, not because I could really be of much use to him but because he told me I could help him in his businesses. I think he did this to make me feel good but also to give me some kind of role in his work. He felt I had his drive for business, unlike my other brothers.

Friday night, we arrived in the little town of Guane. We had dinner at a small family restaurant, and after dinner we went back home. The house seemed empty and I was missing my mother and siblings. We went to bed early and I was anxious and excited; I knew I would be able to play with my friends the next day. At 2:00 a.m., my father woke me up and helped me to dress quickly, as I was half asleep.

He told me, "Get in the car." He drove on a dirt road up into the mountains. I noticed the car was full of clothing and medicine and all kinds of supplies, like flashlights, batteries, and so on. The car was so full of stuff that there was barely room for me to sit. We drove for a long time, and I fell asleep until I heard what I thought were firecrackers. I stood up in the front seat, and one of the "firecrackers" passed so close that it made a hole in the windshield. My father put his hand over my head and pushed me down abruptly.

"What is happening?" I asked.

He yelled in a very commanding way I had not heard before from him, "Stay down! Keep your head down in the seat until I tell you to get up!"

I kept hearing the sound of what sounded like bees flying by but at a very high speed. From my seat I could see the lights flashing by and smoke close to the car. My father floored the accelerator pedal and was driving the mountain roads at an excessive speed. I felt that at any moment we might roll over one of the cliffs. This went on for a while. Finally, the noises diminished and then stopped. We got to a place where my father stopped the car, and to my surprise, there were hundreds of men there with long beards, long hair, and intense body odor greeting us. They helped my father unload the car and the one who appeared to be in charge tried to convince my father to leave me there because he felt if my father were captured on his way back, they would use me to make him talk.

Without me, they knew my father would never reveal their location, even if it meant his death. My father refused to leave me, and told them that he felt no one would suspect him of doing rebel activity with a child in the car. He would just say they had lost their way. We came back okay, but the next day my father was arrested by Sosa Blanco, one of Batista's military leaders. Batista was the president who had taken over the country in 1952 with a military coup.

I spent the rest of that day with my Uncle Gollito, my mother's brother. In the evening, he took me home to my mom in Pinar del Rio. When we arrived, everyone was crying as they had heard my father had been arrested and they feared for his life. Fortunately for my father, his brother, the doctor who was the mayor of the little town of Managua in Havana, had a great deal of political influence and friends in the right places in the government. He immediately became involved and was able to arrange my father's release. They had not been speaking to each other for a while, since a political discussion turned bad in our home during one of our family gatherings, yet he interceded on my father's behalf. He did not agree with my father's defense of the rebels. He felt that violence was not the answer to resolve the political problems we had in Cuba, and said that the medicine, or what one might think is the medicine, might be worse than the disease. However, they were still family, and they loved and respected each other, so he responded rapidly to help my father.

Thanks to him, my father was released almost immediately and was not subjected to physical or emotional torture, for which my family was grateful. Many Cubans were not so lucky and had died after terrible suffering in Batista's prisons at the hands of his interrogators.

Later that year, I was having breakfast with my mother, two brothers, and one of my sisters. My mother looked at me affectionately and said, "Julio Antonio, aren't you excited? You get to go on the ship today!"

My mouth was full of food, so I didn't say anything but indicated my excitement by nodding my head vigorously and finishing my food quickly. When I was done, I ran to my room and over to my bed, where my school case lay. I opened the latch and looked inside to make sure that everything I would need for school that day was packed inside. I frowned as I saw the dullness of the pencils, and headed towards my father's office to sharpen them. As I approached the door, I could hear that my father was listening to the radio again. I knocked quietly and respectfully on the door and waited. After a few moments, my father answered the door and motioned me in. He walked back over to his desk, sat down, and continued listening intently to the shortwave radio.

"I'm sorry to interrupt, Father," I said.

He signaled me that it was okay and to be quiet as he continued to listen intently to the voice on the radio. "This is the voice of the Sierra Maestra," it said. "The Revolution is advancing more every day toward glorious victory for the people. Commanders Che Guevara and Camilo Cienfuegos are moving forward fearlessly." I listened while I watched my father. Patriotic music began playing under the voice as it continued, "We will be on the air at the same time and frequency tomorrow, Stay tuned for more from the voice of the Sierra Maestra. Signing off."

The off-air tone sounded, and my father turned the radio off. As I went over to the desk to sharpen my pencils, my father took me by the arm and looked into my eyes. "My son, we will be free very soon."

"Yes, Father," I said, not really understanding what he was saying.

"Are you ready to go on your school trip?"

"Yes, Father!" I exclaimed animatedly. My excitement grew as he got up to get his coat. We walked out together through the kitchen. He continued outside while I paused to give my mother a hug before leaving. She kissed the top of my head as I said, "Goodbye, Mima."

"Goodbye, my son. Have fun today!"

I ran out the door and climbed into the front seat of the Buick. My father drove us toward the marina and noted my excitement. "You must be happy," he commented, "your first time out on the ocean in a real ship." I smiled at him and nodded happily. "So, you want to be a captain, my boy?"

"Yes!"

"Then, my son, you have to learn the good and the bad the ocean has to offer. But I thought you wanted to be an attorney?"

I cocked my head to the side as I pondered the question. "I can be an attorney, and a captain, and a Mason too!" I said with boyish enthusiasm.

My father smiled at that. "Okay, but remember, the ocean is like a beautiful woman. You must give her love, admiration, and much respect. She is also very temperamental. You must remember this."

"Yes, Father."

The Buick pulled to a stop at the marina, and I hopped out. I ran to my teacher, Ms. Sophia Garcia, who was surrounded by about twenty other students. She called out to me as she saw me coming, "Hello, Julio Antonio!"

Captain Marrero, a hearty, black-bearded man in his twenties, came out and addressed our group. "Ready to board? Let's go!"

"Come on, children," Ms. Garcia said, "let's get on the ship."

We got in line to go aboard. I noticed something on the ground and picked it up. "El Capitan!" I called. "El Capitan!"

Marrero turned around. "Yes, young one? What is it?"

"I think you dropped this." I ran up to him while the other kids watched. Marrero took what I had and looked at it.

"My wallet," his eyebrows went up in surprise. "What is your name, young sailor?"

"Captain Julio Antonio," I replied.

"Well, Captain," he replied, "you should have a reward." He handed me a small compass with an anchor engraved on it. The other children murmured in jealousy.

"Children," Ms. Garcia called, "come along, let's get on board."

We were shepherded into an observation room below the water line of the ship. An entire wall was made of glass, and we could see the incredible sights of oceanic life, as colorful coral and fish danced before our eyes. As I stood near the glass and watched these sights, Sandra, a young girl my age with long, dark hair and beautiful eyes stood next to me.

"Don't touch the glass, children," Ms. Garcia admonished us. "You'll leave marks, and Captain Marrero won't like that."

Sandra looked at me. "Did you know that today is my birthday?"

I returned her gaze shyly. "Oh, really? Happy birthday, Sandra."

My other friends were standing in the back of the group: Yaneba, a girl with blonde hair and who liked to wear black berets; Cisneros, a little black boy; and Arturo, a big-hearted boy with curly hair and blue eyes.

Yaneba frowned at Sandra and said, "I can't see."

"Well," Cisneros said, "move up."

"Yeah, shorty," teased Arturo.

Yaneba gave the pair of them a look and pushed up next to me on the other side of Sandra. I looked at her and gave her a big smile, while Sandra looked on jealously as we greeted each other.

While we were looking at each other, an enormous shark struck the glass, shaking the ship and scaring all of the children. Many of them screamed, and Yaneba jumped and clung to me.

Even Ms. Garcia looked scared, but she said, "Now, children, calm down. It's okay—"

A crewmember spoke up from the back of the room. "It's all right, kids, that shark can't hurt you. Sometimes they can't tell the glass is there since it is so clear. Even a shark twice as big couldn't break that glass."

We all looked relieved, and I let Yaneba go. Some of the kids chattered with each other, while Sandra's brother Julian, a dark-haired, mean-looking kid with a mole on his upper lip taunted another friend of mine, a short, scrawny kid named Kinqui. "Ha! You almost peed your pants!"

"Shut up, Julian!" Kinqui said.

Another friend, Pablo, a big, dark-skinned boy, loomed up behind Julian. "Yeah, shut up, Julian." Julian took one look at the big kid and wisely shut up.

"All right, children," Ms. Garcia said, "let's go up on deck."

We all filed up the stairs. I saw Yaneba sit down by herself to watch the ocean. A few moments later, Julian walked over to her. "You want some candy?" he offered as he pulled some out of his pocket.

"No, thanks," she declined politely.

"You would take it if Julio Antonio was offering," he said. She didn't reply, but looked at him angrily. "Why can't we be friends?" he continued. "That's all I want." Yaneba looked up at him suspiciously as he closed in on her. No one else was around. "Close friends."

I was elsewhere on the deck near the rail, walking along and thinking about life on the ocean as a captain. I heard Yaneba scream. I looked around as she screamed a second time, and I ran towards her. Yaneba was on the deck floor with Julian on top of her. He was trying to kiss her as she struggled against him. She screamed once more as I ran up. "Leave her alone!" I commanded. Julian got up, looked embarrassed, and ran off. Yaneba sat on the bench, crying. I noticed her necklace, a Caridad del Cobre (a pendant believed to offer protection,) lying on the deck. I picked it up and held it out to her, but she didn't notice. "Here," I said to get her attention, "you dropped this."

She looked up at me but didn't take the necklace. "Thanks. You should keep it."

I looked at it again and at the face of the Virgin on the medallion. "You are the one that needs it."

She smiled at me and pointed at the cross hanging around my neck. "I can take that."

I looked at it. "This?"

"Yeah."

I slowly and reverently unfastened the cross from my neck and handed it to her. "Here." She took it and put it on as I wrapped the broken chain around my hand and studied the medallion for a moment.

"Now we both will be safe," she said. She smiled, kissed me on the cheek, and ran off to join the rest of the kids at the fore of the ship.

The next day, I was riding my bicycle through town. A group of Batista's army trucks drove by. One of them would have hit me but for an old man who pulled me out of the way. "Esbirros!" the old man yelled at the truck. A soldier turned and looked from inside the truck at the old man as it drove away. I waved to the old man and kept on riding.

I reached my destination of the Pinar del Rio bakery, jumped off my bike, allowing it to fall over, and ran inside the bakery. I grabbed a loaf of bread, brought it to the counter, and paid for it. As I emerged from the bakery, I saw Ms. Garcia, my teacher, across the street, waiting for the bus. The street was mostly empty but for a few pedestrians and parked cars. "Hi, Ms. Garcia!" I called out to her. I walked over to her, holding the bread, as she waved at me.

"Did you do your homework last night?" she asked.

"Yes."

"Good."

"I have to hurry and take this bread home."

"Run along home, then! I'll see you tomorrow."

I crossed the street to pick up my bike. "Bye!" I called. I started to pedal away down the street.

Suddenly, the storefront behind Ms. Garcia exploded. The windows blew out with incredible force, sending deadly shards of glass flying towards her from behind. She didn't even see the one that took off her head. I hit the ground until the glass settled. I looked up to see shards of glass and blood all around me, and my eyes settled on Ms. Garcia's head, lying just a few feet away from me on the ground. Sprayed with blood and dirt, I slowly got up. I could not take my eyes off of her head. I suddenly had to get away from all of this. I struggled to pick up my bike, leaving the blood-splattered bread behind. In my rush to pedal away from the grisly scene, one of my shoes fell off. I didn't stop to retrieve it, but kept pedaling, my legs pumping hard to get away as fast as I could.

Weary and terrified, I finally arrived at my house. I ran inside, calling for my mother. "Mima! Mima!" I ran down the hallway to where I could see my mother. "Mima!"

"You made it back early, for once," she commented before she beheld the state I was in. She noticed soon enough, as I ran up and grabbed her, holding on as if my life depended on not letting go. "What is it, my son? What is wrong?"

"Her head, it rolled across the street," I said, verging on hysteria.

"What? Julio Antonio, where is your shoe?"

"Mima, listen! Ms. Garcia, she's dead!"

My mother knelt down to face me. "Julio Antonio. Tell me what happened."

"I told you. By the bakery, she was there waiting for the bus. The store blew up. The glass, it cut her head off."

"Where did you get such a crazy story, Julio Antonio? Stop this nonsense!"

I looked up right into her eyes. "It really happened."

For the first time, she took in the blood and dirt. She gasped and crossed herself. "Oh, no. Poor Sophia! Poor Julio Antonio!" She held me as I finally broke down and cried.

A couple of hours later, I had come out of the bathroom. I needed to clean up, but felt a need to thoroughly shower, as if the water could wash away the memory as well as the blood and dirt. There was a knock at the front door. Pablo, Sandra, and my other good friend Yaneba were outside. "Julio Antonio," Sandra called in to me, "come outside and play with us!"

"Hey, Julio Antonio!" Pablo called.

Mother looked up the stairs at me. "Julio Antonio, get dressed and go play with your friends."

"I forgot the bread," I replied.

"That's okay," she assured me. "Go on." I ran off to get dressed while she walked over to the door. "He'll be out in a minute," she told the kids waiting outside.

"Okay," Sandra said.

I ran back out with my baseball glove and out the door, seeming to forget all about the tragedy. As she watched me go, my mother prayed, "Thank you, God, for protecting my boy." As she watched us run off, her fists clenched at her side. "And damn you, Castro. Curse you, you bastard. You almost killed my boy!"

CHAPTER II: THE DECEPTION OF YOUTH

In late 1958, the newspapers started to report on the political turmoil in Cuba. Fidel Castro's forces attacked government soldiers on mountain roads. People fled their homes as bombs exploded and the soldiers were pursued by rebel forces. Batista was forced to flee, boarding a plane to leave Havana. With the ouster of the dictator, Castro and his forces paraded victoriously into Havana as the people celebrated wildly, breaking parking meters and windows, and generally rioting through the streets.

January 1, 1959, marked the start of the Castro regime. My father was driving a blue and white Ford Ranch wagon, which he parked in front of our house in Pinar del Rio. We were all outside, watching the people parading by and celebrating the arrival of the new era. My friends, Arturo, Sandra, Yaneba, Julian, Pablo, Cisneros, and Kinqui, and I were all very happy, with little Cuban flags waving in our hands. We all went inside the house, and after a while my father arrived. My mother greeted him with a kiss, and took the briefcase from his hand. I said goodbye to my friends and went in to talk with my father. My father said, "Oh, that Fidel! What a great man he is. Do you know what he did today? He took over the bakeries in Havana to give the poor people free bread. Ah, what a great man."

I listened to this with joy, fascinated at the radiant face of my father. I said, "Finally, Dad, your friends, the bearded men, won the Revolution. Are you happy?"

"Of course," he replied. "You'll be happy, too. Even your mother likes Fidel."

My mother turned away to hide the rolling of her eyes.

I followed my father and said, "Fidel is going to be a great leader for Cuba. He is going to help the poor and bring justice."

My father nodded and said, "Yes, he is going to end the abuses and corruption in our country."

I said, "I think I can help the Revolution, too, like you did. I've got an idea."

"What idea? Tell me."

I took my books and started to walk away. "Let me think about it, and I'll tell you in a while." I lay down on my bed, deep in thought. I rolled over, pulled out some paper, and began to write a letter. After I finished my letter, I came out and said, "Papi, Papi, I finished my letter to Fidel, and I want you to give it to him, since you're his friend."

"Sure," my father said. "What is it?"

"Well, I want to get all the children and teenagers, all the young generation, to create a new, clean, and decent army for the future of Cuba, that will replace all the old, indecent, and corrupted army we used to have."

My father said, "That is a great idea, my son," and patted me on the shoulder.

A few weeks later, my father came home with a big smile on his face. He looked closely at me and said, "I've got something for you from the Office of the Prime Minister. I think it's the answer to your letter from Fidel."

My face lit up.

It was cold on that morning in late January of 1959. I walked towards the sentry box at the Rius Rivera Military Camp. Two tall, bearded soldiers shouted from afar.

"Halt! Who is this?"

At close range, one of them examined me with great curiosity while teasingly asking, "What is it that you want, sir?"

I didn't bother to answer. Instead, I pulled the communiqué out of my shirt pocket. "Present yourself on January 26 at the General Command of Rius Rivera Camp. Your request has been accepted and we wish to interview you in that Province," read the message.

The soldier hesitated for a moment. Without a word he again looked at me in disbelief, as if my tiny body and light reddish hair were a strange apparition. It was hard to believe the thin, nearly twelve-year-old boy with the mischievous countenance had an appointment with the Revolution's Commander-in-Chief. After managing to suppress his mocking expression, but not his amazement, he kindly asked me to wait a few seconds.

The soldier turned on his heels and rushed to the cabin which protected his companions from the sun. As he initiated a phone call, he showed his companion my communiqué. Very impressed, the soldier offered me a seat.

My optimism was increased when, in five minutes, the jeep driven by a soldier with an officer stopped in front of us. The officer looked untidy and smelled of perspiration. However, he was extremely polite. Patting my head affectionately he said, smiling, "Do you know something kid? When the Commander sees you, he won't believe you wrote that letter. How old are you?"

It bugged me to be labeled "kid," so I answered, "Well, mentally, I'm not much younger than you."

"I see, I see," he said, astonished.

We boarded the jeep. Moments later, we arrived at the military fortress. It consisted of huge installations and microwave towers, war tanks, anti-aircraft guns, soldiers moving back and forth, and ditches designed to become trenches as I learned later. The complexity of the place was quite a sight for a boy my age.

Suddenly the vehicle stopped in front of a building set in the center of all the other installations.

"Let's go, the Commander is waiting." said the officer.

When I stepped off the Jeep, I saw two huge black men dressed in olive green, stiff as starch in postures of exaggerated attention. They saluted the officer without batting an eye. It occurred to me that although slavery had officially been outlawed, the spirit of enslavement lived on. These black men, imposingly attired with their olive green striped white helmets were an unhappy symbol of modern slavery.

On passing, I gave them such an indiscreet look that one of them winked at me, and I responded with a smile. I climbed the steps, trailing the stinking officer and thinking how nice it was, after I raised my arm to check, that I smelled differently.

At the end of the hall, leading to the stairs, was written on a glass door: Rius Rivera, General Command Headquarters. The officer knocked softly and asked if we could go in. A voice reminding me of an old drunkard in my neighborhood answered from inside.

"Come inside, comrade."

We went in. As the blacks had done before, the officer stood at attention before sitting down. Behind a desk sat Fidel Castro holding a big cigar in his mouth. His dirty, unbuttoned boots were on top of the table. Bacardi bottles and assorted snacks surrounded him. Commander Dermidio Escalona, the Provincial Chief, stood nearby and resting in a chair was Commander Vallejo. Several escort soldiers leaned against the wall.

Fidel stared at me. Then, slightly amused, he asked the officer, "Is he the man, Benito?"

"Yes, my Commander, he's the man."

Castro stared again, carefully. His beady, piercing eyes were trying to read my mind. I held his gaze. He was tall and mildly corpulent and stooped a little, as I could see when he got up to put his hand on my shoulder.

"Frankly, I thought you were older," said Castro. "But this isn't important, really. This Revolution has been made by young men. It is for children and youngsters like yourself. You're a young revolutionary with the ideas that perhaps mature men are lacking. Your plan to gather all the young people of your same beliefs in a Military Youth Brigade is simply grand." He raised his right hand and pointed with his index finger high. "Let it be understood with this organization we're going to eliminate the Boy Scouts, the Explorers, and all the rest. Their members are mostly a bunch of spoiled brats."

He offered me a drink. Then he handed me a letter giving me full authority to form a Military Corps, requesting I be given necessary facilities. This document, issued at the offices of the

Prime Minister was signed by Ortas, then Director of these offices, and by Fidel Castro himself. He took from his desk a magnificent .38 pistol and handed it to me.

"Always carry it with pride...I wouldn't give a pistol to just anybody."

I smiled and thanked him. Being at that moment so close to him, I felt the alcohol smell of his breath upon my face. I was appalled. The man in charge of the country, who could order or stop executions, was drunk! With uncertain steps, he returned to his seat. The effort to keep himself standing made him collapse heavily on the chair, wheezing. This was the man who had become the idol of so many youngsters! This was Fidel Castro!

He leaned over his chair and said, "From now on you'll be the Little Commander...You're so very young! Too bad you don't have a beard. Let your hair grow. People will look at you with more respect."

"Beard or no beard people have to respect me." I said, "Because I'm accustomed to respecting others."

Castro laughed heartily. "That's a boy! Of course they have to respect you. You're quite a man!"

Vallejo asked how old I was.

"I'm eleven, but in a few months, I'll be twelve," I proudly said.

They chuckled. Then we took our leave and the officer executed the customary salute. While walking to the jeep, Benito asked to see the document Fidel had just given me. He glanced at it. "Kid, you can't even begin to realize what you have in your hands." He handed it back to me. "I don't understand these people." He said, before pulling out a big cigar from his pocket.

After riding in the jeep for a long while, we stopped in front of a building at the opposite end of the compound guarded by two soldiers dressed in the uniforms we'd seen before. We got off the jeep and I followed the officer. Here also, the soldiers saluted him. Inside, the offices swarmed with people. Among the many desks and file cabinets the soldiers busied themselves, carrying papers and portfolios.

When they saw us, one of them shouted, "Attention!" and everybody stopped. Those who were standing remained rigidly still. Those that were seated got up. Advancing, the officer made a vague gesture resembling a salute. Everything returned to normal.

We crossed a room at whose end there was another glass door. The officer stood in front of it and knocked respectfully. The sign in green letters read Military Control, Commander Jose Algibay Rivero. A young woman told us to go in.

The office was in perfect order, with beautiful drapes, and nicely decorated, unlike any of the offices I previously visited. A pretty blonde asked me to sit and then she and the officer went through another door in the back.

Benito returned after a few seconds, this time accompanied by a tall, distinguished-looking man, as out of place as a modern piece of furniture in a home decorated in Renaissance style. He looked refined in spite of the faded olive-green uniform. It didn't surprise me. Nothing could, after seeing Fidel drunk. Anything could be expected from this army. The man shook hands with me.

"I'm Commander Jose Algibay and I'm at your disposal."

After saying goodbye to Benito who saluted him, Algibay took me into his office and asked me to sit. "You must feel very confused," he said, noticing my eager interest in the surroundings. I nodded, in agreement.

The understanding, smiling fellow called his secretary through the intercom. Once again, I saw the pretty, slightly freckled, blue-eyed blonde. The Commander handed her some documents. "Type it as it is and make a copy for Commander Dermidio Escalona."

When his secretary left the room, Algibay settled comfortably in his chair. "I've ordered a letter typed giving you unlimited powers from this Provincial Command so you won't experience problems organizing your army," he informed me. "Starting today, you'll have a military jeep and two soldiers as your escorts, and you won't have to pay for movies or any other public show. What do you say?"

"Fantastic. Terrific."

"Start thinking of how you want the uniforms of soldiers to look—and of course, yours, I'm going to order them from Major Staff."

"I've thought about it already," was my quick answer. He was taken back.

"And how do you want them?"

"Olive-green pants, light beige shirt and black berets. Oh, and helmets like the ones outside are wearing." I pointed to the guards.

"You're a born lawyer, kid. How did you like Fidel's present?"

I didn't answer. The brand-new pistol absorbed me completely. It was like a dream. I had never seen one except in pictures. Guardedly, Algibay asked if I knew how to use it. He'd caught me red-handed. I had not thought of it. However, I said decidedly, "I don't know how to use it, but I'm sure you'll teach me."

"Of course I'll teach you!" He took the gun from me and put it on his desk. "Watch me carefully," he said.

My two eyes were busy watching. For about three quarters of an hour he repeatedly loaded and unloaded the pistol until he asked me to do it. He was satisfied when I did it.

"Very well, you are a pro. But, also being an intelligent young man, you must remember, this weapon can cut off the life of a friend as well as a foe. That's, of course, if one doesn't know how to handle it carefully." My sudden grim face made him add, "All right, don't get so solemn. You don't have to take it so seriously. Come, you have to meet the Major Staff officers."

Algibay gathered his cartridge belt, adjusted his olive-green cap and gave some instructions to his secretary, who still was intrigued by my presence. The soldiers got up when we crossed the hall, something that I was beginning to like. It was funny to see so many men stand up in attention for us. The salutes were going to my head!

Outside, Lieutenant Benito was whispering to other officers. In the middle of curious stares, we climbed into Commander Algibay's car, a beautiful Ford convertible. Algibay asked if I liked it.

"I sure do. It's smashing. How much did you pay for it?"

My candid question made him swallow hard. At my insistence about knowing how much money it might have cost, he frowned. "Not much," he answered briefly. Afterwards, he took me to see the camp and meet the officers. We had lunch in one of the dining rooms for the Major Staff officers; with Algibay indicating to me that soon, old customs such as having the officers eating in different dining rooms than soldiers and enlisted men would be abolished.

"All men are equal, regardless of their social class or rank," he observed.

I scratched my head, puzzled. He noticed it.

"Don't you believe so?" he added.

"Sure," I said, "but there's something I don't understand."

"What is it? Tell me. I'll try to explain."

"Well, if we are all equal, how is it that not all the soldiers in this regiment have a car like yours, Commander?"

He didn't like my question.

"You're too young to understand these things. You will someday," he said in earnest.

After lunch we went to the Department of Military transports. He told them to give me a jeep with military label and a siren, while he explained he would let me have one of his drivers until I organized my army corps. We said our goodbyes. On my trip home, I wondered about the kind of ideas occupying the mind of a fellow like Algibay, an average man who had probably escalated in rank because of his courage, not his intelligence.

I issued my first orders to the chauffer assigned to me, a sour-faced, grotesque-looking man. Very firmly I told him to drive me to the Department of Recovery of Misappropriated Funds, which is what they called the wealth expropriated from the people who had opposed the Revolution and left the country. My first official visit was memorable. I arrived punctually at 1:00 p.m. and filled out a little form given to me by a young girl. The form asked my name, address, and time of arrival in the building. Hours later, I still had not been received by anybody.

Finally, I got up and asked the employee if the head of that department was not present.

"Of course he is," she said, a bit annoyed, "but he is very busy and cannot receive anybody right now."

It was evident the young woman had taken me for a kid. I addressed her again, this time with feigned courtesy.

"Will you please tell your boss that I was sent here by Fidel? I'll see him some other time when he's not so busy."

Precisely at that moment, the driver entered the room in complete military attire. "Commander, you left these papers in the jeep," he said, handing me the letters of identification I had received from the regiment.

DEDICATORIA DE LOS COMANDOS JUVENILES
AL AUTOR
NOTESE AL CENTRO, EL CUÑO OFICIAL DEL
CUERPO MILITAR

*Dedication from the Juvenile Commandos to the author.
Notice in the center the official stamp of the military corps.*

"Commandos Squad" Juvenile Commandos of the Rebel Army – 1959

"Wait, please," said the now nervous employee. She went into her boss's office, and a minute later, a tall man appeared. He cordially extended his hand to me.

"I'm Daniel Solana, Head of this Department. What can I do for you?"

I told him about my army, and he insisted I would need more than a hall for my Commandos Headquarters. Against my protest, since I considered it excessive and superfluous, he let me have a three-story building. Knowing he was anxious to please Fidel and wash out the incident of my long wait at his office, I agreed.

Similar incidents followed this debut. Everywhere I went I was received immediately and my requests were resolved in a flash. Fidel's letter was a magic wand that opened all doors with the chiefs in the various bodies or departments created by the Revolution.

CHAPTER III THE LITTLE COMMANDER IS BORN

Approximately five months later, my organization comprised 18,000 youngsters from fourteen to twenty-four years of age. This armed body had its military rules and discipline, including saluting superiors according to rank.

I myself had prepared the regulations, taking as a guide the military regulations of the regular army, handed to me by Commander "Che" Ernesto Guevara at the Major Staff in Havana. Che also had given me a book written by him, *Guerilla Warfare*.

Che Guevara was a strange man—very conceited, constantly bragging about past and future feats. Nothing in this world was acceptable in his estimation. Everything had to be changed. I wouldn't have been a bit surprised if he had remarked the sun should come out at night and the moon during the day. He wanted to reform the universe according to his own fashion. He seemed to be out of his mind. I arrived at the same conclusion about Commander Algibay. Countless mental asylums would be needed, should either of these men be allowed to rule the world!

For my army, I received four hundred rifles, seven thousand small arms and about fifteen thousand commando knives. The bill was footed by the regular army, and its members enjoyed the same benefits as the other military men. For instance, we didn't have to pay for any public show. Every month we held meetings at headquarters, attended by captains and municipal chiefs who submitted their monthly report of the work done in the civil sector, transit, and the military, especially in reference to the training of the youth with the regular army. The Army Band came and played the national anthem. I was in charge of the closing speech. Some neighbors were allowed to participate.

By the end of 1960, things began to change, as did my feelings. At the monthly meetings Commander Escalona or Algibay would give us pep talks including worn-out slogans, such as "Workers of the World, Unite" or "Up with the Poor of the World." Meanwhile, they drove the newest cars and the poor continued to be poor after almost two years of Revolution.

Daniel, my chauffer and orderly, replaced my original surly driver. He was a huge black man, and very kind. He once asked me a rather difficult question. After Escalona had finished one of his rants against landowners and capitalists (national and foreign) Daniel asked me if the Commander really believed what he was saying. He couldn't understand how Escalona could repeat at the end of his speech a phrase Fidel had said, "Big cars for what," and yet drive a 1960 Oldsmobile as well as owning two more of the same for his escorts. This was common with all the Commanders who were provincial chiefs. Since I didn't know the answer, I said to Daniel, "I think these people are a little mixed up."

One morning when I was heading to the Rius Rivera Military camp, I saw something unusual. In the first post, they had doubled the camp vigilance. Several armored tanks and equipment were stationed in the vicinity.

"Commander," said Daniel, "something is wrong here."

"Yes, I think so, Daniel," I replied. "We shall see."

As he slowed down, we saw a helicopter trying to land. Helicopters were only seen in the provinces when some big shot in the Revolution was being transported. Several men got off and one of them had a beard. We thought it was Fidel. Immediately a jeep picked up the passengers and sped towards General Command Headquarters.

Daniel left me in the building and took the jeep to be serviced. Inside Commander Escalona's office, I could see that the man who had stepped off the helicopter was Commander Che Guevara. He was of average height and physically strong in spite of the asthma from which he suffered. It was imperative for him to always carry a little respiratory device. The spells occurred when least expected. As I was discovering, his apparent charm hid the most dubious character.

That day, Che showed me a lot of respect. In the presence of officers, he got up and gave me his hand, even though it was common for him and the other men to consider me Fidel's pet. He also talked about his youthful travels to various Latin American countries when he was about my age. He said it was done without consent of his parents, to verify the abject poverty in which other South Americans, on account of Yankee Imperialism, lived. He was smoking a long cigar as he spoke and between puffs told Escalona, "Well, Dermidio, I promise you, in less than forty-eight hours you'll see before you a traitor, Clodomiro, dead or alive."

Escalona frowned. "Listen, Che, I'd prefer not to have bloodshed here." Che stirred restlessly in his seat letting the other man talk. "We must consider that Captain Clodomiro fought for four years with me in the Revolution and used to be one of my trusted men," continued Escalona.

Then Che interrupted. "Dermidio you should check your troops. If Clodomiro is one of your trusted men..."

"You may not believe it, Che," Escalona insisted, "but Clodomiro is a brave and good man. His troops respect him and love him. The only trouble with Clodomiro is that he's an ignorant farmer, almost illiterate."

"He may be ignorant," Che put in, "but you're the one who told me, Dermidio, that he had told you he didn't like Socialism. He also said if what we were going to have was Socialism and Communism, he was going back to the Sierra to fight against us. That he didn't fight to overthrow a tyranny to make room for a worse one. He can't be as ignorant as you are trying to make me believe. He's what I called him before: a traitor. And traitors have to be eliminated!"

Overcome by rage, Che crushed his cigar fiercely in the ashtray muttering under his breath. Escalona sensed he was not scoring points. He made an effort to smooth the conversation. "Look, Che, all I want is to be permitted to talk to Clodomiro and see if we can avoid spilling blood among our own people. Most of the men with Captain Clodomiro are rebel soldiers of humble origin, peasants as ignorant as he is."

Che lost his patience. He stood up and slammed his fist on Escalona's desk. "Listen to me, Dermidio Escalona. Never, never again call these men 'rebel soldiers'. They were rebels. Now they're traitors and we're going to drag them out of those hills with bullets, dead or alive. We are going to bring them here so everyone can see what we do with traitors. I don't have to tell you that these are Fidel's orders." He sat back, his face mottled red with fury.

We witnessed this argument silently. Then Escalona lit a cigar and told Che, "Very well, if it's so, there's nothing more to say."

He went to a small refrigerator inside his office and pulled out a bottle of Bacardi, telling one of his orderlies to prepare drinks.

"Here, have a cigar..." Dermidio said to Che. "They were given to me as a present. I don't believe I've ever smoked such fine cigars."

Che took one, smelled it and tacitly approved. An officer rushed to offer him a light. When the drinks were ready, Che raised his glass and said, "I propose a toast to the physical destruction of all the enemies of the Revolution and especially to the capture of the traitor Clodomiro Miranda."

I snuck out, sickened by the bloody toast. I ran downstairs and met Benito, who was gloomy. "What's the matter? Is there anything wrong?" I asked.

"Nothing at all," he answered dryly. "Can you take me to the Armory? My jeep is broken."

"Yes, of course, let's go," Once in the jeep, he signaled me with his eyes, looking towards Daniel's direction.

"No problem. You can speak freely," I assured him.

"Do you know about Captain Miranda?" Benito asked.

"Yes, some."

"Well, I'm sure you don't know all the truth," he added visibly angry.

"That's right. I only know what was said minutes ago in Escalona's office."

"Look, Little Commander, a few days ago Captain Clodomiro went to see Escalona on behalf of his troops. They were grumbling about the psychological Communist indoctrination that had been going on in the Armed Forces for months. Escalona didn't think much of it. He leveled with Clodomiro and admitted that this system was turning towards Socialism or Communism. His exact reply, actually, was that if he didn't like it, he was welcome to go back to the Sierra and fight against it. Clodomiro returned to headquarters and explained to his soldiers what they were trying to do in Cuba. The first step was indoctrination of the Armed Forces, the strongest support of the Revolution. Results of the meeting between Clodomiro and his men were that they would return to Sierra de Los Organos, this time to combat Communism, which they agreed was not good for Cuba."

"Fine," I said, "but why are you so upset?"

"I'll tell you why. My brother-in-law was under Clodomiro's orders. He's one of those rebels. This kid and I grew up together. We're like brothers." Benito's voice cracked. "He probably won't escape alive, though I'll try to intercede on his behalf."

In the next few days there was a constant movement of troops. One of the usual tactics of the Revolution was to overstate the number of its enemies. For instance, a few troops of the regular army would have been enough to capture Captain Clodomiro's small and badly equipped troop. In a frontal encounter with the army their ammunition would not have lasted over twenty minutes, and no one was going to replenish them. However, Che mobilized nearly 2,900 militia men, utilizing heavy equipment and helicopters for the capture of Clodomiro, as though he were preparing for an invasion.

For two weeks, the hectic pace at the Rius Rivera Regiment was constant. Military ambulances all the time were coming and going with wounded men they were rushing to the Military Hospital. Apparently, Clodomiro's troop had not surrendered. They were resisting to the end.

Cuba: Russian Roulette of the World

One afternoon I bumped into Lieutenant Benito as I was leaving the hospital. "Too many dead and wounded men," he bitterly remarked.

I didn't dare to ask him about his brother-in-law but said: "Yes, too many indeed. And to think there was a time when they were all friends. Has Che already return to Havana?"

"Yes, after the slaughter," he answered, sardonically. "Do you know that only twenty-nine of the 120 in Clodomiro's group are alive? They are inside there." He pointed outside to the hospital. "Most of them are critically injured, and some are dying. It's better for them. If they survive, they face a thirty-year sentence or the firing squad as soon as they recuperate."

I couldn't help it any longer. "Benito, is your brother-in-law wounded?"

"No, my brother-in-law was not captured and he's not dead," Benito said with pride. "He and four more escaped the siege Che had put around him. One of the escapees is his best friend. They call him 'Cara Linda,' Pretty Face, because he's a handsome man. I don't know who the others are."

"Was it hard to capture the group?" I asked Benito. "Che spent over two and a half weeks here, and yet five men have run away."

"Sure, it was hard, what do you think? Those men are brave. I'll tell you how it went, so nobody can fool you with tales."

He explained that Che had cornered Captain Clodomiro and two of his men in a small cave. Five hours later, he still had not been able to capture the group. One hour before rounding them up, Clodomiro had destroyed one of Che's detachment squads, and killed a great number of soldiers. Later on, he captured ammunition and a .30 caliber machine gun. With this weapon, he'd caused many casualties during Che's repeated attempts to reach the cave. Seeing the strategic position occupied by Clodomiro, Che warned him to surrender, promising safety for the group if they gave in.

They answered with bullets.

Che, furious at the rebels' courage, ordered bazookas brought to him. Afterwards, he went by jeep to a landing field improvised for the helicopters, and he and two of his henchmen flew over the cave and shot bazookas at close range while at the same time dropping hand grenades. The cave was filled with smoke and dust and the place smelled like burned flesh. When Che returned, everything was quiet, but Benito said many of his men felt revolted by this spectacle. Che grabbed the loudspeaker and repeated his warning to surrender. This time no shots were heard, only silence.

They went in and found Captain Clodomiro lying on the ground, motionless. His lower limbs were shattered. Next to him, in pools of blood, two of his trusted men were lying face down. Che moved one of them with his foot; then pulled his pistol and one by one gave them a coup de grace. When it was Clodomiro's turn, he put the gun against his temple and the wounded man moved a little. Reacting nervously, Che lowered the gun. One of the soldiers noticed this and remarked that the man was still alive. Che looked at him cynically. "He's dead, comrades," he said. "Those movements are the normal reaction of the human body when the blood is still warm. I'm a doctor, I know about these things." Then he fired into Clodomiro's skull twice, this time with no hesitation.

"That's how they killed Captain Clodomiro Miranda," continued Benito. "They did not even bother to check his pulse before finishing him off."

Early the next day, Daniel and I cruised around the city in order to inspect work done by a group of Commandos. They were supposed to label the avenues and the parking zones and signs, warning drivers to avoid the newly painted marks. Once in a while, we stopped and got off to check closely.

At one of the avenues we saw a driver crossing over the freshly painted strip. He didn't pay attention to one of my soldiers signaling him that the zone was blocked. The car continued on, doing further damages to the recently completed work. Meanwhile, another Commando chased the car that had taken flight.

I jumped into the jeep and told Daniel to follow the fleeing car. Daniel shared my fury at the driver's stupidity. He sped until our car almost overturned in maneuvering the first corner. I told him to use the siren, but the car was already heading for the outskirts of the city, to the highway, where our jeep couldn't catch up with it. Fortunately, a police patrol car encountered on one of the avenues helped in the chase. Ten miles from the city the patrol car intercepted the car, and we pulled up next to them.

I confronted the driver, an old man of aristocratic bearing. I reprimanded him harshly. "What kind of citizen are you, shattering everything that is in your way and then taking flight?"

Looking at me with disdain, the old man dismissed me with a motion of his hand. "I've nothing to say to you, you little shit."

"You're an insolent man!" I answered.

The lieutenant in charge of the patrol car grabbed him by the arm. "Listen, my friend, you should respect this boy even more than you respect me. And you're under arrest for disrespect to authority and also for causing public disorder."

He was escorted to the police car. "I'm taking him to First Division," said the lieutenant, saluting.

"Fine," I said, "We'll follow."

At First Division they also saluted us with an "Attention!" which I answered. In the office to greet me were the old man, now a bit more subdued, the lieutenant, a desk sergeant, and several policemen. They gave me their statement to read. In addition to other charges, the man was accused of causing public damages by driving excessively fast and other aggravating circumstances. Only my signature was necessary to put him in jail.

I made a wry face, staring at the accused man who stared back at me as though trying to guess what the statement said. I told Daniel to read it aloud. When he finished, the old man was drenched in perspiration.

"How do you plead?" I asked him. "Do you have anything to say?"

"No, I don't know what came over me," he mumbled nervously, shaking his head. "I'm sorry."

"He's an old henchman. I bet he was Batista's follower," said the desk sergeant. His remarked irritated me.

"That's irrelevant," and I began to tear up the statement in front of the astonished sergeant and the lieutenant. Then I threw the bits of paper into the basket. "Free this man. He's sorry, and everyone deserves a second chance." Without further conversation I turned my back to them and left the room with Daniel. The black man had a beatific smile on his face.

"Why are you laughing?" I asked him.

"Oh, it's nothing, my Commander. It just occurred to me that you're a softie, like my mother. She never could bring herself to punish us, can you believe it? She used to say it hurt her more than it hurt us."

"What a preposterous comparison!" I said, bursting into laughter.

That evening in our garage, I found a car that was not my father's. I thought nothing of it. I was surprised, however, to see my father in our library talking to the old man involved in the morning incident, who was now apologizing for his past behavior. He looked at me as I entered.

"Here you'll have a real man," he said to my father.

"Yes, but I'm still a little shit," I retorted, teasingly.

He lowered his head. "Look, son, I've two brothers in prison for opposing this regime. You must understand how I feel. I'm an old friend of your father's, although he has his own ideas and I have mine. But we must have mutual respect for each other."

I walked through the house at peace with myself. My mother followed me. Suddenly, she hugged me and kissed me tenderly. "Never harm anyone," she said. "You won't be sorry."

The next morning, I received a phone call from Commander Escalona. "A matter of extreme importance is going to be discussed," he said, "and we are waiting for you at the Camp." I was not unduly curious. The revolutionaries were fond of calling meetings so I thought this would be a routine gathering.

An important figure was present at Escalona's office. His name was Commander Piñeiro, and he was one of the leading bosses in the G-2, the State Security Department (the Intelligence Service). He was accompanied by the Provincial chief of the same body. Escalona asked me to sit, and Piñeiro extracted papers from the briefcase on top of his bureau.

"Well, Little Commander, what we have to tell you is that Fidel, our Commander in Chief, has given us orders to turn your Military Command into a body for the indoctrination of the young. It will be called the Communist Youth."

I was dumbfounded. Clearly, Captain Miranda had given his life to avert a worse dictatorship: Communism. I remained silent, thinking and listening to the man. He was, I knew, one of the organizers of the G-2. Later, he would gain notoriety for his bloodthirsty crimes and persecution of the Cuban people. Piñeiro went on talking.

"Fidel sends you this scholarship," he said, handing me a paper. "He's set on making you an officer of the Cuban Intelligence Agency; but, in order to do this, we must send you to the Soviet Union. What do you say?" he asked, pleasantly expectant.

I was stunned. Naturally, I didn't want to go to the Soviet Union. In my childhood, I had read about the massacres perpetrated by the Soviets in Hungary, and the impressions were indelible. Confronted with this outrageous proposal, it was urgent to make a clever decision that wouldn't betray me openly as an enemy of the communist farce. So, I got up and said firmly, "Very well, I'll go to the Soviet Union."

Commander Escalona became euphoric. "Didn't I tell you this Little Commander is quite a man?" he said to the others. I had to refrain from shouting my defiance and doubts that had been more insistent after learning of the death of Captain Clodomiro and his brave men.

Piñeiro gave me pointers on filling out the instructions, reminding me it had to be signed by my parents since I was a minor.

Daniel noticed an involuntary shadow crossing my face. "Anything wrong, my Commander?"

"Nothing, Daniel," I said, avoiding his gaze. "It's been an interesting meeting,"

We immediately started dismantling our military body with all arms returned to the Rius Rivera Military Camp. During one of our trips to camp I met Lieutenant Benito. He was glad to see me and invited me to lunch in the Viñales Valley where his parents-in-law lived. They had prepared a roast pig. I gladly accepted and so did Daniel, a big eater. The food situation was deteriorating; everything was scarce. It was a treat to eat roast pork. The farmers preferred to fry it and use the fat, one of the items at the top of the shortage list.

As we drove to our luncheon, Benito began referring to the massacre of Captain Clodomiro and his brother-in-law's fate: "Do you remember I told you my brother-in-law and four more men were able to escape the Che's siege?"

"Sure, I remember," I said, "Now what's happened?"

"Some weeks ago, my father-in-law told me he'd gone to the hills to take supplies to these men. I warned him not to do it again. He'll be shot if he's caught. You can understand, I was worried." I couldn't help but to smile in admiration for the courageous man ready to risk his life in order to take food to his son.

"My father-in-law wants me to talk to Che and Escalona," added Benito. "If they vouch for the lives of these men, he says they're willing to surrender. They're starving and not likely to get help from anywhere else. Che moved almost all of the area's peasants and sent them to prison for collaborating with the rebels. The few remaining *guajiros*[1] are terrified. If they're detained under suspicion of helping the rebels, they are instantly shot by the militia men. This is all under a direct order from Che before he returned to Havana."

"What do you intend to do?" I asked.

"I don't think they'll be shot if they want to surrender," he said with bravado.

---

[1] Cuban peasants

His face, however, betrayed concern. He looked at me as if he wanted to be reassured. For my part, I concealed my own doubts and said nothing.

Benito lit a cigar and puffed before confiding. "I'll tell you why I'm worried. I went to see Escalona, who referred me to Che. In Havana, Che told me to bring the rebels. He guaranteed their lives if they surrendered. Trusting him, I went to the mountains with my father-in-law. That same day I brought the men in my jeep and presented them at Headquarters. They've been in prison for two weeks. Yesterday, when I went to visit them, I was told they'd been moved to La Cabaña prison in Havana, on Che's orders. Frankly, all this is very odd. If these men are executed, Che and the rest will hear from me, I swear. I won't forgive myself for having been instrumental in their deaths, no sir. I have Che's personal promise to have them tried in court and perhaps sent to prison, but spared their lives."

My blood curdled, remembering Che Guevara's words at the bloody toast before the death of Captain Clodomiro Miranda: "I propose a toast to the physical destruction of all the enemies of the revolution." Knowing the familial tie existing between Benito and his brother-in-law I felt saddened but did not inform him of my pessimism. Instead, I changed the subject.

"I'm sure we'll have a splendid lunch. Roast pig, yucca, rice, beans and fried green plantains."

"You like them, don't you?"

"They're my weakness."

He was amused. "I'm very fond of you. Many mature men should have your qualities." Then he glanced through the rear-view mirror at the other jeep, driven by Daniel. "That black man is going to kill himself by driving so fast, and he must eat for ten men."

"He eats like a horse," I said, also jokingly, trying to relieve the tension.

"I bet he thought he'd been screwed when he saw you climb my jeep. Did you notice his face when you told him to follow us?"

Behind us, Daniel smiled without knowing why we laughed, displaying his perfect white teeth.

Unfortunately, we never ate the feast. Upon arriving to the Viñales Valley, we found every one of Benito's relatives crying. His mother-in-law clung to him, sobbing and reproaching him. "They shot him, Benito, they shot my little boy. And you said he would be safe!"

Gently, her husband pulled her aside trying to calm her. They received official notification that the rebels had been shot the previous morning and that their bodies would not be delivered to their relatives, following military court orders.

Benito's eyes filled with tears. He pressed my arm with all his might and said, "Learn from this so the bastards won't lie to you as they did to me."

He rushed to his jeep and I followed. I was anxious to know what Commander Escalona would say about this incident. We virtually flew to the Rius Rivera Camp. Benito, silent, occasionally dried his eyes with the sleeve of his shirt. He ran up the stairs of the offices leading to Command Headquarters and I did the same. He kicked open the door to Commander Escalona's Office, who was there with Commander Algibay.

Brandishing his gun, Benito hurled insults at him. But Escalona, scared as a mouse, did nothing. "Benito, I had nothing to do with it," he merely protested. "It was Che who ordered their transfer from here. I didn't order their execution!"

Benito grabbed Escalona by the neck and lifted him from the chair. Algibay made a motion to pull out his gun, but Benito turned quickly to him. "Stay put, you pompous ass, or I'll put a bullet through your head!"

Algibay paled. In the meantime, Benito had pushed Escalona violently back on his chair. The man missed it and fell to the floor where he stayed, not daring to move.

"Can you see what kind of lice they are?" said Benito. "I am going to show them they cannot play with men, much less with human lives."

I thought about the incident and felt revolted long afterwards. Escalona had not dared to get up and fight. Algibay, petrified by fear, kept close to a window. When I left the room and went downstairs, Benito was not there. Daniel informed me he had sped off in his jeep.

The dismantling of our headquarters took several weeks. I did not see Lieutenant Benito again, but I thought of him often. However, in view of this incident, I chose not to inquire about him at the regiment. I handed my badge and the gun Fidel had given me to my commander. Escalona insisted I keep it as a personal gift from our Commander in Chief, but I claimed I was not going to need it since I was not a military man any longer. As a student, I would need books.

It took some ingenuity to try to get rid of the gun and the badge, but Commander Escalona insisted that Fidel would take it as an insult and encouraged me to keep both. "In their eyes," he said, "you will always be the Little Commander. And you should keep your uniform as well, because everywhere you go, people will recognize you was the Little Commander." I had no other choice than to agree with him and go along with his suggestion.

That same day, on my way home I bumped into Benito's father-in-law. He was the bearer of big news. After leaving Escalona's office, Benito went to see Che and was not admitted. Going completely berserk, Benito had killed two Cuban militia men guarding the door of a nearby embassy and had asked for asylum.

I told the poor old man that Benito should have killed that bastard Che, not the two Militia men, but I understood his motives. With that action, Benito had wanted to settle accounts with the murderer of his brother-in-law and the others. Then the old man said with amazing calm, "Don't worry, there's a God up in Heaven. Che Guevara is not going to die of a heart attack, I can assure you."

One day in April of 1960 I visited the home of Captain Eliseo Reyes Rodriguez, alias San Luis, ex-fighter in the Sierra, and one who would perish with Che Guevara in the Bolivian adventure. I was accompanying Lieutenant Guerrero, head of the Police Traffic Department and a G-2 Agent. The purpose of our visit was to pick up some hunting rifles San Luis was supposed to give him. In the course of that visit I heard something intriguing.

"Yesterday I arrested two CIA agents in the North Coast of Pinar del Rio," San Luis told Guerrero.

Guerrero smiled. "Are they really from the CIA?"

"Well, compañero," answered San Luis with ill-concealed craftiness, "they're counter revolutionaries and their probable starting point is the U.S. coast, so we consider them CIA agents."

"Are they going to be shot?"

"Of course, buddy, but right now we are working on them psychologically. Fidel wants them to be shown on television as confessed CIA agents. You know the impact that has on citizens and the world opinion."

"And do you expect them to declare themselves agents?" asked Guerrero.

"Look, Guerrero," said San Luis, again brazen, "we've told them it's the only way they can save their skin. Of course, some of these counter-revolutionaries do not make deals. But others do and since we're going to shoot them anyway, we lose nothing for trying."

I felt a compulsion to strangle him. It was incredible, but true. The scapegoat for all problems that happened in Cuba had a name: the CIA. If they arrested a man whose only crime was not to believe in Communism, he was accused of being a CIA agent. He was shot without further verification. Many of the men arrested were humble people who disliked the regime. They were arbitrarily sentenced to death as "agents of the CIA," although in many instances, they were too unsophisticated to know the meaning of those letters, much less the machinations of the organization.

In Cuba, when trucks broke, it was sabotage by the CIA. If cows died, they surely had been poisoned by the CIA. Yes, the CIA was even blamed for the mistakes made by the Communists. In short, so many patriots have been shot in Cuba under the accusation of being CIA agents that, if such charges were true, the CIA had as many members as a small city.

While I was writing my monthly Juvenile Commando report for the military command, my friends Sandra, Julian, Yaneba, and Arturo came to see if I wanted to go over with them to the Theodore Roosevelt Baseball Park to play. Like a good brother and sister, Sandra and Julian usually played together on the other team, and this happened to be a day when they won. Sandra liked to play catcher, and I was usually second base. Julian was at bat and hit the ball deep. Sandra was already on base and was able to score the winning run. I came in from second base, and as we were walking away with our equipment, Yaneba came up to me.

"Here," she said, handing me a small tin.

"What's this?" I asked.

"It's for your lips," she replied. "They're really chapped."

"Oh." I took some and applied it to my lips. "Thanks."

We had walked by a paved area of the park where some other kids were playing marbles. One of them, Tité, was a larger black kid who was a little slow mentally. Everyone liked having him around because of his easygoing, congenial personality.

"Hey, Julio Antonio!" he called out. "Arturo!"

"Hey," Arturo replied. "Can I play marbles with you guys?"

"You can take my place," Tité responded. "I want to go fish in the river."

The other kids playing marbles laughed at him. Arturo didn't care, and started playing marbles as Tité stood up.

A mean, dark-haired kid named Trimiño pointed at Tité. "Hah! What are you going to catch, Tité, a cold?"

The other kids laughed again, while Sandra frowned at them. Tité got angry and began to stutter. "I'll show you! I'm the best f-f-f-fisher of fish there is!"

They laughed at him again as Trimiño mocked him. "F-f-f-fisher of f-f-f-fish...."

"Be careful," Julian teased, "you might fish up a shark!"

"Hah!" I said, coming to Tité's defense. "You don't know what you are talking about. Sharks are in salt water!"

"So?" Julian said. "Tité doesn't know that, either."

"Fine," I said, coming to a decision, "you guys play with your dumb marbles. Leave Tité alone. I'm going fishing with him."

"Yeah," Trimiño said, "Go play with stupid Tité and the sharks!"

They all turned away, and the other baseball players turned to go. Sandra waved goodbye to us as Yaneba walked up to me. "I'd like to fish, too. Can I come?"

"Yeah," I said. "Meet us at the water by the bridge. I'll go get some fishing poles."

When I met them at the river, they were seated on a rock. Tité smiled up at me as I approached. "Hey, are you ready, Tité?" I asked.

"Yes, yes!" he replied excitedly. He picked up one of the fishing poles with a big grin. I handed Yaneba one, and we all settled down by the rocks to fish.

In three hours, we had no luck. The sun was getting low in the sky, tingeing everything with a rosy color. Two kids walked by with fishing equipment, clearly done for the day. Yaneba began to reel in her line.

"I guess it isn't a good day for fishing," she said, looking back us. As she did, she dropped her pole in the water. "Oh!" she exclaimed in surprise.

I stepped out to try and retrieve it, but it was too far away for me to reach. I put my pole in the sand, hook still dangling in the water, and rolled up my pants to the knees in preparation to wade out into the river to get her pole. I waded out between rocks, leaves, branches, and shallows. Yaneba's pole had caught on a small mud island in the middle of the river. I grabbed the pole, smiled proudly, and started to wade back. "Hey, I got it," I called out.

But they weren't paying any attention to me. Yaneba and Tité were looking over into the water. Yaneba gave out a tiny scream and Tité loudly cried out, "It's big! Dios mio! It's big!" A large fish had caught on my hook while I was away, and Tité was very excited.

"Well, get the pole!" I called back.

Tité looked confused for a moment, so I dropped the pole I had saved from the river, bounded ashore, and put my foot on my pole before the fish could pull it away. I then grabbed it and tried to reel it in.

"It's a monster!" Yaneba exclaimed.

"It really is a shark!" Tité added.

"Help me get it!" I yelled. With their added strength, I was able to reel in my line and properly land the fish.

The sun was even lower by the time we had returned to the baseball park, the three of us bringing our catch to display in triumph to the other kids, who were still there playing marbles. Trimiño and Julian looked up from their game to see many of the kids running up to us to look at the three-foot-long fish Tité was carrying on his shoulders.

"I told you I'd get a shark!" Tité said proudly to the other kids. I patted him on the shoulder and smiled as the other kids came up to wonder over the huge fish.

Dr. Julio Antonio del Marmol

CHAPTER IV: COMMUNISM: THE DESTRUCTION OF THE FAMILY

I had started to observe how the Revolution was twisting towards an extreme leftist ideology as despair increased among my friends and their families. My disillusionment with the Revolution grew greater. The first of my friends to leave was Tité. He came to me to apologize for having to leave, and I told him that I couldn't blame him at all. His father was an English teacher, but by the middle of 1960 had been unemployed for months, as Castro had determined that no one on the island would learn the English language. His grandmother was already in Florida and was able to obtain a visa so that they could leave Cuba legally. My other friends, however, were not so fortunate, and they had to take whatever opportunities they could to escape from the Communist regime.

On an evening in September of 1960, Yaneba's father, Josue, had decided he could no longer take what the Castro regime was doing. He and his wife, Maria, owned a wedding planning business, complete with dressmaking and cosmetic lines. Castro had appropriated almost all of the money they had saved when he took over the banks and now had told them that they had to work for the government for free for two years doing agricultural work in order for them to even obtain a passport, let alone a visa to travel to other countries. Josue had obtained a small boat, and I was helping them load it with provisions while Yaneba's ten-year-old younger sister, Elena, looked on.

"Yaneba," Maria said, "get that box over there."

"Yes, mother," she replied.

The box looked fairly heavy, so I went over to help Yaneba carry it into the boat. Elena was settled on a seat, looking cute in a frilly dress. We put down the box, and Elena smiled at me. I ruffled her hair, which made her giggle. Josue brought a bag into the boat and stowed it away.

"That's it," he said decisively. "Let's go, let's go!"

We walked back to the shore. I gave Yaneba a hug. "God bless you and keep you safe."

"I will miss you," she said, bravely fighting back tears and hugging me tightly again.

"Yaneba," Josue said, "let's go! Now!"

She ran on to the boat, turned and waved at me. "Bye! Goodbye!"

I waved sadly. Josue started the motor and the boat pulled away. I watched until it was out of sight. I pulled out the Caridad del Cobre she had given me and looked at it. I learned years later from Yaneba what had happened in sad detail.

As they were heading out to sea later the next afternoon, they did not notice a small fishing boat. Unfortunately, it had spotted them; trying to catch fish was only the appearance of this particular craft. The reality was that it was fishing for people like Yaneba and her family.

On their boat, Yaneba was opening a sack with Cuban sandwiches and handing them out to everyone. From the boat, all that could be seen was blue sky and blue water in every direction.

"Thank you, Yaneba," Josue said as he accepted a sandwich. He did not hear the faint sound of an approaching aircraft.

Yaneba started to hand fruit out to her family. Maria beckoned to Elena. "Come here, Elena." The little girl came and sat by her mother. Maria handed her some fruit. "Eat your fruit."

"Okay, Mama." Elena began to eat, and then cocked her head, listening. The sound of the aircraft was louder now, and the entire family started to look around for the noise. "What is that sound, Mama?"

Maria didn't answer, but searched the sky. Yaneba spotted the MiG fighter, and pointed. "There!"

The fighter bore down on the boat, and Elena screamed as it opened fire. Bullets tore holes in the small boat, splinters flying everywhere. The family all ducked for cover, but there was nowhere to hide. Blood sprayed through the air as they fell down, motionless. The fighter passed overhead but broke off the attack. It had sighted a U.S. Coast Guard ship, pulled away, and flew back to Cuba.

The Russian-designed aircraft had caught the attention of the Coast Guard ship's commander, who had set an intercept course, even though the incident was occurring in international waters. Seeing that it had broken off, he ordered a boarding party to look for any survivors. As they approached the boat, they could see that the fighter's work had been thorough. The boat was ruined and listing, and blood covered the rails. There was almost an inch of blood on the bottom of the boat, and the bodies of Yaneba and her family lay in contorted positions.

That blood, of course, attracted something else: sharks. Elena's body was hanging over the rail, her arm over the water, dripping blood into the ocean. Shark fins broke the surface around the boat, and one of them started swimming towards Elena's hand. A Coast Guard lieutenant pulled out his pistol and started firing into the water near the surface and ordered a boat to be sent over immediately. He commanded the boarding party that ran over to the boat, and went on board with two crewmembers. Just as they arrived, a shark reached up, grabbed Elena's arm, and dragged her body under.

"No!" exclaimed the lieutenant as he fired into the ocean. "Damn sharks!" He turned around as he heard one of his men retching. It looked like there were no survivors, as the entire family's bodies lay over the blood-soaked deck, twisted at various angles. "My God!" was all he could say.

The other crewman was over by Yaneba, and noticed her pulse fluttering in her neck. "This one's alive!" he said.

"Stretcher party, on the double!" the lieutenant commanded. "Hurry up—this boat's sinking fast!"

The crew lifted Yaneba onto a stretcher, the cross necklace I had given her dangling out from her shirt. Covered in blood, she groaned slightly. Once on board the Coast Guard ship, she received medical attention.

It was shortly after Yaneba left that I lost the company of Arturo. His father had owned a business that specialized in manufacturing the tin cans used for sardines and other preserved foods. It was one of the first businesses Castro took over, as they largely supplied the containers for the army's MREs. Arturo's father, Marco, had had enough, especially once his wife, Rosa, had given birth to a second son, Marquito. Marco's brother, Arturo's uncle Guillermo, and his wife, Anita, also decided to leave with them. Rosa was breastfeeding Marquito while the rest of the family loaded the boat, chatting with each other quietly as they hurried to finish. Marco had to apologize to his brothers who had to remain behind because the boat was too small for all of them.

"Don't worry," he was saying to them, "if we can't come back for you, we'll arrange to get you out of here. Isn't that so, Arturo?"

"Yes, Papi," Arturo said.

"Are we ready yet?" Marco asked.

"Almost, almost," Guillermo replied.

They said their goodbyes to the family, and Arturo took his backpack and threw it into the cabin. Marco checked around one last time to see if anyone was watching. He then led Anita and Marquito on to the boat. "We go," he said. "We go!" The engine started and the boat began to move away from the shore. The shore slipped out of sight behind them.

Several days later, at sunset, they were growing concerned. Arturo said, "We should have been there by now. It has been too many days."

"It's so hot," Anita moaned. Even though the sun was setting, the rays were still intense and beat down on the little boat. "Guillermo," she said to her husband.

He lay there, eyes closed. He did not move. "Guillermo, wake up." She walked over to him, calling his name once more. She shook him. He didn't move. She touched his face, and realized that he was dead. "Guillermo!" she shrieked.

Everyone in the boat stood up and came over to see. The baby started to cry. Marco did what had to be done, while the women cried. He got a plastic bag, managed to get his brother's body into it, and slipped the bag over the edge of the boat into the sea.

Several days later, Marco called Arturo over to the bow of the boat and spoke to him quietly. "We are lost. Out of gas."

"But I thought..." Arturo began, but his father interrupted him by pounding on the controls of the boat.

"None of the equipment works! Not the radio, the compass, nothing!"

"It's okay," Arturo reassured his father. "We will make it."

"Listen, son. Take care of your mother and baby brother."

"What are you saying?"

"Here, I've saved the food for you and the others." Marco gestured toward the food. Arturo and his father stared at each other for a moment. Arturo nodded in understanding, and they embraced.

The sun came up on another morning. By now, everyone had lost track of the days, and the morning sun greeted another body entering the ocean, this time Arturo's aunt, Anita. There was no crying this time. They settled back to sit in the hot sun, with nothing but sea surrounding them.

"The food is gone," Arturo noted as he stared off into the distance at the sun.

The sun rose higher, and hours later Marco noticed something dreadfully wrong. He tried to pull the baby away from his wife.

"No, no!" Rosa screamed.

"He is gone, Rosa," Marco said gently.

"NO!"

Marco finally got Marquito away from her as Arturo watched, completely empty of all emotion. "I will prepare him," Marco said.

Rosa's arms reached out to follow Marco as he walked away. She collapsed into the bottom of the boat, sobbing and wailing. The sun beat down. Hours later, Marco slid a smaller bag with a body into the ocean. Rosa, now completely drained of all emotion, watched. Arturo sat with his head hanging down, weary from grief and the sun.

Near sunset, Marco handed a bottle to Arturo. He spoke very weakly. "This is the last of the water." Arturo started to argue, but Marco cut him off. "Take it." Arturo nodded in resignation and took it.

The next morning, everyone was lying motionless in the boat. Arturo stirred and stumbled over to his mother. He held up the water to her mouth. She woke a little and drank. He then went over to his father to give him water, but Marco did not respond. Arturo rested his head on his father's chest and started to quietly cry. An hour later, Arturo slid the bag with his father into the ocean, showing no more emotion.

Around noon, Rosa had taken an empty tin can and was squirting her breast milk into it. Arturo was staring blankly into the distance. She came to him and held up the can. "Here, son," she said. "Here." He did not move. She put the can up to his lips. "Drink, son." He mechanically drank from the can held to his lips.

Days later, Arturo and Rosa were lying motionless in the boat. In the distance, a shore was visible with sand and trees. Arturo finally woke up, raised his head, and saw the shore. "Mama," he croaked.

She stirred and opened her eyes to slits, squinting in the sun. He pointed to the shore, and she barely raised her head. They had arrived at Florida, but the cost had been too high for both of them. They did not smile, but only stared. The sound of a boat horn sounded far away. In the distance, they had been spotted by a Coast Guard vessel, which was now coming up to them.

That year, I moved to Havana. Fidel Castro wanted to interview the young men selected for the important mission of studying abroad to be trained as Intelligence Officers. We were lodged at a beautiful home in the Vedado section; one of the many mansions that were or had been the property of the dissidents leaving the country and whose possessions were confiscated by the Government. In my growing disenchantment with the regime, I wished to remain in that environment as little as possible. Consequently, I asked and got permission from my immediate superiors to stay during the day at the home of relatives, returning at six to spend the evening in the Security House where we were living.

At my uncle's I found great moral support. They did not approve of the Revolution or of Castro and his ideas. For six months, he had been waiting for the opportunity to send his family out of Cuba. I spent many pleasant hours with them until it was time to go back to my lodgings. The Vedado seemed different now from how I had known it. Most of the homes were closed; the gardens abandoned and the window panes broken. The government could not keep up the expensive mansions left behind by their inhabitants.

Cuba was experiencing the worst wave of crime in its history. Robbers marauded near luxurious residences and at night broke windows to get into and take as much as they could. This was easy. In many areas no person was visible along a stretch of several blocks. Their former residents had expatriated except for a few old people who remained out of love of their homeland. Frequently, these helpless people were murdered by bandits when they were found living alone.

Families were going through chaos. The young ones, fearing their future in Cuba, longed to leave the Island. The old ones could not reconcile themselves to the idea of forsaking everything, money, cars, homes, and above all their country land. They were sustained by hopes that the Castro government wouldn't last and that it was their duty to stay and help to overthrow it. This argument divided the Cuban families in two. Those who chose to stay had to bear a life of sadness and anxiety for departed relatives and friends.

I would go to bed as soon as I returned to our residence, feeling increasingly restless and helpless in trying to untangle myself from my predicament. One day, in spite of my worries, I slept until 2:30 p.m. to be awakened by one of the house guards. He shook me, and I jumped to my feet. "What is it?" I demanded irritably.

"Get dressed immediately," he said, cheerfully. "Commander Fidel is here. He wants to speak to all of you."

I got dressed and met all the others in the living room. We were all seated on a long sofa and the smiling Fidel Castro occupied an armchair, smoking his familiar cigar.

"Kids, you're the future of the Revolution," and he continued on that speech for over an hour. Among other things, he had conceived a gigantic, nationwide literacy campaign. His goal was to teach every person to read and write correctly. We were his hope, he said, the pillars holding up the Revolution, its safeguards against numerous enemies. He finished, and after a brief pause, he stood up. "Have any of you anything to say? Don't be bashful, ask anything you wish." He watched us closely as he exhaled.

Nobody said anything, too overwhelmed by the communist leader's presence. Finally, I broke the silence. "Listen, my Commander, in my opinion, I would be much more useful here in Cuba, helping with the literacy campaign. After listening to you, I feel very enthusiastic about it. I've never been in the Cuban mountains, and before I leave the country, I'd like to see the places where the Revolution was born. Yes, up in the mountains, living with the humble people who helped create it." I said this long speech without stopping to breathe, hoping to grab this precious opportunity to evade the scheduled trip. Fidel himself had given me the excuse. However, I had to be cautious. He was a distrustful and shrewd fellow.

Obviously displeased, he pulled his beard and fixed his beady, now severe eyes, on me. "I truly think you'd be more useful in the mission we've assigned to you, but if that's what you wish, you can stay and participate in the Literacy Program. Of course, I personally will be very happy if you went to the Soviet Union with the entire group, and achieved the goal we've set out for you."

I remained silent. Fidel had said it all: "If you want to stay," and that was enough for me. I would not go to the Soviet Union! Fidel again became cordial, expecting we would grant him his wishes after he said his piece. Then he jokingly added we shouldn't get too accustomed to the luxury of living in a mansion, or we might turn into bourgeois. Then he was gone, followed by his bodyguards.

After breakfast, the next day, we had a visitor: Commander Piñeiro of the G-2, accompanied by an orderly who carried his briefcase. After general greetings, Piñeiro, to my surprise, addressed me in particular. "Little Commander, we want to talk to you privately."

"Very well," I said right away. "As you wish."

We went to a little room and he ordered the doors closed so nobody would listen. "Commander Fidel is very displeased," he said, with a dramatic overtone, pausing long enough to force me to ask why. When I didn't, he added. "Do you know why Fidel is so displeased?" I shook my head. "He's upset because you backed out on us."

I had to feign anger. "Look Piñeiro, I haven't failed you. Men can change their opinions, and I have. I don't want to go to the Soviet Union just yet." I said, knowing I wouldn't gain anything by openly confronting them. "Perhaps I'll go the USSR," I falsely promised, "but at the present time I'm very excited with Fidel's idea of teaching the farmers to read and write. Yes, I'll go to the most isolated mountains. Where nobody wants to go, I'll be there!" While delivering my emphatic protest I looked at Commander Piñeiro with the corner of my eye. He smiled. My acting had been convincing. I had managed to save myself without causing direct problems for me or my family.

"You're a devil of a rebel! You go to where you want to go and do as you please and not what anybody else tells you to do!" said Piñeiro, again beaming. He left soon after with the papers I had signed canceling my scholarship.

That same evening, I went back to my parents' home. I was quite determined to persuade my old man to leave Cuba with the family. In childish expectation I almost was sure I'd succeed in convincing him. I had grown up in a happy home where all decisions were resolved harmoniously. Furthermore, my father and I were extremely congenial. *He'll understand when I tell him all this is a farce*, I thought to myself.

The possibility didn't occur to me that we were about to have our first and most serious domestic rift.

Julio at 13 years old

I told my mother first of my dissatisfaction with the Communist Revolution, how I'd extricated myself from the Russian obligation, my determination to persuade my father to send me out of Cuba and later leave with the rest, before I joined the Literacy Brigades. My mother agreed and encouraged me, but she also warned it was not going to be easy to persuade my father.

After supper, I went to meet father who was alone in our library. "Dad, do you know something? I feel awful in Cuba."

He looked surprised. "Why? What's the matter?"

"I think this government is not a revolutionary one as they say," I said looking at him straight in the eyes. "It's a dictatorial communist regime and Fidel Castro is a paranoid and egocentric tyrant. In short, he's a fake. He's taken advantage of the Cubans' good faith and the common unrest the citizens felt under Batista's dictatorship."

My father leaned on his rocking chair. After a brief, scrutinizing stare, he closed the book he had in his hand and spoke. "Who's told you this is a communist government? Do you know what this government has done? It has given some justice to the poor classes. In fact, it has done the will of Jóse Martí, Antonio Maceo, and your great-grandfather Donato del Marmol, all of whom gave their lives for Cuba's independence from Spain. And this nation, for which they died, was for many years plundered by unscrupulous rulers who only had in mind to become rich. They didn't care about the poor or desired to help them!"

Anger swept over me. My father had completely swallowed Fidel Castro's clever propaganda and I had to tell him what it grieved me to say. "Look, old man, you said the other rulers were only concerned with their own profit. Maybe you're right. But don't forget this: you and the others helping this political delinquent with your capital and your moral support don't know the enormity of what you're doing. Have you any idea of what you're helping Castro to accomplish?"

My father didn't answer. He rubbed his chin.

"You don't know? Then let me tell you."

I took a paper from his desk, tore it in many pieces and said. "You're contributing to the destruction of the Americas, and if you keep helping this maniac, the American continent will be shattered into pieces, just as I've done with this paper." Opening my hands, I let the pieces scatter on the floor. "Unfortunately, when you realize your mistake it will be too late. He will have no need of you. To those who will not share his Communist views he'll do what I've just done with this sheet of paper. I've heard them and you haven't. Castro's idol is Adolf Hitler. Imagine what they will do with his ambitions for power. They won't stop with the Americas; they will continue until they control the entire world unless we stop them."

My mother interjected, "Julio Antonio is right. We're swimming in an avalanche of dirt. The bums and the drunkards are ruling the nation and enjoying what other people built up through fifteen or twenty years of hard work and sacrifice.

"Who's this city's commissioner[2]?" she asked. "Is he the man who has sacrificed himself all his life, working to raise a capital as his reward? No! Is he the man that has killed himself studying to pursue a decent career? No! Who then is this Commissioner but a loafer, a drunkard, whose only merit is to have killed a policeman from Batista's government? He's either the kind that kills a man for a political ambition and a public position, or a paid thug. In any case, he is a delinquent and this is the Commissioner of our City!"

My father got up and refused to listen to the unassailable truths my mother was telling him. His final comment was emphasized by a strong blow on the desk with the book he had in hand. "That's enough! Quit making stupid remarks! This is my home and everybody has to do what I say." He screamed then. "Enough is enough! You are not only talking like a traitor; you *are* a traitor! Who brainwashed you? Your uncle?"

I didn't reply. These words pushed me to a sudden decision. "Very well, Father. This is your home and you're the boss. But only to those living under your roof. I'll move today." I kissed my tearful mother. "Don't worry, Mima, God is always on the side of the truth. Old man, I hope you think things over."

From the doorstep I could hear my mother sobbing, but I had to leave. Choking in my tears, I closed the door and hit the street. My once happy home had turned into hell.

I went directly from my house to my uncle's house in Miramar, Havana, still wearing my military uniform and sidearm. He was in his late forties, with a placid demeanor and distinguished appearance. He was clean-cut, always impeccably dressed. He received me with a smile like always, but he could see that I was distressed. "What is wrong, Julio Antonio?" he asked.

---

[2] A Commissioner is the equivalent in the communist system to a mayor

I replied, "I just had a big fight with my father, and I cannot go back to the house. Do you mind if I stay here for a while?"

"Of course," he replied. "Come in. Tell me, what happened? I know my brother can be hard-headed sometimes. But you are his golden child, and you are a Revolutionary. How can he have a fight with you?"

We went into his library. His house was a beautiful one, and the library had a wonderful ocean view. He pulled out a pipe, filled it with tobacco, and lit it. He was a very intelligent man, deep in political knowledge, and superb at reading people. He looked at me with curiosity as I said, "I don't like the Revolution any longer, and I don't trust these people. I think they're all bandits, and I told my father, which made him very upset with me."

"Why have you changed? What has been happening to you? I believe you're in Fidel's First Ring of trustworthy people. What happened to you?"

I told him, "I see what these people are doing. They have hundreds of people they've been training, getting them ready to take over every single business this country has: the electric company, the banks. They're going to nationalize everything and take away every single bit of wealth everyone has and place it all under government control. This only has one name: communism!"

He sat back in his chair, looking me up and down in an appraising fashion, especially at the pistol at my waist and the uniform I was wearing, and hesitated before answering. He leaned his head against his hand, his finger to his forehead and asked, "Did you tell this to your father?"

"Yes," I answered. I grew emotional and a few tears escaped my control. "He said I cannot stay under his roof if I'm thinking like that, and that I'm a traitor."

He reached out to me and placed his hand on my shoulder as he realized what I was going through. "Of course, of course; I bet he got very upset when you told him that. Your father is a complete fanatic for these people. For a long time, I've been telling him that this was going to happen, but he wouldn't believe me. I wonder how you, at such a young age and in such a short time, manage to figure out what your father hasn't picked up for years."

I tried to defend him by saying, "Well, I've been seeing all of this up close, and Dad hasn't. I would love to show him these things, but they won't let anyone know until it is too late."

He puffed on his pipe and smiled. "You are a good son; you're still defending your father," he said as he touched my shoulder with a certain amount of pride. "What do you plan to do?" he asked.

"I will arrange to leave Cuba," I replied instantly, "one way or another."

He reclined again, crossed his legs, and told me, "You took a big chance to tell me this. Why? If I tell anybody, you could be in deep trouble. Look at you; you're even dressed in uniform with a gun at your waist. You're one of Castro's favorites."

"He makes me feel sick," I replied. "He is a traitor and will destroy Cuba, the whole continent, if we let him do it. He's a maniac, and he's got a Napoleon complex. He wants to control the Americas and then the world. I've heard this in the conversations he has with the people around him."

"Well, since you've been honest and straight with me, I'm going to take a big chance with you."

He stood up, walked to the little table, and made a phone call. He had a short conversation with the person on the other end. "Yes. I want you here as soon as possible. My nephew is here, and he is inside Castro's First Ring. I want you to hear how he feels about the Revolution and the new leaders."

He hung up, came back, and sat down. "I'm part of an intelligence cell from World War Two. My mission was to keep the Nazis from taking over in Central and South America and the Caribbean Islands." He stood up and looked out the window to see if anyone was loitering outside. He closed the curtain. "What I'm going to tell you, you have to take with you to your grave. Even to your father, even to your shadow, do not share what you are going to hear now. I'm a master spy, and I can make you a master spy as well. Don't leave Cuba. Stay with us, and we will train you so that you can help us to bring this regime down."

I looked at him in astonishment. "Are you a spy for the Americans?"

He took another puff on his pipe. "Let's just say I work with international intelligence to defend democracy, freedom, and the human rights of people around the world. I've proudly done this all my life, and I will continue to do so until I die. But remember: you cannot tell this to anyone—even to your father—because you will die, and I will die." I hesitated for a few seconds, thinking about what he had just told me. "You will make an excellent intelligence officer, because you're very bright. I just called my contact so that you can meet him. If you agree, you can come to be a part of our team."

"Okay," I replied with determination, "I will do it."

"You have to pretend to everyone that you like Castro and the Revolution. Do you think you can do that, even though you don't like them?"

"I think I can do that. Actually, that is why I've been doing all this time: pretending."

He smiled and put his arm on my shoulder. "I know you will. I always say you're the brightest and bravest of all my nephews."

Cuban Military Base, April 17, 1961

On the day of the Bay of Pigs invasion, there was the sound of a falling bomb, followed shortly by an explosion. The pavement was littered with the bodies of many dead and wounded soldiers. Che Guevara and I ran along with my brother-in-law Canen, a tall, distinguished military officer in his early twenties with black, curly hair. Canen was trying to keep very calm as he squatted and ran. I was in my Juvenile Commandos uniform, and Canen had been showing me around the base when all of this started to happen.

Guevara led us over to a jeep. A young officer was hanging out of the driver's seat, covered in blood. He dragged the body out of the way and picked up the jeep's radio microphone. "This is Commandante Guevara, get me the commanding officer!"

There was some static from the radio, and an unclear voice asked, "Who are you?"

"Who am I? It's Che, dammit. Commandante Guevara! What the hell is happening?"

The voice on the radio came through more clearly. "Commandante, we don't know! There is shooting everywhere, the planes...they have friendly markings but they are bombing...." The voice was briefly overwhelmed by static. "...be enemies," was the only part that got through after the static cleared.

"Listen to me," Guevara said, "call the TV, the radio stations. Rally the people, we need support to survive! Where is the main point of the invasion?"

A bomb exploded nearby, showering us with debris. I exchanged a nervous glance with Canen as we crouched next to the jeep. "We don't know, Commandante," the voice on the radio replied. "Will advise of any new information. Hold on...." There was static as the line was cut.

Guevara disconnected. We waited by the jeep, surrounded by the sounds of gunfire, explosions, and screams. After what seemed like an eternity, the radio came alive again, and the voice on the other end spoke. "Commandante, are you there?"

"Yes, yes—go ahead."

"They are coming in from Playa Giron. I repeat, Playa Giron! They are moving fast, already miles inland...." The voice abruptly ceased as Guevara killed the connection and dropped the microphone.

"No," he muttered to himself. "I knew they wouldn't swallow this pill. If only I had more time...." He pulled the bloody body all the way out of the jeep, callously dropping it onto the ground. He looked up at a passing young lieutenant covered in debris and blood. "Lieutenant!"

The lieutenant turned, clearly dazed, and hesitated for a moment before speaking up. "Yes, my Commandante!"

"Get in," Guevara commanded. He glanced at Canen and me. "All of you, get in!" He got into the driver's seat as the confused lieutenant, Canen, and I jumped in. He drove away quickly, carelessly, flying wildly down the road in a panic. The sounds of the attack were still not far off, and as he drove, Guevara turned to the lieutenant beside him. "You! You have to make sure you hide all, everything to do with those missiles. All the parts, all the boxes, everything." The young officer looked frightened, but nodded. "They must not find proof of what we are doing!"

This last comment caught my attention, and I looked at Guevara from my position behind him with great curiosity.

"Turn here to the base, Commandante!" the lieutenant said. The tires squealed and the jeep made the sharp turn. As we swerved around the corner, the road immediately ahead of us was littered with bodies and more debris. As he turned the wheel hard, Guevara slammed on the brakes, and barely stopped the jeep without rolling it over.

All four of us got out of the jeep and began clearing the road of the grisly scene. There were hundreds of bodies lying around both the road and the surrounding terrain. We were astonished at this sight, and Guevara grew angry.

"My God," he exclaimed, "how many brave men died like this? How many of these are the enemy?"

Canen and the lieutenant worked together to clear bodies, while I helped Guevara. As we started to move a corpse, he looked up at me. "It doesn't matter what we do, we will still kill them in the end. We will kill all of them!"

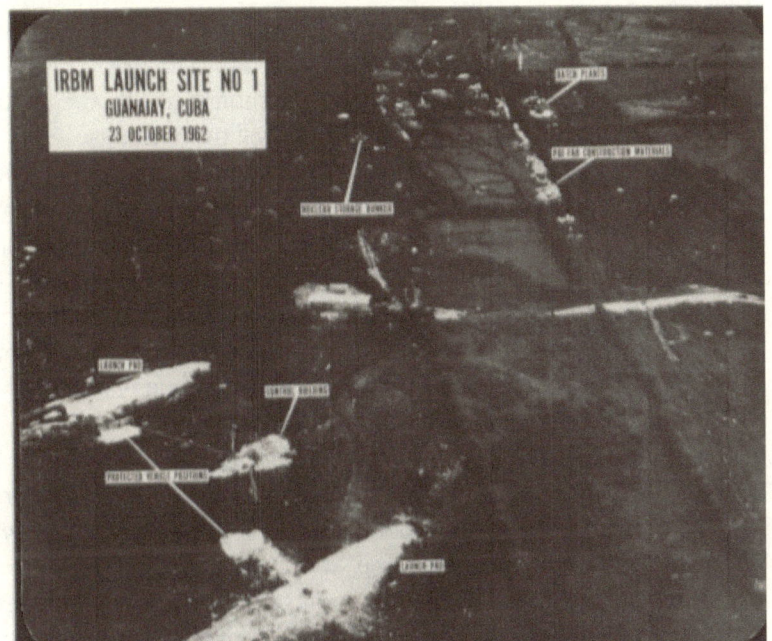
Aerial View, Secret Cuban Missile Base

ICBM in Cuba, part of the secret installations

I was sickened by what surrounded me. "I have never seen...." I couldn't finish my thought.

Guevara mistook my revulsion for dismay and tried to cheer me up. He indicated the dead man we had just picked up between us. "Hey, don't worry, Comandantico. It's these guys that are dead, not you and me. That's all that matters."

I was still in a mild state of shock and so did not answer. Guevara immediately returned to what was apparently foremost in his thoughts. "If they find those Russian missiles...."

After a while, we took a break from clearing the road. The two of us went over by the jeep to relax for a bit. I pulled out my canteen to take a drink of water, only to find it empty. Guevara's was empty, as well. "I'll look for some water," I said. He nodded at me and waved me off.

I walked over to another jeep that had been abandoned by the side of the road. I searched it for water and, finding none, started to remove the spare gas tank from the back. I was disturbed by a groan below me, and looked down to see a young black man, dressed in the camouflage uniform of the invaders. He croaked out a plea for water. I went over to a nearby body, made sure it was dead, and took the body's canteen to the wounded man. I tilted the water into his mouth, and he opened his eyes. As he looked up at me gratefully, his eyes widened in shocked recognition and he grabbed my arm, speaking in a weak voice. "Julio Antonio...is that you?"

"What?" I asked in puzzlement. "Who...?" I broke off as I looked closely at the man. "Tité?" I said in astonishment. "My God, why are you here?" I looked down and saw that his legs had been nearly destroyed by the blast.

"Is there...more water?" he asked.

I shook the canteen I had gotten for him. It was empty. "I...I'll find you another one," I said, choking back emotion. I searched all the other bodies, all of them dead and dressed as freedom fighters. I found another canteen, this time almost full. I stood up to see where Tité was lying about thirty feet away from me, and saw Guevara standing over him by the jeep.

I got up and walked towards them. Guevara was laughing, and it sounded slightly insane to me. He turned toward me, his pistol in his hand. "Can you believe this nigger piece of shit?" He looked down at Tité. "After all we did for you, this is how you repay us? You son of a bitch, nigger bastard!" He raised his pistol and shot Tité in the head, once, twice, angry but still laughing.

I stood there in absolute shock, the canteen dropping from my nerveless fingers. It fell to the ground, leaking out water onto the pavement as Tité's blood poured from his head.

"He was still a human being...."

Guevara cut me off with a jovial laugh. "You grow up, Comandantico! Our enemies aren't human! They are dogs...worms!" He called out to the other men, who had managed to clear off most of the road. "Hey! Let's go! We have to hurry!"

We walked back to our jeep. I carried the spare gas can I had taken from the abandoned jeep. Guevara stopped next to another dead man, this one dressed in fatigues identifying him as one of Castro's soldiers. One a piece of broken wood beside him, he had written out in blood Cristo Rey (Christ is King.) Guevara knelt, and with his fingers wiped the letters to change the C to an F. He continued so that it spelled "Fidel" instead. He then picked up the board and said to me, "Can you imagine that? This man, with his dying blood, wrote 'Fidel.' They will love this, wait until we show it on television!"

I was utterly speechless. Numbly, I followed the other men as they climbed into the jeep. We drove away towards the base.

A few weeks later, I was in a luxury mansion in the Miramar suburb of Havana. The place was lavish with champagne and hors d'oeuvres, delivered by servants. Many happy people were in attendance, men in military uniforms and suits, the women in fancy evening gowns. Near the center of the large reception area, Fidel Castro was surrounded by his cohorts: Raul, Piñeiro, Che, and the other commanders.

He stepped out to address the crowd. "Today, we celebrate our victory; a victory for freedom, for the people. But there are other victories, future victories to come!"

Che stepped forward with two men, Daniel Ortega, a shorter dark-skinned man with a mustache, and his brother Humberto

Ortega, a short man with a paunch. They stood with him as he spoke.

"In Nicaragua, the Revolution is imminent. These comrades of ours will bring freedom to that land with our support."

The crowd cheered this speech. There was a pause, and a short American man with short, greasy hair and a nerdy look was shaking hands with the Ortega brothers, Fidel, and his comrades. I had noticed Che had been talking with him, separate from the group for a while. He came back to the group. "Hey, hey, hey! I want to announce something big here. You see this man here? He will be instrumental in changing the course of history."

The man, Lee Harvey Oswald, looked modest and embarrassed at so much attention.

"What those worms don't know is that the Revolution is great! It is bigger than one man, bigger than us all. They've been trying to kill Fidel several times. We will cut off the head of the snake, and show those gringos not to fuck around with us. Our socialist ideas are the only route to end poverty in this world, and this man just arrived from the Soviet Union with great training from the Russian comrades." Che pushed Oswald forward to speak.

"Uh, mucho gusto," he said in broken Spanish. "Yo soy Lee Harvey Oswald. Muera el imperialismo yankee." He nodded at them as Che applauded, and the party went back to its festive mood.

I was standing next to Canen, my sister's husband. He was the military commander of the Occidental side of the island. As the applause finished, we turned to each other. He told me, "Boy, things happen so fast! Now we are not only concerned about our Revolution, we're concerned about the Revolution of the whole continent."

Che and Oswald went out to one of the terraces to smoke cigars, smiling and talking. At the entrance, a young woman entered the room. She had long black hair and wore a long, ivory dress that accentuated her small waist and large breasts. Canen watched her entering from behind me and grinned. "Looks like trouble," he said.

"What?" I said. I turned around and saw her, and she absolutely took my breath away for a moment. Then I recognized her as Sandra, one of my childhood friends that I had played baseball with. I quickly recovered as she approached me to say hello.

"My," she said, "how handsome you are in your uniform. I almost didn't recognize you."

"God, Sandra! How long has it been? At least three or four years?"

She smiled, looking down for a moment through her long eyelashes. "Only two years and three months." He turned to Canen. "Who is this?"

"Ah, yes," I replied, "my brother-in-law, Canen."

He took her hand and kissed it gently. "I will leave you two alone to enjoy your reunion."

I walked her out to the terrace, which overlooked the ocean. On this clear day, the waves broke gently over the beach. I stood close to her, both of us holding our drinks. I looked at her surreptitiously. "How long have you been back?"

"A while now. You just missed my birthday." She smiled as she noticed I was admiring her figure. "You have grown as well. Look at your arms." She squeezed one of my arms. "All that manly military training."

"Speaking of which," I said, "you have been training as well, I see."

"Yes, I and my brother Julian both got scholarships to the superior naval academy for intelligence."

"Wow! That sounds really mysterious," I said jokingly. She smiled, and I thought to myself, if she only knew! Aloud, I added, "It's nice that you can be with your brother so he can take care of you."

She smiled at me. "I think it is more like me taking care of him." She winked at me, and then looked at me more seriously. "Have you ever heard from Yaneba?"

"The last I heard, she and her family were all killed, trying to leave Cuba to Florida in a boat."

"That is the fate of the traitors."

I grabbed her arm and turned her towards me. "She used to be your friend."

"She used to be my friend. Now she's joined the worms."

I turned serious and obviously upset. "You don't know why she did it, Sandra. Maybe her parents took her and made her come with them. Does friendship mean so little to you, like so many others these days?" I let her go, staring out sadly at the ocean. I said to myself, "Revolution first, friendship second, family last."

She took my arm. "I'm sorry. Every day, I hear my instructors speak this way...and I am starting to repeat it. I have forgotten to think for myself." She squeezed my arm and stared into the ocean with me as tears filled her eyes. "That is what I've always liked about you. You are different: you call the bread, bread, and the wine, wine."

Inside the salon, Fidel, Che, Oswald, and the Ortega brothers were all having a good time, and we heard them all screaming, "Enjoy!"

I turned to Sandra, and asked, "May I kiss you?" She nodded, still with tears in her eyes, and we shared a long kiss.

Through the salon glass, her father, Ortiz, a short, squat man dressed in a minister's uniform, was looking around for someone. Occasionally, people stopped him in greeting and to shake his hand. He extricated himself quickly to keep looking. Canen stood outside, and noticed Ortiz looking for his daughter. He rushed to the terrace door and broke us up. "I think her father is looking for her," he said.

Sandra hurriedly handed me a piece of paper before leaving. "My numbers, at the academy and my phone at home." She gave me another quick, tender kiss, and went inside. As Canen closed the door behind her, Ortiz appeared.

"Sandra," he said, "I was looking for you."

She smiled at her father and said, "I just was looking at the ocean and enjoying the breeze."

The next week, we were in the Revolution Plaza in Havana as Fidel Castro delivered another speech to the mandatory crowd. He was saying, "We love our fatherland; we love the well-being of our people; we love the wealth we create with our hands; but mankind comes before the fatherland. Eternal life to the heroes who fell in Giron fighting for the fatherland and fighting for mankind. Fatherland or death, we shall win!" He turned and entered the room in the house where the Inner Ring were all seated while he made his speech. As he shut the door, the sound of people weeping and cheering at his speech was muffled.

Che and Raul clap lightly for him, smiling. Che said, "Excellent, Commandante!"

Fidel smiled broadly, and said, "Baa, baa!" We looked at him in astonishment for a moment before he continued. "These morons are just like sheep. They believe whatever shit I tell them!"

A few weeks later, I accompanied Canen to the site where they had started to build the missile base at San Cristobal. The loud sound of bulldozers was heard as they busily moved and cleared dirt as other men in military dress ran around, moving boxes, carrying equipment, and working other construction jobs.

We walked up to the top of a small hill as we watched the men. I put a small pen in my pocket. A detail of men with crowbars and bolt cutters popped the metal latch on a large green crate labeled with Russian markings. They extracted parts of a large missile from the box and some men hauled it off, while the detail moved on to open the next crate. A pair of high-ranking Soviet military advisors walked up to observe the work, frowning.

Canen, Julio Antonio's brother-in-law (Zenen), Miramar Gardens, Havana, Cuba

I said, "Fidel Castro must trust you a lot, putting you in charge of this installation."

"The reward of hard work, my brother," Canen replied. "Wait until it is finished, what power we will have."

I looked grimly at the preparations, subtly clicking the pen over the open crates, secretly taking microfilm pictures of the missile parts. Later on, we sat at the table in a luxury mansion, one of those left behind by the wealthy that had left the island, disaffected by the communist regime and appropriated by Castro and his men. We were finishing dinner, and my sister was clearing the table, and I wiped my face and put down the napkin. I looked at her and said, "A delicious meal. Now, I should visit my uncle while I'm in town."

We all stood up, and Canen said, "Yes, of course. My wife is a great cook." He walked me to the door, and he said quietly, "It's nice of you to compliment my wife's cooking. You know it was overdone."

I smiled and said, "Yes, well, she's my sister, too, and I don't want to get her mad." We clapped each other on the back, and I left for my uncle's.

It was late evening as I reached his house, everything tinged orange by the setting sun. I pulled up in a black Volga, one of the Russian models now in frequent use in Cuba. My uncle hugged me in greeting and ushered me into the living room.

"Ah, Julio Antonio. I've been waiting for you. Sit down, sit down. We've got a lot to talk about."

"Yes, I've got a lot for you, and a big surprise for our friends." I took out my pen and handed it to him. "The whole installation. Russian designed missiles. And this is only one of many locations they are setting up."

"Good job, Julio Antonio. If only our friends believe the danger."

"They could hit the United States within a few months. It would kill so many people...."

"Then," my uncle said with determination, "they will have to listen." He looked at the pen grimly.

Nineteen sixty-one was the third year of the Revolution. Castro was gathered with his commanders in a conference room in the Prime Minister's office. He slammed down a newspaper with the headline, "Russia Brings Cutting Edge Military Technology to Cuba." His advisors looked startled for a moment. Che, Canen, Piñeiro, Raul, and Ramiro all looked worried. Piñeiro, a thin, middle-aged man, stroked his red beard.

"First," Castro said, "he released secret documents about the air force. Now, our enemies know about our secret weapons from the USSR!"

"The Lightning," Piñeiro observed, "has struck again."

"Who is this man?" Castro demanded.

"He must be someone high ranking, in our military or higher circles," Piñeiro replied.

"The U.S. is sending in U2 spy planes," Canen said, "they are finding all the bases."

"We will have to relocate them all," Piñeiro said. "It will take months."

Castro's face was mottled in fury. "How do we get this man? This...traitorous pig!"

Piñeiro looked up calmly. "Commandante en Jefe, I have a plan. We will put out the bait, and see if the fish bites."

Fidel said, "Make sure all of the military bases with the new weapons are relocated immediately. And this time, let's put them underground where the gringos can never see them with their spy planes!"

Office of the Prime Minister, Vedado, Havana 3:45 am

I was driving in my Soviet jeep. I got to the guards at the entry to the compound. They recognized me at once, and gestured me through as they raised the barrier gate to allow me to pass. I drove into the compound and headed towards to parking area near the buildings which housed the Economic Department. I parked the jeep and walked towards the building in the center and rang the buzzer by the double glass doors. A few seconds later, Huberto, one of my colleagues at work, came and opened the door, a smile on his face. He looked at his watch, and remarked, "Wow! You're really early today. It's only fifteen minutes until four!" He passed to me the Soviet PPSh-41 that was the duty weapon.

I said, "Well, it's better to relieve you fifteen minutes early than when you relieve me thirty minutes late."

He grimaced, not happy to hear that. He straightened his uniform hat and his pistol, and replied, "Thank you for not trying to get even with me. I need to go home early today. I'm really tired." He made a gesture with his hand, and said, "See you tomorrow," and headed out to the parking lot.

I waved to him in reassurance and locked the door behind him without a word. I went directly to my office. I removed the machine gun from my shoulder and placed it in the reclining chair. I sat down, took out my keys, and unlocked the bottom drawer in my desk. I opened the drawer, leaned slightly to my right, and removed a round plastic baby powder container. I put it on the edge of the drawer, closed the drawer halfway, and then twisted the tube in an attempt to open it. The bottom half was actually a secret compartment containing a device, while the top inch or two of the tube remained full of powder, to disguise the real nature of the container. I removed the top half, placed it on the desk, and removed the device. It detected electrical current: a green light meant that the room was clear, but if the red light was lit, that meant there was some kind of surveillance equipment in the room, whether a camera, microphone, or other bugging device. I turned the button on. Both lights came on; after a couple of seconds, the red light flicked off, while the green light remained on. I got up from my desk, walked around for a few minutes, passing the detector by every lamp, light, and wall in my office. The light continued to be green. I went back to my desk, placed the other half of the container in the drawer, and closed and locked the drawer. I picked up the detector and my rifle, and walked out of the office.

I went to the end of the corridor, where there was a double door marked Prime Minister's Office. Private. Do Not Enter. I took my keychain out of my pocket, selected the master key, and opened the doors. I slowly entered the room, and closed the doors, taking great care not to make any noise. I started to go around the large, luxurious office, checking every fixture and wall in the room. This took me quite a while. In the second office, the light turned red by a painting of a typical Cuban landscape. Slowly, very carefully, I moved the picture up, watching the growing intensity of the red light, until I saw the tiny wires connecting the picture to the wall. The safe I was looking for was concealed by the picture, so I left the picture slightly inclined to remind myself where the wires ended at the picture, and then followed the course of the wiring.

Sometimes I missed it, and the red light flickered, went out, and the green light came on. Then I would have to backtrack until the red light came back on and grew bright with the actual track of the wires. It took me a while, back and forth, to follow the signal to a small room at the end of the last office with metal doors and deadbolt locks. It took me some effort to unlock this door, but at last I found the appropriate master key. When I opened the door, I noticed at the end of the room a metal panel like those used for an electrical fuse box. I opened it, and saw different small, tiny breakers in different colors. It looked like a very sophisticated alarm system for the different rooms inside the entire complex of the prime minister's offices. To avoid confusion, I switched off all the breakers. I got out of that room, leaving everything open, including the panel on the wall. I went back to the office with the picture.

I removed the picture from the wall, taking care to avoid breaking the delicate connection of the cable. I placed the picture on a nearby executive chair, the kind of revolving office chair with a long back. I pulled out a small plastic container from the pocket of my uniform a pair of latex gloves. I put them on and pulled out a stethoscope from another pocket. I placed my device against the wall, and the light turned green. I felt good, since that meant that one of the breakers on the panel had disconnected that particular alarm.

Using the stethoscope to hear the clicking of the tumblers, I started work on the combination of the lock on the safe. After a couple of failed attempts, I managed to find the right combination and opened the safe. My forehead was drenched with perspiration, and I wiped my brow with the sleeve of my shirt. Perhaps the air conditioner had been turned off or was broken yet again.

I removed from the safe a few folders, and selected the one I was looking for: one sealed in wax and marked with the national emblem of Cuba and marked on the front in large letters Three Continental. Classified. International. Official Use Only. Office of the Prime Minister.

I took out of my shirt pocket a small piece of paper, unfolded it, and picked up the razor blade that was concealed in it. Very carefully, very slowly, I cut the border on the bottom of the envelope.

I removed the contents and withdrew from the inside of my shirt some papers, which I then slid into the envelope. With a tiny tube of transparent glue, I slowly sealed the envelope back up. I tucked the real documents under my shirt, and proceeded to replace everything in the safe, meticulously ensuring that everything was in the same order as I had found them. I closed the safe, and again taking care not to break the contact with the wires, replaced the picture.

I went back to the small room in the other office. I closed my eyes and fervently prayed that nothing was disconnected and then turned all the breakers back on. I stayed still for a few seconds, and was greeted with silence. All was well, and I smiled, closed the box back up, and carefully made my way back out, closing and locking the doors behind me. After I confirmed with my detector over the picture that everything was in order, I got out of the office, again taking care to close and lock everything behind me.

I came back to my office, took the documents from my shirt, and placed them next to the documents in my portfolio. I unlocked the drawer, opened it, returned the detector to the tube in the drawer, rejoined the two sections, and relocked the drawer. I went to the bathroom, removed my shirt, and washed the perspiration off under the faucet. I finished refreshing myself and my brain after the adrenaline rush I had just gone through.

The first part of the plan was done.

I dried myself, put my shirt back on, and had to wait until 9:00 a.m., when everyone else started to come back to the office, and my once-weekly, five-hour shift on guard duty was over. I sat down behind my desk, and tried to relax, hoping that everything would go well, and that the next day, everything would be okay.

Evidently, I relaxed too much, because I fell asleep. A few hours must have passed, and I was awoken abruptly by a sound like a gun shot and voices outside the building. The alarms started to sound loudly, and I grew nervous, thinking it might have had something to do with my activities. I tried to pull myself together, because I knew what pains I had taken. There was no reason for the alarms to start ringing after so many hours. I looked at my watch and went over to the window to look out at the parking lot and the front gate.

I saw the soldiers at the gate pulling out, and it looked like a man had been shot. Another had his hands up, and they were searching him. They were arguing with the man. I couldn't hear very well, between the thick glass of the window and the distance between where I was and the front gate. The guards tried to disarm the other man, but he was resisting. One of the guards got close to him to try and wrest away the pistol from the man, but he instead was trying to grab the guard's rifle. The other guard shot several times, hitting the man in the chest. He collapsed, I assumed, dead. The soldiers, officers, and other official civilian personnel started to come out of the other buildings.

I was glued to the window, paralyzed for a few minutes, hoping the whole ordeal had nothing to do with me. I reacted by picking up my portfolio and started to walk out into the corridor. I expected at any minute to hear a voice behind me to command me to halt. I felt a little more comfortable when I saw some of our workers coming into our building, full of confusion and asking what was going on.

I replied to them, shaking my head, "I don't know. I was just in my office and heard the shots and the screaming. I don't know what happened."

Everything was in confusion, and the military police started to arrive in jeeps, closing off the entire compound. One of the soldiers, the one who had fired the shots, had blood on his face. He screamed, "These are spies. I received orders to search them, and they resisted."

The MPs grabbed the bodies and dragged them to the wet grass near the exit off the parking lot. They started to check for signs of life and started to question everyone that was there. The scene was very confused, with people coming in to work, people coming out to see what was going on.

Cuba: Russian Roulette of the World

When I heard the word "spy," my spine froze, and I asked, "Lord, please don't let these people start to search everyone here." I started slowly to make my way towards my jeep. I got into the parking lot, got inside my jeep, placed my portfolio on the seat, and slowly started to drive out of the compound towards the gate. When I was almost there, the relief soldiers opened the barrier to let me out.

I was almost clear of the barrier when one of the MPs yelled at the soldiers, "Don't let anybody out until we secure the area and know what's really happened here!"

I ignored that command and kept going. In my rear-view mirror, I could see the guard bring the barrier back down. I kept driving, hoping that they wouldn't order me to turn around. As I put some distance between myself and the compound, I breathed deeply and thanked God a million times to be able to get out one more time out of that situation without a problem.

CHAPTER V: "FREE" COMMUNIST SCHOLARSHIPS

Fidel called 1961 the Year of Education. In reality, it was another year of complete failure and tremendous propaganda to the detriment of the Cuban people and the world. I personally saw from beginning to end the so-called "Literacy Campaign." I was in charge of the Rio Frio area, in the municipality of Mayari, Oriente Province. The person responsible for the program in the Eastern Zone was Maria de Los Angeles, Commander Agibay's sister.

The impudence displayed by the Communists in deceiving others and even themselves was outrageous. For instance, the farmers did not want the literacy squads in their homes. First of all, they had to feed them; and secondly, most of these farmers were adults no longer interested in going back to school. Some had unmarried daughters and were not keen on housing strangers with whose background they were unfamiliar. In other cases, they were newlyweds who resented intruders. In short, it was a chaotic, undesirable situation.

Of course, the opposite was also occasionally true. The farmer would accept the volunteer feigning enthusiasm for the Revolution. Later on, he would put him to work as a beast of burden, until the volunteer, fed up with so much manual labor, abandoned the campaign. Sometimes these disgruntled volunteers complained to the Communists in charge, but they would do nothing. Hadn't Fidel said the volunteer would not be a burden for the farmer and should help him during the day, as much as he could? Castro did not envision the farmers putting unwanted visitors to work as slaves, hastening their departure.

In spite of these difficulties Fidel Castro was mailed a million letters, prepared on orders by the Communist leaders. The Machiavellian idea behind this was to deceive the world, by having the literacy volunteers write on behalf of the farmers, stating: "Commander Fidel Castro, I have learned to read and write correctly." Properly armed with this "proof," Castro then declared to the world that Cuba was the first country in America that had succeeded in stamping out illiteracy.

My mission was accomplished, and I returned to Havana and a new apartment in Vedado. I felt lonely, especially since my estrangement from my parents. I practically became a hermit. Nothing interested me. I only wanted to be alone. My usually happy disposition had been deeply shaken by separation from my father, whom I loved and had considered my best friend.

1961-Photo of the Author

One morning I awoke thinking the day was perfect for underwater fishing. Collecting my equipment, I readied to go when I heard a knock on the door. It was the mailman bearing a telegram. "It's very important," he announced joyously, "from the Prime Minister's office!"

The mailman departed, and after some hesitation, I opened the envelope. The telegram simply read: "Present yourself at the office of the Prime Minister, located at 11 Street in Vedado. We want to interview you." It was signed by Celia Sanchez Manduley, Secretary of the Prime Minister. The telegram took away my desire to go fishing.

Fidel's offices were enclosed by fences with soldiers everywhere. It resembled a military headquarters more than government offices. I was led to a small receiving room. A few minutes later Celia appeared, thin and plain-looking, carrying some papers in her hand. She greeted me kindly. "Fidel and I have talked to a great deal about you. You're an intelligent boy and we think you have the makings of a first-class revolutionary leader." Then she sat by me, asking what I would like to study. She did not give me time to answer. "Wouldn't you like to study in the Soviet Union?" she asked.

I faced a serious dilemma. If I told her I didn't want to study under the Communist education system I would declare myself an enemy of the Revolution. To gain time, and free myself from the prospect of going to the Soviet Union, I improvised naïve delight. "Actually, I would like to study music here in Cuba," I replied.

Celia looked at me astonished. "Music?" she repeated, managing to repress a displeased frown. "Well, if that's what you want…." She had no other alternative but to agree.

"Yes, that's what I want," I confirmed with a smile.

"All right, I'll give you a scholarship to study music at the Cubanacan Conservatory. You'll like it. It's in the former Country Club, a really beautiful place."

She gave me a handwritten note introducing me to the director of these schools and we said good-bye. How funny: a simple note from this woman was enough to have me admitted at the Conservatory, and a different little note from her would be enough to send someone to prison for twenty years like my friend, Commander Huber Matos.

At the Country Club where the National Arts School was located, the director's fawning attention made me uncomfortable. Once the interview was over, I was installed in my new home, a grand mansion expropriated from God knows whom, Building number 1103. There I saw my old friend Pablo, who studied the saxophone while I studied percussion. We bumped into each other under strained circumstances. One day, at lunch time, he and a very tall black man stared at me in the dining room. The black man was telling Pablo something, and he smiled. It didn't affect me. The rumors had spread that I was a special student with a scholarship sent by Celia and Fidel. This intrigued them. Almost all the students sent there had been enrolled by the Education Council. I was the only one placed by the Revolution's top leaders.

Barely had I started to eat when I saw a dark hand grab my small ration of bread. Raising my eyes in surprise, I gazed into the eyes of a black man who had been staring at me. "Put it on my bill," he said shamelessly, returning to the table where he sat with Pablo and two others.

I got up calmly and went to their table. "What did you do that for?" I asked.

As I had wanted him to, he answered defiantly, beginning to get up. I didn't let him. With my left hand I grabbed his shirt collar, and with my right, I grabbed his hair, banging his head repeatedly against the tray, breaking the glass top into many pieces. The students rushed to break up the altercation. His face was covered with blood.

The people in charge of the dining room discipline took him to the Infirmary. I was taken to the School Director's office, the monitor told me I was a savage who was to be expelled from the school. I didn't respond. In the presence of the Director, he continued his tirade, but fortunately, the Director insisted on hearing my version. Then Pablo appeared, not to accuse me, but to verify and testify I was not to be blame for the incident.

From then on, Pablo and I became best friends. I learned from him that the man had required four stitches in the right eyebrow and had lost two upper teeth. I felt sorry for his injuries, but justified because he was a bully.

My father sent me a modest weekly allowance, a bourgeois gesture, according to the Communists. All the mail passed through the hands of the monitor. Often, I heard comments about my father being a bourgeois and a capitalist, a rumor that probably spread because my old man sent me a check in envelopes imprinted with his business letterhead.

I stayed in that school for a long time, applying myself to my music studies. In addition to percussion, I was receiving general music education, composition and harmony, voice lessons, corporal expression or dance, and other subjects required for a bachelor's degree. If I were to eventually leave the country, it would be advantageous to have a good education. Naturally, being a minor, I couldn't travel without my parents' permission: adulthood was years away. I had decided to graduate as a symphonic orchestra percussionist, but very soon I had to change plans.

One morning, several trucks loaded with militia men arrived at school. They assembled us in front of our respective rooms and read to us a new manifesto declaring that the school would be operated by military instructors. We had to awaken at the sound of a whistle and go to bed in the same manner. We also had the obligation to perform military drills, joining in the sugarcane cutting and other farm work on all weekends and any weekday required by the Agriculture Plans.

The situation was worsening day by day. We spent more time marching, doing military training practice and working in the field than taking lessons. This hard work left us too tired to do more than sleep right after dinner. There was no time to study.

Every morning we were awakened by a disagreeable militia man, who we nicknamed "The Dandy," because he spent the entire day combing his hair. Plump and short, and quite ridiculous in his uniform, it was a laugh even to see him walk.

For weeks, his hateful signaling whistle made us jump from bed at six a.m. After the whistle came a shout: "Up, Up!"

Pablo and I, of course, plotted to play a dirty trick on him. We talked to the rest of the fellows in 1103 and the day of reckoning was arranged. That evening, Pablo and I sneaked out of school after roll call, and the usual evening whistle call to silence.

We climbed out a window leading to the patio, and unseen, reached the bus stop in front of the Country Club and headed by bus to Havana's downtown section. With some effort, we found what we were looking for in a children's store. It was a whistle.

We returned to school (and to bed) happily anticipating the prank to be perpetrated on the Dandy. Our dormitories were on the upper floor and my bunk faced the front window. From my bed I could watch the street where we lined up for military drills.

Usually, when the militia man blew his whistle, we had to be in formation within fifteen minutes. That morning, I woke up before it was our turn, and from the window saw all the lodgings being emptied of the occupants, already lined up military style in front of their houses. The Dandy could not believe his eyes when he realized no one in residence 1103 had gone down to formation. He blew the whistle again, now furiously, then got closer to our house and said some foul words. He had hardly finished when from upstairs somebody shouted to him. "Shut up, pig!"

The militia man, completely petrified for a moment, asked himself, "What the hell is that? Is that a rebellion?" His surprise grew even greater when he heard from upstairs a whistle, which grew even louder as someone blew it furiously. It was the same kind of whistle he carried, and heard a bunch of boys crying, "Postman! Postman!" In Cuba, when the postman had important mail he was delivering, he would blow a whistle as he deposited it in the box. In the Castro-Communist system, being a postman was considered the lowest form of work.

The militia man flew up the stairs, hurling insults and threats. Realizing, however, that this attitude was taking him nowhere, he retreated with his troop to the dining room leaving the unruly squad in 1103 behind.

Taking advantage of the fact the professors and the rest of the staff were eating breakfast, Pablo and I went to the conservatory where the musical instruments were stored, wrecking dozens of them. That afternoon we were visited by the director of the school and two officers of the G-2.

We were charged with sabotage of state property and being counterrevolutionaries. They even insinuated that among us there were CIA agents. For ten hours they questioned us individually, but we all maintained that we didn't know what happened in the conservatory. Our excuse for having not gone to formation that morning was being totally fatigued after spending the previous day cutting sugarcane. At midnight, the director and the agents left the lodging, warning us as punishment we couldn't leave the school for several weeks, and to expect further questioning.

While waiting for our detention to end, our school activities continued. For months there had been advertised with great fanfare throughout the island an international festival of modern music. Headquartered in our school, the festival was to be attended by delegates from Asia, Latin America, and Africa.

The director of the school asked me to compose a number for the festival based on musical protest and wanted to offer our guests a sample of the new youth and his creativity as developed in socialist Cuba. After a few hours, I had completed a song whose nature nobody suspected! On the appointed day, the club appeared beautifully decorated, and a magnificent stage had been improvised at the end of the huge swimming pool. National media visitors were there to interview the visitors and film live television coverage.

Various foreign groups were introduced and performed. As our turn neared, I felt my hands get sweaty. Finally, they called on us and, after other students performed, I was summoned to the stage and presented to the applauding public by the master of ceremonies. I sat at the piano to play my protest:

JULIO ANTONIO'S AVE MARIA

This song sprang from me
As an ardent protest
Against those who in the world
Who try to kill the faith in God
And in the lives of men...
Ave Maria, Ave Maria,
Mother of Baby Jesus.
They say once upon a time
The Lord saw a child in the road.
One little leg was lame
And the child Jesus saw.
"Come to me, little child,
And his hand caressed...
The child ran away...
Ave Maria.
And I ask myself,
Those who do not believe at all,
What do they live for?
What do they want to live their lives for? (bis)
And I say, Ave Maria...

Dr. Julio Antonio del Marmol

Cuba: Russian Roulette of the World

"Ave Maria" Music Score

When I finished my song, my eyes were wet, and the public was stunned. First, I heard the isolated applause, then a deafening ovation. Many Spanish-American students asked for copies of the score and lyrics. I agreed, gladly, but I never had a chance to fulfill this request. The director of the school and two G-2 members, always smiling, pulled me away from the crowd and almost forcibly took me to the director's office. There, they pestered me with questions that I tried to answer as cleverly as I could.

"I believe that there are people who are trying to kill faith in God," I explained, "and they are wicked and greedy men. My protest is against them. Socialism respects religion and tries to do justice. Frankly, you've misinterpreted my protest....."

One of the fellows cut me off and said, "Yes, but even though socialism respects religion, we don't believe in it. Religion is a fraud against society."

"Very well," I said, "you are entitled to your own opinion. But I've composed this piece in good faith, because the director asked me."

The director hastened to clarify. "All right, we believe there's been a misinterpretation."

After a short pause, they indicated I could leave. I was asked to return the original paper of my composition "Julio Antonio's Ave Maria" and forbidden to reproduce it, in order to avoid further misinterpretations. I only hoped that my message would remain in many hearts forever.

The Castro regime oppressed many who believed in God. In fact, there were many riots in Jewish neighborhoods where "good" communist citizens destroyed and burned Jewish family stores and property. Many Jews were sent away to work camps just for displaying their faith. Some families had even fled to Cuba in the 1930s and '40s to escape oppression by the Nazis, only then to be oppressed in the next generation by the anti-religious movement inherent to Castro's communism.

The quarantine imposed on us eventually gave me the excuse to present my resignation to the director, still declaring myself innocent of the incident that had brought it about. He flatly told me I couldn't leave the boarding school before the period of punishment had elapsed. Furthermore, I had to submit a letter signed by my parents or tutors.

I was aghast. My parents' authorization had not been required when I entered the school. Now it was needed in order to leave the place! My protests were in vain. I had to wait for the quarantine to be lifted.

At least I was allowed to get out with a 48-hour pass and I wasted none of my precious time. Since I could not produce a letter signed by my father, with whom I had not spoken since I left my home (though my mother and I wrote frequently), I went to see my uncle explaining the situation. They accompanied me to the boarding school and signed as my tutors. The director had to give me credit for the studies I had completed in that institution.

With this letter and a test, I was accepted in the University of Havana, in the School of Veterinary Medicine. I would have preferred to study civil law, but that school was closed. "Attorneys for what?" Fidel had asked. There were no more attorneys in Cuba.

Before leaving the school, the director gave me a letter from my mother. Its contents made me happy. Two militia men had visited and invited my father to organize a Revolution Defense Committee (CDR) to watch his neighbors. This had outraged my father, who had replied that if the Revolution fulfilled Fidel Castro's promises to the people, there would be no enemies and it wouldn't be necessary to watch anyone. According to my mother, the militia men took their leave without even saying good-bye.

In 1962, I was sitting in my uncle's living room. My uncle was holding his head in his hand. "They knew," he said, "and they did nothing! They just let them build the sites!"

I shook my head. "I gave them the photos...they saw the missiles. Even gave them locations."

"The deal with the Soviets is a fraud," my uncle observed. "Kennedy agreed to no inspections of the missile removal."

"And the Soviets transported loads of fake missile parts," I replied, "while leaving the real ones here."

"And they moved them!" my uncle exclaimed.

"Don't worry," I reassured him, "I will get pictures of the new locations and prove the fraud."

"Kennedy's name is a joke," my uncle said in disgust. "The Yankee Donkey." I put my hand on my uncle's shoulder sympathetically.

A year passed. The great hypocrite Castro had thrown off all the false pretenses and finally declared himself a communist, though he had told his people his revolution was as green as the Cuban palm trees and only his enemies wanted to dress it in red! A communist, the man who had declared he never would break bread with the murderers of the Hungarian people! What a blow for my father and many others who, like him, had cooperated with the revolution in the belief they were helping to establish a democratic and honest government in Cuba!

CHAPTER VI: SABOTAGE

I decided to apply myself to organize a clandestine group within the University of Havana to combat Fidel Castro's Government. I met many anticommunist young men, and among them the most memorable were Eduardo and Chino, as well as my old friends Kinqui, Cisneros, and Pablo. We met at the home of a professor on C-Street, Vedado, to plan a method of underground sabotage. We decided to first sabotage the public telephones in the capital, then burn sugarcane in the areas adjacent to Havana City.

We also acquired a small manual press and printed proclamations exhorting the students and people, asking them to open their eyes to Fidel's treason and the true nature of his communism. To carry out this project we needed many recruits. I suggested a plan that could not be subverted or infiltrated by the G-2.

For instance, Kinqui would choose two people he completely trusted and would not have any relation with members of our group. Each individual, in turn, would choose two others following the same procedure. In this way the origin of orders for action was unclear. In case of denunciations, no one would positively know the mastermind of strategy. The maximum penalty would be applied to informers. Following this procedure, each of us only directly knew two individuals, in whom, of course, he trusted implicitly.

By this method, we successfully sabotaged Havana bus routes 60, 76, and 31. We even managed to set fire to some buses in the heart of Havana and in suburban neighborhoods, making them appear to be accidents due to faulty automotive parts provided by the government and poor maintenance rather than the personnel. We wanted to protect the brave men in charge of these operations.

We destroyed sugarcane and we disabled telephones. This almost resulted in a jam one time when I urgently needed to make a telephone call. I was trying to stop an act of sabotage, and the first three telephones I tried were out of order. Fortunately, I was given permission to use a private phone is a restaurant. After I made my call and anxiety passed, I laughed. I had almost fallen into our own trap!

That same night, Kinqui's people wreaked havoc with the telephone receivers. They were cut off and thrown into a basket. Not even the crowded Havana Libre hotel, formerly the Havana Hilton, was spared.

We lacked live phosphorus and other incendiary devices to burn the sugarcane. We had to prepare Molotov cocktails, bottling gasoline, putting cotton waste into the neck and lighting it up at the moment of throwing them. We were taking a huge risk because at night the lighted bottle was visible within a large radius, and this sometimes resulted our being shot at. They started to place watchmen in the sugarcane plantations, and we had to attack closer to the city. Eventually, this activity also had to be suspended.

At a meeting between Kinqui, Cisneros, Pablo, Eduardo, Chino, and me, we toyed with the idea of asking for help from abroad. We desperately needed arms and explosives. Kinqui, a slender, dark-complexioned fellow, a brave and great pal, told me, "Julio Antonio, do you think we could leave Cuba, make some connections, and find a way to smuggle explosives and detonators onto the island? We've got to wipe out this communism, once in for all. What we're doing now, burning some sugarcane here and there, won't overthrow Fidel."

The others laughed, but I took him seriously, "Kinqui is right. We can't go on fighting without the necessary means."

At that moment, there was a knock at the door. Kinqui jumped from his seat by the window, from where he could see the street through the curtain corner. "It's the police," he whispered.

There was a patrol car outside. The mere fact that we were gathered in a house loaded with proclamations and a printing press in the den was compromising. We locked ourselves in the bedroom while the Professor opened the front door. We listened to voices from our hiding place. After half an hour we heard the door slammed.

Our friend came to give the all clear, annoyed by the unnecessary scare caused by a triviality. The government had given the house next door to a communist family. Before our arrival that night the Professor had walked around the garden in the same attire in which he had received us, white shorts and a white pullover. The neighbors, who had girls, had called the police to complain that the man next door was walking around indecently dressed.

"Can you imagine?" our host said. "These trashy people telling me how to dress in my own home? This is too much, too much," he kept repeating bitterly.

Eduardo, tall and thin, made light of everything. We called him "slow poke," to which he invariably answered, "Yes, slow but sure…" That evening, after the police had gone, he turned on the TV. Coincidently, Commander Raul Castro was on the screen. People whispered that Fidel's brother was a homosexual. To amuse us, Eduardo mimicked him. He walked around with mincing steps and effeminate gestures, until Chino, who owed his nickname to his Asiatic features, but had a fiery temperament, stood up and scolded Eduardo.

"Look, buddy, stop clowning and take the son of a bitch off the screen!" Chino exclaimed.

"Wait, Chino, let's hear," I butted in. "I think they're talking about the Compulsory Military Service. This is important." After we listened to the most important information, I said, "Okay, let's turn it off. We've heard enough rubbish."

The following hours were spent assigning tasks and discussing our plans. We had to pick up materials the next day and take them to the Professor's home, to be distributed to the various groups. Fresh events prevented it. Prior to my rendezvous with others, a guard delivered telegraphs dictating that I be medically examined, that same evening, before joining the Compulsory Military Service.

I lost control when my uncle showed me the demand at breakfast. I hit the dining room table hard with my fist. No doubt I would pass. I was seventeen years old, strong, although of medium height, and in training at school camps, at the gymnasium, in Cubanacan, and most recently at the University.

"Remember who you are," my uncle said. "Remember what we trained you for. Continue your fight that your mission will never end. All the survival skills and training will be useful for you now to maintain your fight for the freedom of Cuba."

"I could lead all my friends to burn all the recruiting telegrams in protest," I suggested.

"Are you out of your mind?" exclaimed my uncle. "What would you solve by doing it? Are you going to liberate your country by being incarcerated? Is that how you are going to topple Fidel Castro? All you'll achieve is destruction at the hands of psychological and physical torturers. Listen, it doesn't pay to confront a more powerful enemy. Use your common sense. Go to Military Service and, once established, study the possibilities of getting out without any problem and go on fighting."

Leaving my breakfast unfinished, I walked through Infanta Street. In the movie house Astral, a Russian war picture was playing. I wondered how much longer God was going to allow this situation to continue. Next to me, a lady and her two small children were looking at the billboards. I also wondered what kind of future awaited these little ones in Cuba. At the Malecon, I leaned against the old, decayed containing wall by the waterfront, staring at the sea and reflecting on how nearby was freedom, the U.S.A., a land where youngsters could study and have good times without being harassed by anyone. In my country, merely being well-groomed was considered a crime. It classified you as a good-for-nothing bourgeois.

I thought of my uncle, a lawyer and university professor, demoted to errand boy, humiliated for not being a revolutionary. After four months he had been forced to quit his job, in spite of Fidel Castro's protestations to the world that unemployment would not exist in the new Cuba! Of course, a single person could not oppose the system. Mere mental opposition was enough to send anyone to the farm if the person was not too old, or to prison if he refused to work for the Castro-Communists. The crimes were to not be a communist, to believe in God, and to love democracy and freedom.

All of my friends already had their telegrams when I arrived on C-Street. All except the Professor, who, of course, was past the age of recruitment. Despite our sadness at the prospect of being separated for the first time, and perhaps forever, we made jokes about the situation, shook hands, and said good-bye.

Returning home, I found that my aunt had prepared a satchel with changes of underwear and other necessary items. I showered and had an early supper before leaving for the medical examination, scheduled at 8:00 p.m. in one of the countless recruiting offices recently opened all over the island. About a thousand youngsters from ages sixteen to twenty were there already. After handing in my paper and being asked to wait outside in line, I sat on the curb, feeling very lonesome. The street resembled a dispersed army. There were packages and satchels, boxes tied with rope, and people sleeping on their bundles in the sidewalk.

Five hours later, at 1:00 in the morning, many military trucks arrived. We were made to line up and they called our names. One by one, the trucks disappeared with loads of people and the street became empty. I was one of the last to be called, so I had an opportunity to see how they covered the trucks with sailcloth. For about three hours we drove around, unaware of our destination.

In complete darkness, we arrived at a place of exuberant vegetation, and judging by the continuous bumping over rugged and sloping roads, a rather mountainous area. We got off the truck, formed lines and were taken to the huge barracks. Each of them had rows of three superimposed bunks, and a capacity for three or four hundred men. I lay dressed in the bed assigned to me with only my shoes off, so tired I didn't notice how hard it was.

At 6:00 in the morning we heard a whistle (I thought to myself, *Oh, no— not again!*), followed by the sound of an unpleasant voice shouting, "Up, up!" I shuddered at the thought of having to listen to him daily. The pedantic, tuneless voice belonged to a plump and ruddy corporal, thirty-five or forty years old. He had no neck and resembled a tortoise. After lineup, walking like a penguin, he'd march us to breakfast, deliberately avoiding a glance to the side where the troop composed of boys taller than him were marching.

Prison cells confirmed my suspicions that the place had been a Soviet military camp. There were eight barracks in total, and a paved practice ground stood in the middle. The recruit dining room was at the right. Yes, the segregation of officers and recruits as far as eating and sleeping facilities continued, despite what Commander Algibay had told me in my first interview with Fidel Castro when I was twelve.

Nearby was the outdoor movie theatre and infirmary. At the left were smaller barracks that served as dormitories, offices, and the Office of the Major Staff of the Military Unit, along with the dismal prison cells.

That first morning, after making us wait under the sun for over two hours, they gave us watery chocolate, the worst I had ever tasted. We were so hungry we gobbled it up with small pieces of bread. Twenty minutes later, the latrines were being overworked. As the lines were endless, the smart ones did their business behind the bushes. Those who patiently waited in line had "accidents" and had to change clothes. A cook with whom I later became acquainted told me recruits brought to the training camp were given jalapa, a very strong laxative, in their breakfast snack, ostensibly to demoralize rebellious spirits. That's why the chocolate served to us had tasted so bitter!

We spent that day racing at full speed to the latrines or bushes. By afternoon, my neighbors in the lower bunks had been taken away. In total, fifty youngsters from my barracks were gone and some from other barracks. At nine in the evening, I was not sleepy. I restlessly walked through the barracks. At the entrance, there was a little table and a stool to accommodate the guards. Over the table, a small clipboard was kept for writing down the watch hours. The signed sheets were picked up in the morning by the corporal, who in turn would take them to the unit Major Staff. This gave me an idea.

At 10:00 p.m. I went to bed like the others, shortly after whistle call. That night, at 2:00 a.m., I heard a bustle of trucks, people moving and shouting. In the half-light I saw newcomers being assigned to bunks. I went back to sleep, feeling sorry for them.

In the morning I didn't hear the whistle. While the rest of the fellows hurriedly dressed, washed their faces, and went to formation, I slept. Since my bunk was the highest, those occupying lower ones did not notice my absence. When they called roll and I did not respond, the corporal asked about me. The others did not know what to say. Suddenly, I felt someone pulling me to my feet, yelling at the top of his voice, "You won't have any breakfast! Get up and sweep the barracks. Get up!" I raised myself with difficulty, staring at him in puzzlement. After all, I was there against my will. He must have read the hatred in my eyes, because he warned me, "Don't look at me like that. In the army, we put tough guys to cut down sugarcane and then eat it."

He made sure I jumped from my bunk and was dressed before taking his leave. I felt tempted to follow him and wring his neck but remembered my uncle's advice. Instead I grabbed the broom and started to sweep.

When my buddies returned from the dining room, the corporal found me still sweeping. "That's enough," he said, "but try not to oversleep." He left with some papers he took from the table to the Major Staff.

By nine in the morning the sun was strong. Taking shelter under the shade of a tree, I heard voices calling to me. It was Kinqui and Eduardo. We hugged and I asked them how they had recognized me from the back with my new crew cut. We all looked alike in our shirts, pants, olive green berets, and boots. My friends knew I was there because they had slept in the same barracks, and in the morning had heard my name called at the formation. They had waited for the corporal to leave before coming near me. If the officer had noticed we were friends, we would have been separated immediately. I inquired about Chino, but they had not heard from him.

"Okay, no more chitchat, let's get you some breakfast," said Kinqui.

"Are you crazy?" I answered. "Whoever doesn't go with the troop doesn't get breakfast or dinner in the dining room."

"That's what you think!" Kinqui said, signaling Eduardo in amusement.

"Hey, guys, what's the matter with you? You just got here last night and already are far too clever," I said.

Kinqui left, but Eduardo stayed with me. Ten minutes later, he came back carrying a pitcher of chocolate and a piece of bread. In the dining room they'd been told to eat as much as they wished. So, Eduardo had smuggled a third helping for me. As I hesitated, touched by his kindness, but fearful, Kinqui said, "Well do you want it or not? Because if you don't, I'll take it!"

"No, Kinqui, we're not going to drink it." I said, spilling it on the ground. "You don't know what you've done. Eduardo, did you drink two rations also?"

"No, I only drank a half portion," he answered.

I told Kinqui this sudden generosity was suspicious. However, he insisted they were doing it to make us happy, sort of preparing us psychologically before giving us arms, so I said, "Oh, I see. Well, Kinqui, did they also give you enough toilet paper?" He didn't have time to answer. He put his hands to his belly and ran to the bathroom.

As the months went by, it became harder to endure the harassment and hard labor to which we were submitted. The short-necked corporal hated me. He would make me squat for two hours or run three hundred times around the practice-ground at double step as punishment for things like having one shirt button unfastened or not shaving closely enough.

One evening, we were taken for the third time to the unit movies. It was not a fun pastime. They ran Soviet films chosen by the Army intelligence: movies of psychological indoctrination with a pointless plot. It was over before it began to make sense. Furthermore, sitting in the open air we were the prey of gnats, mosquitoes, and other biting insects.

That was the evening Kinqui, Eduardo, and I started planning our escape. We agreed that before retiring we would approach the only new person with whom I had started a friendship, my bunk neighbor Miguel Angel. He was fat and short but was a moral giant, as we had the opportunity to appreciate later. We discussed the escape, but he didn't favor the idea of leaving with us.

"A few days ago, five kids attempted to escape and were captured immediately," he said. Captain Valle, who was the Unit Chief and another martinet, had presented them to the rest of the company and sentenced them to five years in La Cabaña prison, serving as examples to any imitators. Furthermore, after completing their sentence, they would have to return to Military service for three more years.

Miguel Angel insisted he was not afraid. But his mother was dying of cancer and she begged him to behave in the Military service. However, he would say "Present" in our places when the roll was called at bedtime. In this way, we would have the night's advantage to get away, making it difficult to catch up with us. I objected, because of the promise to his mother, but Miguel Angel wanted to help us. The roll call was done outside of the barracks, under scanty light. It would be hard to find out who had answered for us. We agreed to escape the next evening.

That night, after roll call and the whistle's blow, I let two hours pass. The guard in the front sat under a small electric bulb which hardly shed light over the table. He held a newspaper up to read but it didn't look as if he could. I got out gingerly, and crept into the next barracks, barefoot, of course because partitions between the barracks were metal sheets that made a lot of noise when one stepped on them. Under the first bunk at the rear I found what I was looking for, grabbed it, and returned to my place. Fortunately, the guard was in the same position. I went to sleep quietly, holding the boot I'd taken from the other barracks, laughing to myself at the thought of its owner's face when he missed it.

When the corporal came into the barracks the following morning, I had been awake for a while. I gave him time to blow his whistle, which he did with the satisfaction of a virtuoso, but before he could shout the usual "Up, up!" the stolen boot flew into the air hitting him in the mouth. He put his hands to his bloody face and yelled, "You criminals! Sons of bitches!" Then he ran to the infirmary.

It's easy to imagine the subsequent confusion. Having waited in vain for the order to get up, everybody asked what had happened. As none could answer, they went back to sleep except for me. I got dressed and washed myself quickly, as if nothing was wrong. The corporal came back twenty minutes later, his upper lip all bandaged, and accompanied by the Unit Captain.

The corporal was hysterical. He started lashing out at those who had gone back to sleep. Between insults and secret grumbles from the recruits, the barrack was a mess. When order was regained, he indicated to the captain the direction from which he believed the boot had been thrown, thus involving three kids from the bunk in front of mine. Their punishment would be to spend three months digging ditches. One of them was Miguel Angel's brother, a sixteen-year-old boy, puny and thin, almost a child. Miguel Angel stepped out and pleaded guilty, to save his brother and the other two.

Captain Valle asked Miguel Angel where he had found the boot, which he couldn't answer. I in turn, stepped out. "What do you think you're doing?" said the captain. "Go back in line!"

"Yes, Captain," I replied, "but before I do, I have a confession to make. I threw the boot… I took it from the barracks on the right and from the last bunker."

The captain checked my claim. A little later, the corporal returned informing the boy whose bunk I had indicated had a missing boot. "Very well, little friend," the captain said, "Take a pick and a shovel. Your lunches and dinners will be taken to you every day to the site where you happen to be working…until I remember." This meant I would be working until his resentment passed.

By 3:00, my hands were bruised. I was not used to this type of work. Once in a while, the corporal, with his broken lip, would come to check. "Come on, bastard, dig until you find oil. Dig deeper!"

I simply stared at him until he was out of sight.

One day, Miguel Angel saw me drying the sweat of my brow with the back of my hand. "I'm sorry, Julio Antonio...it's my fault."

"No, Miguel Angel, it's nobody's fault. You tried to protect your brother without implicating us, and that was very noble of you. But I would have felt even worse, seeing you doing this and knowing you're innocent. Anyway, I'm escaping tonight. The corporal won't have his fun tomorrow. And he'll have to order someone else to blow his whistle, because with his broken lip he can't."

"I wish you luck," said Miguel Angel, laughing in spite of himself. "I wish it with all my heart. And whatever the outcome, remember, I'm your friend."

"Thanks Miguel Angel. Tell Kinqui and Eduardo to try to take out extra bread and food from the dining room, in case we need it for the trip."

The military unit was in the middle of Cayajabo, in the Artemisa area. Our plan was to foot it from there to the town of Artemisa. Dressed as we were, in army greens, any vehicle would take us to Herradura, the small junction between Artemisa and the City of Pinar del Rio. Afterwards, we'd find someone to take us to the town of Herradura, where an old friend of my father had a farm. The next step would be to hide there and try to steal a magnificent yacht owned by my sister's husband. Canen was a Commander, and at that time he was in charge of the armored body of the army major staff. That's how he owned the yacht.

Shortly after I would leave Cuba, friends would write me that he was imprisoned in La Cabaña, stripped of all military rank. There they put him through the hell of all kinds of physical and psychological torture. I am still, as of this writing, uncertain of his whereabouts under Castro's regime.

The night of our intended escape, ready to depart from a previously agreed-upon point, Kinqui expressed anxiety about Eduardo's delay. I did my best to calm his fears, but an hour had passed and our friend had not come. We decided to go back to the barracks before the roll call, and Eduardo was not there, either. Miguel Angel told us he had not seen him.

Suddenly, we heard the alarm and ten minutes later, a shot. We rushed to formation, and when Eduardo's name was called, he did not answer. Kinqui and I figured out that Eduardo, not having seen us, had assumed we had already escaped and had tried to do the same on his own. We went to bed sick with worry for him.

The following morning, before breakfast, we were assembled in the practice-ground. The captain informed us that the night before, some coward had sneaked into the armory and killed himself with a machine gun. The coward, as Captain Valle referred to him, was our dear friend, Eduardo. Kinqui, at the other end of the line, looked at me with eyes full of tears.

After saying a few more absurdities, the captain warned us not to attempt suicide, because if anyone failed to accomplish his purpose, he would be sentenced by a military court after recuperating. The recruits belonged to the army. No one had the right to dispose of his own life; that faculty was reserved to the army and the revolution!

Later, we heard that before committing suicide, Eduardo had left a note for his parents. The captain had read it and destroyed it. Kinqui and I knew our buddy was not a coward but always wanted to have a machine gun or any other weapon. Considering we would be executed if caught possessing arms, we had not let Eduardo steal any guns. But Eduardo had probably slipped into the armory. The alarm rang, and he heard the guards rushing to the place, lost control, and aimed the weapon at himself. In any case, there is the unknown factor of that note addressed to his parents. We shall never know for sure what happened to Eduardo.

That evening we talked to Miguel Angel and reminded him to answer the roll call for us. After dinner, Kinqui and I started out for the city. We continued silently, with quick steps, and at the fence we dragged ourselves through the grass to the other side. After walking all night, we thought we were approaching the town of Artemisa, but new difficulties were ahead for us. Suddenly, I heard a cry of terror. I looked for Kinqui but he was not around. After calling his name repeatedly, he answered faintly, and I followed the sound of his voice.

"Be careful, Julio Antonio, walk with care," and when I stopped, I noticed his voice was coming from beneath my feet. "I'm here in this hole. I think it's an abandoned water well. The water comes up to my waist. I'm holding up but don't know for how long I'll be able to stand it. My hands hurt."

The water well must have been deep, because Kinqui's voice seemed very distant. In desperation, I looked around for something to lift him out with, but in the darkness, I only saw trees.

"Hold on, Kinqui, I'll get help," I said, giving him the courage I was beginning to lack.

"All right, but hurry up. My hands hurt badly." I walked around, careful not to stray too far away thus lose track of Kinqui. I didn't know the area very well. Not finding houses or signs of civilization, I dropped to the grass and leaned against a tree, feeling discouraged and helpless, muffling with my hands the urge to cry aloud.

At that precise moment, I heard halting steps, repeated long enough for me to locate the point of origin. Unbelievably, it was a horse looking for pasture, tied to a long rope! With nervous hands, I tried to unite the knot, but impatience slowed me down. Finally, I pulled the bush loose, and with the rope in my hands almost dragged the animal, too.

When I thought I was near Kinqui, I called him, but heard no answer. Then a marabou branch hit me hard in the face, and I heard Kinqui again. "Julio Antonio, I can't stand it any longer. I've got to let go!"

I yelled at him with all my might. "Don't! I have a rope with me!" I urged frantically, coming close to the well's mouth, and dropping in the rope's end. "There it goes! Hold on tightly!"

"I can't reach it!" Kinqui said with anguish. Then I urged and pushed the horse closer to the well, until Kinqui shouted, "I've got it, I've got it!" I motioned the animal to go even farther until it pulled Kinqui completely out.

He fell face down on the ground, his hands bruised from holding a metal ring around the well. We had been avoiding the road traveled by many military vehicles, but now, in a fervent desire to get out of that area, we rode the horse at full gallop until we saw the town lights. Then we dismounted, continuing on foot. Later, by the light of a street lamp, Kinqui saw my face covered with blood. The marabou thorns had scratched me deeply. I cleaned it with my handkerchief, which I'd dampened in a puddle. After walking a while, a truck passed by and the driver picked us up. We traveled in the back of the old vehicle loaded with milk jugs. Of course, we drank all we wanted, using our hands as cups. We got off at Herradura, shouting thanks to the driver. We didn't dare get too close in order to avoid later identification. We were covered with milk from hand to toe, a result of the bumpy road.

We arrived in town in the battered jeep of a farmer who stopped and gave us a lift when he saw us in the uniform of the communist army and thought we were going to search him. He couldn't refuse to take us, because that highway led to only one place, our destination.

We jumped off the jeep at the end of town and walked down a slope leading to the coast, reaching my friend's farm at 5:00 in the morning. It was still so early that we decided to sleep in the barn. The hay bundles felt like fluffy mattresses to our tired bodies. Later, a loud sound awakened us. It was my friend warming up the old tractor, ready to start his day's work. At first, he appeared surprised when I called him, but then he came closer and embraced me. "What are you doing here, kid?"

This friend of my family was about forty-five years old, heavy set, and blessed with the kindest disposition. No matter how serious his thoughts might be, he always appeared calm. I told him briefly about our escape as we walked towards Kinqui. I introduced one to the other, and after pumping water to wash our faces, the three of us sat on the hay to talk.

Juan had for a long time wanted to leave the country with his wife and children, but the regime had always found excuses to prevent it. After all, as an expert agricultural engineer, Juan was very useful. After many postponements, he had almost lost hope. On one occasion, in my presence, he asked my uncle, the university professor, to leave Cuba secretly with him, but my conservative uncle didn't accept. Aside from the fact that he didn't like the regime and made no attempt to conceal his desire to leave Cuba, Juan was well-liked by high officers in the system. They'd visit him often, tempted by Sunday meals he'd serve on a weekly basis including roast pig and delicacies such as yucca with mojo sauce along with fresh vegetables. The town was already having food shortages, and officers didn't scorn the tasty dishes prepared by Juan's wife. It was to their advantage to forget political differences, take their mistresses to the farm, and enjoy the feast—all without their wives knowing about it. On the other hand, Juan, through these officers, could get parts when his jeep broke, and other benefits that only these individuals were in a position to provide.

Juan advised us about our escape. "Listen, boys, I think I'll be able to get out of the country legally, God willing. But you can depend on me, whether I go with you or not. I'll help all I can. I'll only ask you one thing: for the time being, please don't go out of the barn for any reason. I'll get you civilian clothes and think of something to explain your presence here. If they see you in that uniform you'll be arrested and sentenced as a deserter from the military service, and you know what that means. So be careful and don't take any chances. Now I'm going to work. Do you know what I'm doing for them now? I'm directing a plan to grow tomatoes for exportation."

The government grew tomatoes to be consumed by foreigners, while our people couldn't even get a glimpse of them!

Two hours later, Kinqui and I were visited by one of Juan's sons, a smart, talkative nine-year-old boy who brought us two hammocks, a pitcher with coffee and milk, bread, and delicious home-made butter. We put everything on top of a palm leaf, stuffed ourselves, and hounded the little boy with questions. He was fascinated with our presence there and had overheard his parents talking about us. He could barely suppress admiration for the feat we had accomplished. At one point, he excused himself, ran to the house and shortly after came back with tooth brushes, blankets, and a jar of milk.

He told us, "Mami says you shouldn't eat too much at once you may get stomach cramps after having been so hungry." The boy spent the day with us, except for brief trips to the house, located half a kilometer from the barn. After bringing us supper, he said good-bye until the next day.

Juan's home was a beautiful chalet provided with every comfort and every domestic appliance imaginable. Although far from town, it was equipped with a motor that propelled water into a huge, concrete tank, providing it for the house. In the barn, a well provided us with all the water we needed. The electricity did not extend to the barn, so we lay down as soon as it was dark. For weeks we stayed liked this, with Juan visiting us for daily briefing on how things were and on further efforts towards helping us leave the country.

One evening, we were unable to resist the temptation to explore the surrounding area. We put on our uniforms, first taking off the recruit emblems. Then, out of an orange peeling, Kinqui cut three captain's bars for me and two lieutenant's bars for him, gluing them to our clothes with resin from a tree trunk. They really looked like emblems of Communist officers. In the moonlight, the oranges shone like metal.

It was a long walk, but finally we reached the town's badly lit edges, always trying to avoid Herradura's Main Street. While walking, we saw the tomato fields, and the vegetables looked so gorgeous that Kinqui took one, almost ripe, and bit into it. He said, with his mouth full, "Honestly, Julio Antonio, it's a shame these bastards eat these lovely tomatoes while the rest of the population can't get a whiff," and he kicked the bush in anger.

"Let's go to that house in the middle of the tomato field," I said. "I want to see what's in it."

From afar we heard the sound of the turbine continuously running, irrigating the valuable field. Next to the old palm leaf house were large numbers of modern tractors of communist make. Inside the house, manure and fumigation powder sacks were piled up. It was ten in the evening.

We discussed finding a way of spoiling the tomato patch without implicating Juan. We discarded the idea of taking all the oil from the tractors so they wouldn't run. The tractors were checked before being put to work in the morning, and all they had to do was replace the equipment, of which they had plenty from the Soviet Union and other communist nations. Furthermore, Juan could be blamed. We gave up the project for the time being. Before we left, Kinqui took with him a sack of tomatoes, to add to our future meals.

All of a sudden, we were startled by a noise at our backs. Ten meters from us, a man wielding a machete shouted at us, asking what we were doing there. We didn't answer. "I bet you are counter-revolutionaries trying to sabotage the plan!" he said, advancing towards us.

My instant reaction was to feign indignation. "What are you talking about, comrade? Do you realize what you are saying? Did you hear that, Lieutenant?" I asked Kinqui. "Where did this citizen come from?"

Kinqui, not quite recovered from his surprise and with the sack of tomatoes in his right hand and one, half bitten in his left, said, "I don't know Captain." Right away he started to behave like a lieutenant. He told the intruder to come near, but the man stood there, paralyzed with fear. Kinqui yelled at him. "Aren't you listening? I've told you to come near!"

The guy lowered the hand holding the machete and came closer, slowly, and visibly scared. "You see, I'm keeping watch. That's why I talked to you like that."

Very much afraid Kinqui would overdo the Lieutenant role I introduced myself to the guard.

"I'm Captain Nuñez, Chief of the Department of Agricultural Investigation and Sabotage," and I extended him my hand. I didn't know if such a department existed, but it was the first thing that occurred to me. The naïve man was impressed. I pointed at Kinqui. "This is Lieutenant Gonzalez, my assistant," and after they exchanged greetings, I asked the guard if he was integrated. He pulled out of his pocket several identity cards: CRD (Revolution Defense Committee), DP (Popular Defense) and other affiliations. He was a communist, all right. I consulted with Kinqui. "What do you say, Lieutenant, could we use the comrade?"

"I think so, Captain," he answered, examining the man.

At that moment it crossed my mind that the worst S.O.B. in the plan, according to Juan, was the political director, named Jésus. I asked the guard this man's name and other personal data, letting him know that we did not have a pencil and paper on hand. Our activities taught us not to write anything down that might fall into the hands of our enemies. "I carry the information here," I said, pointing to my forehead while I continued to question him. Aniceto, thirty-five years old, was short, had very lively eyes, and was shabbily dressed. Half of one of his trouser legs was split to the knee and hung loose. "Do you believe you would do any good at investigating a man we suspect of being a counter-revolutionary?" I asked, as though doubting him.

"Of course, comrade, just try me!"

Kinqui seconded me. "Do you see these tomatoes, my friend? We're taking them to the Lab to be analyzed. We suspect this fellow works for the CIA and wants to sabotage Fidel's plan."

"But who is this worm?" The guard asked, dying of curiosity.

"Unfortunately," I interjected, "we believe it is Jésus, the Political Head of the plan. That's why we have to be cautious, Comrade!"

The man turned pale, rubbed his head and mumbled the name slowly. Encouraged by his obvious puzzlement, Kinqui stressed the point. "With these people there are not enough precautions. As soon as they realize someone is watching them, they try murder. I wouldn't want anything to happen to you." he added.

Aniceto, flattered by so much affection, said, "Don't worry, comrades, from now on I'll keep track of him." He then volunteered information about the fellow we didn't know, the personnel director, who he believed to be a thief. As for the warehouse chief, he was in the habit of taking home dinners allotted to the workers. Another man, in charge of reporting hours worked in the entire plan, noted down extra hours for his friends. Aniceto said he wouldn't be surprised if he was in the racket, for his share. In short, Aniceto was not an educated man but was very sagacious. None of these things had escaped his attention.

"The sad part is," he continued, "all these bandits are milicianos, claiming to be revolutionaries, and they're running the plan. Now it turns out that the only one I believed in is just another worm, a CIA agent, according to what you tell me. Do you know what we have to do? We have to clean this mess up and execute all of them in a single bunch!"

"Aniceto, what do you think of the engineer of the plan, a fellow named Juan?" Kinqui asked.

Our friend Juan also got his share of defamation, so much so, that I cut Aniceto off by asking, "Aniceto, what days are you on duty here?"

"Every two weeks, Comrade Captain."

"Very well, we shall see you then, right here. Now you can go. We're going to pick up some more samples for the lab. Our jeep is on the highway."

On our way to Juan's farm, Kinqui said, "Julio Antonio, do you realize we're living under a system where everyone is stealing? I wonder why the regime has not collapsed by now."

"It's true," I said, "the revolution has created a gang who robs from each other as well from the nation. The people in charge of the revolutionary enterprise are the worst mob Cuba has ever had. I saw that they always had blamed capitalism for their bad luck, calling exploiters those who managed to gain wealth. These loafers never worked steadily except to cover their urgent needs. Did you notice the envy in Aniceto's expression when he referred to Juan? Honestly, if we put all the communists in a boat and send them to a desert reef, I assure you they would devour each other."

The next day we were awakened, as usual, by the cock's crow. I asked Kinqui if he was awake.

"Oh yes, for quite some time," and he started to laugh uncontrollably, until the hammock overturned and he fell to the floor, managing at last to say in the middle of roaring laughter, "Can you imagine what Aniceto must be saying to his family and friends? How stupid these people are! He's liable to swear he saw Fidel last night and talked to him."

Juan and Juanito at that moment came with our breakfast. "What's the matter, chum, are you having a nightmare?" asked Juan of Kinqui, who was still lying on the floor.

Kinqui let him believe so. "Yes, that's what it is," he answered.

Juan had news, but he urged us to immediately eat the delicious potato omelet his wife had just cooked. We begged him to tell us the news without further delay. "Very well, last night Commander Puerta, Chief of the Matanzas Province, and Commander Serguera, Chief of the Cuban Institute of Broadcasting, were here. They want me to prepare a roast pig for next Sunday. They are going fishing on the yacht."

"Did they invite you?" I asked.

"Yes, isn't that something? I'm surprised myself."

"You probably were invited because they felt embarrassed to ask you for a pig just like that," commented Kinqui.

"It's all right," I interrupted, "the important thing is you'll be able to see the condition the yacht is in, if they've guarded its fuel capacity, and other important details."

"Of course," said Juan. "It's crucial. But remember, you're risking your life...don't do anything crazy. Well, according to a good informer I have, yesterday a plan to murder Fidel was discussed right here."

We burst out laughing. The night before, we had contemplated the possibility of eliminating the dictator without jeopardizing the life of the executioners. Little Juan had told his father. Kinqui ran after the child, grabbing him and making mock threats. "I'm going to hang you! That's what we do to informers—we hang them and cut their tongues out with a pair of scissors."

The boy had laughed nervously. After Kinqui released him, he ran to his father's arms for shelter with a restless smile on his face. When they left, we devoured the tasty breakfast, to which we added a salad, prepared by Kinqui, with the tomatoes stolen from the plan. Then, we rested on our hammocks, daydreaming, until I shouted excitedly, "I've got it! I've got it, Kinqui! I know how we can spoil the tomatoes without implicating anyone!"

I then proceeded to tell him about my scheme.

That evening as we were preparing to go out, Juan paid us an unexpected visit. He had something to tell us. It seemed Aniceto had told people in the plan about being visited while on duty the night before by two officers inspecting tomatoes. He had gossiped about how they had talked to him for a long time. He had not specified about what. Thus, we determined that Aniceto simply wanted to appear important in front of others and the matter had been of no consequence.

"I think these officers are the same ones who visited me last night to arrange for the roast pig next Sunday. There's not much food, and most likely they went to the field to pick some tomatoes and when Aniceto caught them, they had to invent that story about the inspection," said Juan.

"Sure," we agreed. We knew that Juan should not suspect we were the visitors. After Juan left, we went across to the tomato field. We were careful because we knew every night there was a man keeping watch. When we tried to enter the warehouse, we bumped into a bundle lying on the doorstep. We almost fell face down on it. As he moved and said something unintelligible, we noticed it was a drunken person. Kinqui smelled a few drops of the liquid from a bottle nearby and said, "What a brute! It's plain, homemade alcohol. It smells like the alcohol used in spirit stoves!"

We left the man in the same position and rejoiced. Things would be even easier! "We can utilize the pipe with the tractor," I said, "but we'll have to work in the dark. If we turn on the tractor lights, they would be seen from afar."

We proceeded to open the sacks of pesticides used for the fumigation of tomatoes against blight. One by one, we emptied them out in the pipe, a big metal tank with 300 gallons capacity, attached by metal rings to the sustaining platform. The guide had a six-inch tube across the tank, and the tube had a series of holes with stopcocks to graduate the liquid coming out of the tank in spray form. Naturally, the proportion of poison and water was one sack to a pipe of water, but we used a barrel of water to a pipe of poison.

It took us two hours to empty the sacks into the pipe and then hook it to the tractor. With Kinqui driving, we went to a huge water reservoir supported by concrete columns. Laboriously, we placed the pipe's central hole under the key of the gigantic tank, filling up our "war tank." Then we began to spray the liquid into the tomato drainage ditches, a repeated operation.

We were in mud to our noses. The excessive amount of powder we had poured into the pipe had clogged the nozzles, and once in a while we had to get out among the muddy furrows and hit the guide hard with a piece of iron so the pressure would unclog them.

While Kinqui drove the tractor, I sprawled in the back of the pipe, took charge of the nozzles. At the end of the operation we rinsed the pipe out and put it back in the place where he had found it, doing the same with the tractor. Finally, we gathered all the jute sacks and stacked them for delivery to a factory for recycling. There was a shortage of containers in Cuba.

As we left the palm leaf house, the drunkard in charge of watching the worms (as Fidel Castro called his enemies) was still lying on the floor.

On returning to our temporary refuge, an unexpected rain cleansed our bodies and made us shiver with cold. Luckily, showers removed traces of the tractor wheels and remnants of poison that might have spilled carelessly. At the barn, we changed clothes and went to sleep.

Everything went as usual. Two more days passed and we began to think we had worked in vain. On the third afternoon, Juan appeared, extremely nervous, greeting us with solemnity that was not customary for him. "You were not at the plan, were you?" he asked.

"No, why do you ask?" Kinqui and I said simultaneously.

Juan looked into our eyes, but our steady gaze and feigned surprise convinced him he was mistaken. He lowered his head and, while holding in his hands the palm leaf hat, said just one word.

"Sabotage!"

"What are you saying?" asked Kinqui the comedian.

Juan sat in one of the hammocks and put his hand to his sweaty forehead. "Yes, sabotage. Of course, all these idiots in the plan believe it is a plague, but I know it is not. I'm convinced someone sprayed too much pesticide on the tomatoes and now they're hopelessly ruined. And to think these people have brought in Bulgarian and Czechoslovakian technicians, believing it was a plague. Naturally, I can't say it was sabotage. I can't involve the people. After all, what do I care? As long as do they do not take it out on me and accuse me of being a CIA agent, I'm glad the tomato crop is ruined."

Obviously, he was more worried than he pretended to be. We felt very guilty. The possibility of Juan being arrested, even without proof, and sentenced, and even shot, wasn't remote. After all, he was directing the plan and was not a Revolutionary. "Do you think they can prove it?" I asked, getting close to him.

"Yes, but it is difficult. It has rained a lot, and besides, this idea has not crossed their minds. Anything but admitting there might have been.... No, there's no problem. They can bring all the technicians they want. They will get bewildered, thinking it is a rare sickness contracted by the tomatoes."

I squeezed his shoulder affectionately. "Then you have nothing to worry about, Juan. Pretend to believe, with them, that it's a plague. Try to appear ignorant in front of them. But you're right. It was sabotage!"

He looked at me with astonished eyes.

"Yes, Juan, we did it. Forgive us if we have caused you to worry, but we couldn't allow Fidel Castro to continue replenishing his account in the Swiss banks at the expense of the people. The least we can do is to cause him a setback."

Juan had a hard time believing we'd done it, but at last he said, "Very well, don't worry about me. I'll know how to manipulate these people, even if they decide it is sabotage. I have no responsibility in the fumigation. Honestly, I'm proud of you. Now tell me, how did you do it? I had a hunch you were involved."

Juan listened to our story with mixed feelings. He couldn't help laugh when we told him about our officer ranks insignia made out of orange peels, and the way we made Aniceto believe Jesús, the most communist in the plan, was a CIA agent, but he warned us to be very cautious.

Nothing happened to Juan. He went fishing with the commanders and had a chance to observe the yacht's condition. It was not guarded. It had been expropriated from an individual leaving Cuba, and since it was used as a floating bachelor pad with a lot of sexy parties, it was not convenient to have a guard there. To prevent boat theft, the officers would take the gasoline tank out of the motor, along with spark plugs and other minor parts, making the yacht inoperable.

Following that visit, Juan started collecting gasoline, pouring it into two 55-gallon tanks kept in the barn. It was going to be a long journey. Once the tanks were filled, and the gear, including compass, navigation charts, water and food were readied, Juan surprised us by saying he was departing with us. He was bringing the family with him. We decided to depart that same night.

At nine thirty he picked us up in his jeep. We were dressed in our olive green S.M.O uniforms, and in that attire, we would be difficult to spot in the darkness. Juan dressed in khaki. It was agreed by all that the we wouldn't pick up the family until we were sure of the situation, which included carrying gasoline to the jeep in five-gallon cans, facilitating its transfer to the boat.

We drove for a long time through inaccessible roads, finally arriving at the place where we could leave the jeep. We could hear the sound of the waves. We cut out some branches to camouflage the jeep and then began to walk.

It was a dark, cloudy night. Kinqui and I carried each carried a machete. Juan carried an old .16-caliber cartridge gun. The sea was farther than we had calculated. As soon as we saw the yacht, we knelt down among the mangroves, quietly observing the scene for several minutes. Nothing moved. Minutes later, Juan told us to wait as he went to the yacht to explore. He returned after a few minutes, whispering that everything was fine and no one was aboard.

"Come," he said, glancing from side to side. We followed him to a big tree close to the coast. He knelt down and searched for something. "Here it is," he said at last. "Please help me. This is heavy."

It was a waterproof sack containing the gasoline tank, spark plugs, and other pieces of the motor. We carried it to the boat. Then Juan pulled out a flashlight while Kinqui formed a funnel with his hands. The light would concentrate on one angle, preventing detection from a distance during the assembling operation. In the meantime, standing in the bow, armed with Juan's shotgun, I kept watch. Everything was quiet.

We made several trips to the jeep, transferring our supplies to the boat. Then Kinqui replaced me at the watch and I helped Juan carry the heavy boxes. We were almost through when we saw lights moving between the trees and heard the noise of motors. We lay down on the deck.

"I think they're jeeps," said Kinqui. It was an odd time for maneuvers, I thought, but said nothing. We waited for them to leave.

Suddenly we heard a voice. "Don't move! You are surrounded, and we have orders to shoot to kill. Surrender!"

Without thinking twice, Kinqui shot Juan's gun in the direction of the voice. This was followed by an agonizing scream, and a rain of bullets whistled over our heads. Kinqui continued loading and shooting.

"Stop it, pal. Those shots are guiding them to our position," I warned him.

Juan, hanging by his hands from the stern and half immersed in the water, shouted, "Don't waste any more time!"

We crawled to the stern. Kinqui continued shooting despite my warnings, and the other side reciprocated. We dropped into the water as Juan had done, and guided by him, we got away from the yacht, following the coastline by swimming in the icy water. It was 1:00 in the morning, more or less. The shots decreased, and by the time we reached the shore, they had stopped altogether.

Now the problem was starting the jeep. If we turned on the motor, the noise would give us away. So we pushed it and put it in a starting position while Juan waited at the steering wheel. We heard scattered shots, but fortunately we managed to start the vehicle without turning on the lights. We moved so quickly that Juan lost control and went off the road. The car almost overturned.

"Turn on the lights, damn it!" said Kinqui. "We're headed towards the cemetery."

Juan obeyed, although speeding like a demon. At the farm, he voiced our misgivings. "Boys, I'm afraid someone saw us and informed the guard."

He put his jeep away and we went to the barn, watching the road. At 3:00 in the morning, we decided to go to bed. We were interrupted by lights as two jeeps approached. They entered the farm grounds passing a few yards from the barn. In front of the house, four soldiers stepped out of jeeps. After a while they came out. One of them was holding Juan by the arm.

We were extremely worried. Under normal circumstances, it would be hard to prove it was Juan at his jeep. It was a dark night, which made identification difficult. But we knew well that under Castro's regime no proof was needed for arresting, condemning, or executing a suspect. In Cuba, there was no longer a Constitution, no lawyers to defend human rights, and no authorities with whom to seek appeal. The G-2 was omnipotent: only abuse, rudeness, and mistreatment could be expected from a body created to suffocate any rebellion and terrify the people.

We started walking towards the house. Juan's wife was approaching the barn with some items for us. The extraordinary woman, still attractive and intriguing, didn't cry. The only signs of distress were her trembling hands and her labored breathing. "You must go right away," she said. "Juan warned me that if something like this happened, to tell you to go to Santiago de Las Vegas and contact a friend of his. He'll help you. I brought you food, and a note for when you meet him. His address is on the back. Good luck, and be careful. Now go quickly, before they come back to search the farm."

We gathered our things, and dressed as farmers, we walked for a long stretch away from the farm. At dawn, we waited on the highway for the bus. That beautiful morning, I thought how nice it would be to awaken on a day when Cuba was free of communism and oppression. With respect for human dignity. But unfortunately, at that moment, we still lived in one big prison— the Island of Cuba.

It took almost two hours to reach Havana. Autobuses passed but were so filled to capacity, people were hanging from the doors. During the trip we toyed with a future plan: to escape via the airport. We contemplated the possibility of seizing a plane. In spite of our recent discouragement, the new project cheered us and was an incentive to continue.

At the Havana Bus Terminal located on Rancho Boyeros Avenue near the National Airport, I noticed an individual observing us for some time. Perhaps our clothes and palm leaf hats had attracted his attention. I told Kinqui.

"I think he's from the G-2," he remarked. "He's too young to have his hair shaved off."

"Let's walk to the rear of the Terminal where it's darker," I suggested. "It will be easier to disappear."

But the man gave us no time. He approached us and asked for identification.

"And who are you?" I asked him.

He pulled the green State Security Department identification card out of his pocket. Not being able to identify us as members of any revolutionary group, he took us to the small office recently installed on the terminal. Then he telephoned headquarters. Soon the patrol car took us, handcuffed, to Villa Marista where the State Security Department was located. For the first time, I saw one of their cells. It was a cubicle as big as a Volkswagen, provided with as many locks and padlocks as if it were the infamous Lubianka. The air conditioning was set so high we actually felt frozen. The only bed available for the two of us was a thin, stinking, bug-infested mattress. There was no need to take turns sleeping on it. We preferred to stand or to lie on the floor. To the left was a water faucet, and directly under it was a hole for our personal needs.

During intense questioning, we routinely denied our intention to escape the country. We admitted to have escaped from the military camp because of the unpleasant conditions and mistreatment to which we had been subjected. Still they weren't convinced, refusing to let us sleep for two consecutive nights. Every fifteen minutes they'd awaken us for another interrogation. Finally, after the military unit confirmed our story, we were returned to unit 3234.

Our hardships were far from over. The same day we had escaped, three other boys from our barracks had also fled, carrying the tommy guns used by the guards. Three days later they were captured near Havana, without the arms, so officials were certain we had hidden them. We were submitted to harsh questioning at the unit, with the usual personal offensiveness, roughness, and humiliation, until they were convinced we had nothing to do with the missing weapons. Unfortunately, they took Kinqui to another cell and I did not see him again. In the morning, I was put to work, weeding, digging ditches, carrying big boxes, and doing other tasks. They would lock me in when I was finished.

At the beginning of the sixth day I woke up with a fever and couldn't get out of bed. When the guard came to get me, I explained my illness, and in spite of his insults, I refused to go to work. Continuing to feel ill, I left my lunch untouched. I fell asleep with my head between my legs on the cell's floor. I awakened in the evening when the guard opened my cell and said, "Hey, get up. You have to listen to your sentence!"

"What sentence?" I asked shivering, my face red with fever.

"What sentence? Yours!" he exclaimed, making me walk with him to the Major Staff Office.

Captain Valle, Lieutenant Lenin, and Lieutenant Barrios were there. Lieutenant Barrios, ex-Lieutenant in the militia, barely twenty-five years old, was the worst of all. His efficient squealing had enabled him to join the Army, but his inferiority complex made him worse. He took sadistic pleasure in shouting, insulting, and punishing the recruits. In a sack of dogs, Lieutenant Barrios was the worst. He stood up, holding a typed sheet of paper in his hands, he asked, "You are del Marmol, aren't you?"

Instead of answering, I smiled.

Barrios turned to the others and said, "Have you ever seen a more cynical jerk?"

"Don't worry," said Lenin, "We're sending him to a place where he won't feel like laughing or anything else."

Then they read my sentence. "This Military Court of Unit 3234 sentences Julio Antonio del Marmol, Francisco Gonzalez, Daniel Frias, and others to five years imprisonment at the Military Prison of La Cabaña for plotting to steal three tommy guns and trying to escape..."

On my way back to the cell, I asked the guard to take me to the infirmary. He put his hand on my forehead. Confirming that I had a fever, he complied. The doctor admitted me despite the guard's protestation that I was under arrest. At last I was able to sleep in a fairly good bed in unit 3234. The next day I was diagnosed with a kidney infection. While Kinqui and the others were taken to La Cabaña, I continued to recuperate under medical treatment. The physician, an excellent person, extended my disability indefinitely.

One morning, about 2:00, trucks loaded with personnel started to arrive. At the combat alert alarm, they made everyone in the unit get up, except those, like me, who were exempted from service. Naturally, we couldn't sleep either because the noise of the traffic continued all night. The following day, I learned that the regime feared that John F. Kennedy, the President of the United States, had ordered the Marines to invade Cuba, a situation so critical that almost all the doctors were mobilized and sent to military units. That same morning, I walked to one of the smoking areas and was greatly surprised to meet Dr. Sanchez, a good friend of my family. His first comment, when we shook hands, was, "What an involvement, my friend!"

I took advantage of our long conversation to ask him questions of a professional nature. I wanted to verify the practicality of a plan I had concocted while convalescing to evade my sentence and get dismissal from the military service. Dr. Sanchez was speechless when I told him I would soon be transferred to La Cabaña to serve a five-year sentence.

The next day I saw Barrios crossing the halls towards the dining room. I dressed quickly and went to wait for him in the smoking area, where at that moment there were six or seven recruits. It was customary that one of the recruits get up and yell, "Attention!" while the others stood up stiffly as an officer passed them in the hall. That was part of military regulations. Disobedience spelled punishment. We did this little ceremony reluctantly. These officers were in charge of a pseudo-concentration camp where we worked all day at various agricultural labors, including cutting sugarcane, digging ditches, and carrying heavy blocks for future military constructions for seven pesos a month—and at that time one dollar got you 37 pesos!

Barrios came near, and our eyes met. A young man next to me got up and shouted "Attention!" and the others stood up, saluting rigidly. All except me. I lay down on the circular bench and folded my hands over my chest.

Barrios stood in front of me. "Hey, who do you think you are? A tycoon? Stand up right now!"

"I don't have to stand up or salute anyone," I replied. "I am a sick man and the doctor has exempted me from service."

Barrios grabbed my left shoulder and tried to forcibly pull me up. "Get up or I'll have to do it for you. Who do you think you are?"

I jumped and while he held my shoulder, I punched him in the face. He fell down into an area where we threw the cigarette butts. It was full of rain water. He stood up, mad as a beast, and was going to hit me when I instead hit him with my right hand, giving him such a blow, he lost his balance. Before he hit the ground, I hit him in the belly with my knee while I punched his face again with my right hand.

He got up with a bloody face and a cut in his upper lip, and more subdued. "Don't think this is the end of it," he warned. "You are going to rot in La Cabaña or be shot by me. You're nothing but a shitty recruit!"

Lieutenant Barrios returned from the Major Staff about ten minutes later, accompanied by Lenin and two more guards. Thus protected, he shouted the insults he hadn't dared to tell me before.

Lenin handed me a machete. "Start immediately to weed the training ground," he ordered. "When he is through," he told the soldiers who came with him, "bring him to the office."

Naturally, these soldiers were not recruits, but were paid guards. None of the recruits had access to the Major Staff. Obviously, they did not trust in those who were paid so little. I didn't move or make any attempt to grab the machete Lenin was extending to me. When he yelled at me, repeating his command, I said, "I'm not going to weed any training ground. In the first place, I'm sick and exempted from service. In the second place, it's the fault of this man who provoked me. All my companions saw it!" and I pointed out to the other recruits in the smoking area, who had congratulated me, although fearing a harsh sentence that was pending anyway.

"You're going to weed because I say so," continued Lenin. "I'm going to count to three. If you don't grab the machete before that, you'll go directly to the doghouse, whether you're sick or not!"

I disobeyed him, and he shouted to the soldiers to take me to maximum security, where I was not to be given food until he ordered it. Then he told Barrios to prepare an act accusing me of disrespect and aggression to an officer. One more charge to add to my sentence papers to be sent immediately to La Cabaña. When the soldiers were taking me to the doghouse, Lenin had the nerve to shout, "Button up your shirt, you lowly worm!" I turned around so abruptly that I got loose from the guard holding me. Lenin put his hand to his pistol threatening me. "Hey watch out, I don't have any qualms about killing you. I'm not Barrios!"

I unbuttoned my shirt and threw it to his feet. "Regulations don't apply to me anymore, stupid!" I said, and walked away to the doghouse. The first part of my plan had been accomplished.

The doghouse was a wire fence, three and a half meters high, placed circularly on the grass. The top was finished with barbed-wire. As it was roofless, the 24-hour prisoner was in the open air all that time. The doghouse was the place where they sent the most rebellious people. Isolated, but in plain view of all others, they served as examples to the other recruits. At the right side of the door, there was a small tent to protect the guard from the weather.

Upon entering the doghouse, I threw myself on the wet grass. As decreed by Lenin, they did not bring me any lunch. I saw the guard eating rice, navy beans, and a candy called matahambre, or marchpane. It was of such poor quality that no one ate it or made it before the revolution. I spent all the afternoon under a strong sun that made my shaved head burn. Although the standard haircut for recruits was a crew cut, at the G-2 they drew blood from our scalp with the electric razor.

Cuba: Russian Roulette of the World

At 6:00 in the evening we had strong rains. I did not feel hatred for the guard who watched me huddled in the ground, my head hidden between my knees and covered by my hands, protecting it from the rain. After all, the guard was nothing but an instrument of the communist machinery. While the water rolled down my face, I thought of my father and my mother; especially the latter, who always took such good care of me. If only she could see me now. All these thoughts made me want to cry. I got up and faced the rain, hatless and shirtless as I was. I walked around the doghouse. After two hours, the rain became a drizzle.

At 3:00, the guard, trusting no one would come out at such an ungodly hour, lay on the floor, asleep, his tommy gun under his chest. I climbed the fence but when I almost was at the top, my trousers got stuck in one of the barbed wires. I pulled the cloth gently, trying not to make any noise with the wires. But tearing the material from the iron, I cut my flesh at the hip. The fiery pain I felt didn't stop me. I began to come down the opposite side, until I touched the ground. The soldier had not moved.

I took flight across the camp mud holes towards the woods. Suddenly, I heard a voice to my left halting me. The guard was ten meters away and he aimed a short arm at me. I ran to the deposits of bricks, sand, and other construction materials, trying to take cover behind the brick piles. The guard shot but missed me—or so I thought. Then I heard voices and hid in the ditch by the unit central road, half buried in grass and shrubs.

Before long, I felt blood running down my left shoulder. One of the bullets had hit me. I blocked the blood running down my arm with an improvised bandage made by tearing off one of the big pockets sewn to my campaign trousers. Then I waited. Finally, two jeeps full of soldiers stopped twenty meters away from my hiding place. They searched the place where the guard had seen me.

More soldiers were coming on foot and in motorcycles—Urals, previously used by the Germans during the Second World War, and copied afterwards by the Soviets. Daylight was coming, and I decided to risk crossing the highway to the other side. The woods were a kilometer and a half away. If I succeeded in crossing, it would be difficult to catch me. Since I didn't see anybody around, I ran almost squatting to the opposite ditch and jumped into it. When I looked up again, I saw first a pair of boots, then the face of a soldier aiming his machine gun at me.

"Don't move or I'll kill you." He shouted to the others, and seeing I was wounded, they took me to the infirmary. A health officer extracted the bullet— without giving me anesthesia— and bandaged my wound. The unit doctor was absent. Fortunately, they didn't take me to the doghouse after treating me. I was told they would take me to the unit prison on Captain Valle's orders. One of the soldiers escorted me with his tommy gun pointed at me while the other held me by the right arm.

The first warned me, "Do you know what happened to the guard keeping watch in the doghouse? He's in prison. So, I warn you not to try anything. If you force me to shoot, I will have to do it, and I don't want to." Actually, he was begging me to behave. This man, who had a weapon, was afraid I'd pull some new trick.

In my windowless cell there was no bed, only a bench, and nothing else. We had no way of knowing if it was day or night. The urine odor was unbearable. After my eyes became accustomed to the darkness, I saw something inscribed in what I assumed was Russian on the bench. The unit had previously been a Soviet camp. Its existence proved that those Russians, most of them very young, had been brought to Cuba to pass the compulsory military service and had likewise rebelled. They had been treated as despotically as we were.

My arm hurt and I was dizzy from blood loss. And yet I could not lie down as I wanted. The cell was only one meter long by half a meter wide and the bench had been placed traversally. I had no choice but to lean on it from my waist down, resting my waist against metal sheets that in the evening were very cold, and in the day scalded at the touch.

Sometime later, I heard steps coming down the hall. Somebody knocked at my door and announced, "Breakfast!"

The person left again. Two hours later I became aware of the slot under the door, built to store food without having to see the prisoners. I saw a rat biting a piece of bread that was part of my breakfast, together with a dark beverage resembling chocolate. I kicked the cup and the liquid spilled out. Later on, I did the same with my lunch. At supper time I didn't wait for the guard to leave. When he shouted, "Dinner!" depositing a tray of dirty water barely passing for rice soup with few floating grains in it, I kicked it so some of the liquid spilled on his clothes. The soldier called me filthy names and swore I would starve. He had no intention of bringing more food to me.

I lost any notion of time, but judging by the usual dinner in the unit, I figured it would be six or six-thirty in the evening. Hunger was giving me a terrible headache. My ears hummed.

Then I heard steps, and when they knocked at my door I did not answer. Lenin opened it. Two soldiers and the health officers accompanied him. "Listen, kid, what are you up to? You will starve, and we could care less. We shall return you to your family in a coffin and we shall tell them you refused to eat. So, it's up to you. But we won't give you up until you are dead. Or better yet, we might bury you and tell them you escaped and we don't know where you are."

While he talked, the health officer changed my bandages. I pushed him aside and grabbed Lenin's neck. One of the soldiers intervened. He held me by the wounded arm, hurled me against the bench, and closed the door when he saw I intended to attack again.

"You don't know what's in store for you in La Cabaña, stupid!" Lenin yelled from the outside.

I hit the metal wall hard until my right hand began to bleed. Then I dropped to the bench and leaned my head against the zinc, biting my lips in fury, feeling the wounds in my body. My soul hurt. That's how I lived for six days and six nights, hardly eating, and throwing away the tray so they wouldn't notice it.

But then I changed tactics. My bandages had not been changed in three days and I was in great pain. When the guard shouted that the health officer was there to change my bandages, I threw myself over the bench and feigned a fainting spell.

They opened the door and saw a part of my body lying on the bench and the other half on the dirty floor of the cell. Then the health officer felt my pulse and put everyone to work. Two guards brought a stretcher and took me to the infirmary.

Then I was given a shot of something that I thought smelled like coramine. I overheard the male nurse say I had a high fever and serious arm infection. They even phoned the nearest town to ask for a doctor in another unit since our doctor was still absent. This doctor sent me in an ambulance to the national military hospital in Havana. I was leaving behind me the town of Artemisa and the hated Military Unit 3234. And it was only a few weeks later, sitting in the military hospital, that I saw the live news coverage of the assassination of President John F. Kennedy, which I'd already known was coming. Through my contact in Cuban counterintelligence I had already seen the details of the operation months ago. I had passed them to my contact for the U.S. intelligence services as an urgent matter. If the world only knew that the power behind the assassin was the same power I was fighting in Cuba. The plan was so perfectly crafted to create confusion that it spawned many conspiracies far from the truth. The unbelievable details of this event remained wrapped in confusion for generations.

But the enigma of JFK's assassination is another story for another time.

CHAPTER VII: SIMULATED MADNESS

At the military hospital, they put me in bed in the emergency ward with an IV in each arm. It was the last thing I remembered as I lost consciousness. I was awakened in a room with three patients. Two new IVs had been connected to my arms. After a while, a young doctor asked me, "How do you feel, comrade?" He didn't wait for a reply before adding, "Now, you have to behave and eat all the food they bring to you."

I smiled. Naturally, I had read the records of my case, always sent in connection with the patients in military hospitals, and I knew mine was bad. My roommates were two kind young men from the S.M.O. (Servicio Militar Obligatorio) and a thirty-year-old black man from the regular Army. I spent some quiet days. Apparently, the orderlies had told them about me, and they were anxious to become friends. One time, I heard the black man say to the others, "This one is really fucked up. Do you know what it means to hit an officer?"

The day I noticed the door custodian's absence, I began to put into practice the second part of my plan to get out of that hell. When the male nurse came to give me the daily shot of B-12 for anemia, I asked him to bring me some 90% alcohol for my acne. The male nurse did what I asked him.

Early in the morning, I got up and opened the window midway. Then I put my boots, the olive-green clothes, my cap, and the rest of my gear about a meter away from my bed. I sprinkled these with alcohol, setting them on fire. Then I pretended to sleep.

In five minutes, the bonfire was blasting full force. The black patient was the first to raise the alarm. The air entering through the window funneled the smoke to his corner of the room. The male nurses and doctors on duty in our ward brought extinguishers and put out the fire, and the bustle was incredible.

A trail of smoke and the strong odor of burned rubber lingered in the air from my boot soles. The patient observed that I hadn't moved from my bed and was staring at all of them. He whispered something to one of the male nurses, who in turn asked me, "Are these clothes and boots yours?"

I looked at him as though I were baffled, and at the same time searched under my bed. When I appeared to have found nothing, I said, "You must be right."

In spite of his scolding, I continued denying I'd set my clothes on fire, but I had intentionally left the empty alcohol bottle where anyone could see it. The male nurse picked it up and talked to the doctor. After a while they gave me a shot something unusual at that time of the night. I slept through until 11:00 a.m. the next day.

When I awakened, the black patient was looking at me apprehensively. We started a game of staring at each other, with him smiling nervously. I looked at him seriously until the moment came when he couldn't stand it any longer and looked to the other side of his bed or at the terrace. I kept him in a state of anxiety all day. The minute I caught him looking at me, I would feign sleep and then jump in my bed in convulsion-like jerks. When he passed by my bed holding a cup of milk, I jerked so violently that he got scared and spilled the milk on his pajamas. He cursed in a low voice and went to change his clothes while I turned toward the wall so he wouldn't see me laughing to myself.

IV serums were applied in the morning and removed in the evening. However, since on that particular day I overslept, they had to apply them later. At 8:00 they had not been used up completely. My roommates had gone to see a movie in the recreation room. I decided to put into action the last leg of my plan.

When the serums were nearly used, I contracted my body, closed my eyes and got up from the bed, pretending to sleepwalk. Two big serum bottles rolled over onto the floor and I felt a great pain in my arms as the elastic cords holding the needles to my veins loosened. The nurses on duty didn't hear the crashing sound so I had to continue walking.

I crossed the back door of the terrace and stumbled about for what seemed an eternity, through the various terrace roofs in the left wing of the building. In one I saw women walking about. I was pleased I'd chanced upon a female ward, because the women were excitable and would provoke the commotion I was seeking. I went directly toward one of the windows, and before I reached it, a woman saw me and gave the alarm. From far away, I saw male nurses, doctors, and others crowding together behind the window. I looked at them indifferently. Then I climbed the small wall of the terrace in front of the building and stared at the distance, from the hospital's fourth floor. Several male nurses came near me, and one asked, from below, "Hey, what are you doing there?"

I looked at him with the eyes of a madman. "My tommy gun, I want my tommy gun," I said.

They looked at each other, perplexed, and one took it upon himself to reply, "Sure, sonny come here, we're going to give you your tommy gun."

He gave me his hand to help me down and while he escorted me away from there, I kept saying, "My tommy gun...I want my tommy gun..."

Once in my ward, the male nurses on duty identified me and put me to bed. My pajamas were soaked in blood from the wounds caused by the needles. When they saw the serum bottles on the floor, they called the doctor, who listened to my chest and gave me a shot. I fell asleep.

I awakened to face a short, dark man with his head shaved and wearing thick lenses. "How are you?" he asked me.

"Not well," I replied.

"Can you walk?" When I replied that I could, he made me go with him to his office. To his many questions, I answered that I hated the army and especially my squad and the clothes I was forced to wear. At the end of the interview he inquired about my clothes.

"I don't know what happened to them," I said.

"Don't you remember what happened last night?"

Feigning puzzlement, I asked what had happened the previous evening.

"Nothing, you can go back to your room. Try to eat all your meals and sleep as much as possible. Don't think about the army or anything else, okay? We may leave you here with us and you wouldn't have to return to Unit 3234."

I didn't like the idea of staying three years in military service, there or in any other place. The thought of doing another sleepwalking simulation crossed my mind, but common sense prevailed. I would wait a little longer.

A psychiatrist's examination was the next step and I was again interrogated. He prescribed chlorpromazine and naturally, the first two doses didn't agree with me. It was designed for nervous illnesses and affected my respiratory tract to the point of giving me asphyxia. I decided to throw the other pills in the water closet or sink. When the male nurse brought me the pill, I would put it between my lips and teeth, and pretended to swallow it.

As soon as he left, I would go to the bathroom and throw it out when the coast was clear. When the psychiatrist asked me if I had slept, I would answer I hadn't completely, although it was hard to believe these pills were not making me sleep. I abstained from eating too much, though I had a perfect appetite. But I'd gorge myself on milk when no one was looking. This way, I could almost leave untouched the beefsteaks or fried chickens assigned to my special diet.

In my last interview with the psychiatrist, he told me perhaps it wouldn't be possible to let me stay at the hospital as he had previously thought. I required good nourishment and rest and it would be better for me to convalesce with my parents. Needless to say, I was thrilled at hearing this, but determined to carry on with my plan in case of a trap.

When I'd walk into the room, my roommates would shut their mouths as if they had seen a ghost. The black fellow would smile, but I'd look at him solemnly, with a fixed smile, abnormally continuing my gazing. My scheme was paying off. I overheard the man telling his neighbor that as soon as there were empty rooms elsewhere, they should request to be transferred. He was afraid to sleep near a loony. They hardly dared to speak to one another in my presence. They slept or pretended to do so. If I fidgeted in bed or went to the bathroom, they kept tracking me out of the corner of their eyes. So desperate were they to see me out of the room, that when the psychiatrist asked them if they saw me eat and sleep, they would exaggerate reality, thus favoring my plan.

At last my parents were permitted to visit me, and the doctor explained the state of my health. His diagnosis was neurotic reaction. It accounted for my past behavior and that I was not in control of my nerves. Naturally, I couldn't be taken to prison, as it was impossible to apply any sentence to a sick man.

The hospital gave me a letter signed by the Commander and Psychiatrist, Dr. Juari, giving me a permanent discharge from the Army. For months I rested at the home of my parents, but I didn't confide the truth. My father and I maintained a certain distance from each other, owing in part to my need for secrecy and in part to his badly wounded pride. Then I realized my mother worried too much when she saw me studying late into the night. I had to tell her the truth when she tried to arrange another visit to the psychiatrist.

While I was convalescing in my family's home, I took that time to form a musical group named the Black Cats (or, in Spanish Los Gatos Negros), every one of us between fifteen and seventeen. We had Elizabeth on the harp, Pablo on the tenor saxophone, Cisneros on the drums, Hernesto on the standup bass, and myself on piano. I provided lead vocals with the four of them providing backup. We would practice in my room on the second floor of the house in Pinar del Rio. It was a recent addition my father had built on to the house, and being very isolated, it was the perfect location for us to practice and play music without anyone knowing about it or being disturbed.

We recorded on a reel-to-reel recorder my uncle, the doctor, had given to me as a present. After we finished a recording, we would play it back so that everyone could listen and enjoy what we had done. We gave each other high fives, and I said that we could bring it to our friend, Lozano, at the radio station. "We don't need to practice anymore," I said. "We're ready to play for the class graduating from the pre-university tonight."

The director of the pre-university, who had invited us to play at the graduation party, advised us to be pretty mellow with what we wanted to play, because the government had started to carefully censor music played in Cuba, especially rock and roll. They started to send communication to the local radio stations to halt playing that particular music, expressing the belief that the music was corrupt and eroded the communist values they were instilling into the youth, even though the smaller radio stations were still privately owned. At this point, the government had only taken over the larger stations.

Pablo looked at me in concern. "You know, these recordings are great, and I love them, but I get the impression that when we bring it to Lozano, he'll tell us that he can't play it because it's a little too much like rock and roll. The rest of the stuff we've brought him is more like ballads, slow rock, and calypso."

Elizabeth said, "Well, he's been playing our music for several weeks now, every Sunday. Mi Sonya and El Bambino are both #1 and #2 at the station, and he hasn't really had any problems."

Hernesto shrugged. "Well, guys, they really aren't rock and roll. Both of them are kind of between a ballad and slow rock. Now these songs that we're doing right now, this is really rock and roll!"

Los Gatos Negros, Julio Antonio's band

Pablo said, "Remember what happened to us at the Academy of Music?" He had a long face as he remembered the fallout from the "Ave Maria."

Hernesto replied, "You know what, guys? We're torturing ourselves. Let's bring it to Lozano and see what he says. Either he can play it, or he can't. That's the worst that can happen."

Since this young generation hated to be restricted by anything, and this music had been censored by the government, we found ourselves being greeted by a loud standing ovation even before we started to play. After we sang a couple of songs recently played on the radio, we played a couple more songs by Paul Anka, and closed with some hard rock and roll from the movie *La Dolce Vita*. All the kids went crazy as I sang the title song in English, and they started to shout for more. The organizer from the preparatory school came and told us that we needed to leave the stage so that they could start the cleanup, in spite of our agreement with them to give us time for eight songs, and we had only performed five. Evidently, the song in English worried them greatly. They even gently placed their hands on our shoulders to guide us off stage.

The kids continued to cheer, and members of my group kept playing, so I grabbed the microphone and said, "Hey, I'm really sorry, but our time is over. We really appreciate your support. On behalf of my group, we thank you, but we need to close it down because the organizers need to start cleaning up. We'd love to keep playing for you all night, but we have to give proper consideration to the people who provided this evening's enjoyment."

At that, the students erupted into noisy protest.

We exited backstage of the theatre, and saw two police cars with some plain clothes men, probably G-2 or local secret police, waiting for us there. They called out to us, and one of the men introduced himself as Lieutenant Lemus. "For your safety, come over with us. We'll take you kids home in safety." We looked over and saw a large crowd of the kids coming out, possibly to get autographs.

I said, "No, thank you. I don't think we need to go with you. These people aren't going to be aggressive or violent with us." I looked at my friends and said, "If you guys want to go with the lieutenant, go ahead, but I want to go greet the crowd." And I started to walk towards the crowd running towards us.

My friends looked at me and then at each other. Clearly, none of them trusted these men enough to want to get into the car, so they followed me towards the crowd with polite smiles and shakes of their heads to decline the invitation. They all knew it could be a trap to send us immediately to re-education camp. We had crossed a line by not only singing American music, but I had crossed another line by singing it in English. Even my long sideburns and the slightly long hair could open up charges of homosexuality or other crimes against the State, and this could simply be a convenient excuse for them to take me someplace for a severe beating. They portrayed such people as Elvispresleyannos, or the imitators or followers of Elvis Presley. The only person in Cuba who was allowed followers was Fidel Castro, so that was strictly forbidden.

After we embraced the multitude and spent the next several hours conversing with them and signing autographs, they started to disperse and we began our walk back home. It was around midnight, and we were full of joy, laughing and talking with each other. A few teenagers followed us home, as well. We lived close to the school, so it wasn't far. As we crossed a dark street, the guards from the party emerged and surrounded us. The teens following us screamed and ran away, as they knew what was coming next.

I said to my friends, "Stand steady and don't run. Don't be afraid; we haven't done anything wrong."

Cisneros started to yank on a supportive post by a tree to pull it loose, and I said, "Don't do that. If you do anything aggressive, you'll only give them an excuse for them to do what they want to do to us." I looked at the Lieutenant. "What the hell do you guys want? We haven't done anything wrong. Why all the batons and this threatening behavior?"

He said to me, "You are a bad example for the future young generations." Without another word, he started to beat Pablo in the head and stomach with his baton.

I saw Pablo fall to the ground, his face a mask of blood. Hernesto fell by us, also struck in the head. I was struck in the head and stomach, and I fell down by Pablo, also bleeding. Cisneros, on the other hand, was not as easy to put down. The large black guy yanked the wooden post out of the ground and began to strike out at the police. He landed a blow on the arm of one policeman in the arm and another in the head, sending both of them sprawling on to the ground.

Lemus pulled out his gun and aimed at Cisneros. "Nigger! Worm! Piece of shit! Drop that at once or you die!" He cocked his pistol. Cisneros saw the gun and stopped, but he didn't drop the post. One policeman took advantage of his pause to hit him in the back of the head. Cisneros collapsed onto his knees. One of the policemen on the ground rolled over and hit him on the jaw, knocking out a couple of teeth and spraying blood all over the place. I saw the blood run freely down his jaw, even as a policeman's boot on my neck held my head down.

Lemus pulled out a small kit and opened it. He held a pair of electric clippers out for us to see. All his cronies started to laugh and make fun of us. "This is what we do to you Elvispresleyannos," he said with a smug grin. "Shave off all your hair and sideburns. You first," he said to me.

Evidently, they had called for reinforcements, as more police cars came screeching to a halt. A large mulatto came out of one of the cars, the chief of the secret police in Pinar del Rio. Lemus said to him, "Capitan Palacios, this group of worms needed to be put down, because they offered resistance to us. We were just about to teach them the same lesson we teach to all the *Elvispresleyannos*."

Palacios looked at me and recognized me. "Lieutenant Lemus, do you know who that kid is? This is the Commandantico, one of Commander Fidel's favorites and the brother-in-law of the commander in charge of the major staff in Managua, and his other brother-in-law is one of the big honchos in the G2 here in Pinar del Rio!" He separated them from me and helped me to my feet. "Come on with me, Commandantico," he said.

"No," I said, "I'm not going anywhere with you, I'm going to go with my friends."

"Listen to me, I'm just going to get you out of this situation."

"Thank you," I replied, "but we're all going to go together. You can't save me from any trouble, because we didn't create any trouble. We didn't do anything wrong."

They bundled us all into the same car, and took us, ironically, to the same police station we had taken that rude old man, so many years ago. The sheet music and instruments remained on the sidewalk, covered in blood. The secret police didn't even bother to pick them up. One of the policemen even stepped intentionally on Pablo's saxophone like he was squashing a bug, irreparably breaking it.

On the way to the police station, Palacios questioned me. "What's the matter, Commandantico? Why have you been playing this crazy music with these kids? You're one of us, a Revolutionary. What's going on with you?"

I didn't respond to his implications but looked at my friends, bleeding and beat up. Elizabeth had a nasty cut on her forehead.

When we got to the station, Palacios called our families. I said to him, "I'm not going to leave until my friends are released." At that, he had no choice but to release all of us.

After this incident, my mother called Canen in Havana and begged him to get me out of Pinar del Rio and bring me to his house with my sister and place me under his protection, because she feared for my life. That way, she believed that I wouldn't create any more problems for myself. My brother-in-law sat me down for several hours and told me that if I didn't like this system, I couldn't resist it because that would only lead to my being killed. In order to live with him, he begged me to calm down and behave while I was under his roof.

Before I left the next day, as I packed my things an idea hit me about how to get back at Lemus and his cronies, a lesson to teach to these abusers. The carnival had started the day before, and they had closed the main street that ran through town all the way to the *Malecón*. All the streets were decorated for Carnival, with vendors selling lemonade, sugar candies, confetti, and other festive items, decorations hanging from buildings. People danced in the streets, each one representing a different ethnicity—this had not yet been nationalized by the government. The sidewalks were barricaded off from the streets, leaving the roadway free for the parades.

In one of the small beer kiosks, Lieutenant Lemus and his two cronies were nearly intoxicated, each with a large pitcher of beer, as they enjoyed their day off. Even though they were in plain clothes because of their off-duty status, they made it a big display to occasionally shift their guns around under their clothing, in order to prove to everyone around them that they were the tough men with guns, the real macho men.

Right in front of them, a coach stopped. It was an 18th century carriage pulled by two horses, decorated for Carnival, driven by a large black man dressed in 18th century attire and a mask. The young man smiled at them without showing his teeth. The curtains in the coach opened, revealing several long-haired women, also dressed in 18th century attire and masked. The most petite one with red hair, leaned out through the window of the coach and asked, "Do you handsome boys want to come with us to a private party? We can enjoy our own private Carnival."

The Lieutenant smiled at the other two. "We should follow you. Where do you live?"

Another girl opened the door to the coach. "Why follow us?" she asked. "The traffic will be too hard with all this crowd. You can come with us right now. The house isn't too far away from here." At the same time, she exposed her leg, revealing the garter on her thigh. The men were too excited to say any more.

Another woman showed them a bottle of Bacardi. "We'll have the best time in this Carnival for ourselves."

Another woman touched her breasts and said, "Come to Mommy."

The three men left their pitcher of beer. Lemus left some money for the vendor, and they jumped into the coach and into the hands of the beautiful, voluptuous women.

One of the men couldn't control himself, and as he jumped in grabbed the exposed thigh of the second woman. Another one of them attempted to unmask another girl, who refused the gesture and teasingly slapped him with her fan. "Calm down," she chided, "don't be impatient. We have all night."

The coach started to move, the young black driver gently nudging the horses to steer them to leave the parade route. A man opened the barricade to allow them out, and they headed towards the suburbs, leaving behind the multitudes of the Carnival. One of the girls closed the curtain for privacy, and the men smiled.

Lieutenant Lemus attempted to grab the breast of the woman sitting next to him. She smiled but gently protested, and pushed his hand away, saying "Don't be impatient. You're such a bad boy." She poured him a glass of Bacardi, adding a small amount of orange juice.

Lemus, intoxicated and belligerent, slapped the glass away and said, "I don't want to drink that crap. Give me the bottle." As he grabbed the bottle, the women exchanged glances. He was already getting out of line, and they may have to do something about that sooner than expected. At that moment, the driver of the coach signaled by knocking four times on the roof of the coach. They were now on the same dark street by the pre-university grounds where they had beaten us up a week earlier.

I pulled a small .38 caliber pistol out of my bag and placed it against Lemus' neck. In my normal voice, I said, "Don't move, or you'll die right here, you son of a bitch."

The other women sitting by the other two men at the same time pulled out a pair of straight edge razors and held them to the throats of the men. All three were completely shocked, not daring to move or even blink. I reclined just a little bit, as the coach was now stopped in the dark street. I gave the same four-knock signal on the roof, and the coach started into motion once more. Everyone remained silent, the three men's eyes almost bugging out of their face, their expressions stunned. After a brief trip, the coach stopped by the bank of the river. The door opened, revealing the features of the young black man, Cisneros, this time smiling broadly and revealing his two missing teeth.

Pablo took the hand of the man sitting next to him and placed it in his groin, and said, "Why don't you hold this? It will probably be firmer than my breasts." When the man realized that this wasn't a woman, he jerked his hand back with a look of revulsion on his face. The question for them remained the same: what was going to happen to them now?

We disarmed them and got them out of the coach. We made them walk to a small overhang by the river and sit down by a huge rock. Cisneros pulled out a small pair of dental pliers, tightly bound their hands and feet, put a finger in his own mouth, and said, "Eye for an eye, and tooth for a tooth." He then removed the same teeth he had lost to Lemus' baton from the Lieutenant's mouth, ignoring his screams of pain. The man's friends looked on in complete panic. He then dropped the teeth into the river and said, "Justice is done."

We all kept our masks on, and Cisneros pulled out of a plastic bag a straight-edge razor. "Tooth for tooth, and eye for eye," he repeated. Both men urinated in their pants as he approached them with the straight edge, as they thought he was about to cut their throats. Instead, he shaved them with soap and water drawn from the river. Their bare scalps shone with reflected moonlight.

Cisneros then pulled out a can of what appeared to be Vaseline and said to us, "OK, my friends, untie their hands and feet. Now we're going to have some real fun with these sons of bitches." All three men looked on with dismay as Cisneros dropped some women's lingerie at Lemus' feet. "You'll look very pretty in these clothes, my love," he said.

Lieutenant Lemus' eyes almost bulged out of his face as he followed every one of Cisneros' movements. At that moment, Cisneros put his pliers down and unzipped his pants. Lemus pleaded, "No! You shouldn't do that to us, that's indecent. Take all my teeth if you want, but don't do this to us."

We all of us laughed as we watched Cisneros take a short walk to urinate on a rock.

Pablo shook his head and said, "Only a sick mind like you guys would even think we would rape you guys. But thinking about it now, maybe that's what you deserve for being bullies and such disgusting people yourselves."

Cisneros opened the can, and with a small brush began to put yellow-colored shoe glue onto the bald heads of the three men. He took three women's long-haired wigs, and did the same inside the wigs. By this time, we had dressed them in the women's lingerie and tied them back up. Elizabeth applied lipstick and makeup on all three of the men. Cisneros blew gently on the wigs and waved them in the air to help the glue to set. After a few minutes, he put the wigs on each man's head, one by one.

We dropped their clothes and weapons into the river, put them inside the coach, and drove the coach back to the Carnival. After we were readmitted to the parade, we dropped them one block at a time. The last to leave was Lieutenant Lemus, who pleaded with tears in his eyes not to be dropped publicly in the street, but instead to leave him in some private, secluded street, where no one would see him. We decided he didn't deserve such special treatment. Pablo gave Lemus the same kick in the rear to eject him from the coach that he had given the previous two cronies.

We drove the coach out of the Carnival and all agreed we had to leave the city, just in case we were recognized. I told them that I would be leaving the city that same night. We hugged each other in farewell, and I walked off into the darkness. Canen and my sister came by later that evening to pick me up, and we left for Havana.

I then moved in with him and eventually, I returned to the university and continued my studies. At the same time, I maintained my clandestine fight against the regime, while changing my outward appearance to conform to the communist ideal.

By then, my father was a sworn enemy of the Revolution. The Neighbors Committee had searched his home and the communists had constantly harassed him. They went as far to denounce him to the police for vagrancy—a man who had worked for thirty years. But after his business was confiscated, he refused to work for the state.

He had some money and it permitted him to continue living in comparative comfort with two cars. This made him a bourgeois. How well I remember that in one of his speeches Castro had said, "Two cars for what? You can only drive one at a time." This, coming from the man who also drove one car and was followed everywhere by three new Oldsmobiles. The difference was that my father had bought them; Fidel had stolen them from the people who had left the country. It was also part of the Castro demagogy: criticize the owner of a splendid residence but don't mention you are living in one of the best ones in Cojimar, or that each time someone leaves the country, your henchmen rush in as birds of prey to grab everything left behind. Enjoyment of luxury and comfort ceased to be a crime if a communist was the recipient.

People left Cuba resigned to lose everything rather than have their children grow up in a morally depraved environment where the mere act of wearing a religious medal or a cross hanging from the neck was enough to mark someone a *gusano*, or "worm," a nickname coined by tropical communists for their enemies.

Father was summoned to the Neighbors Committee and his non-appearance almost caused him to be consigned to one of the farms, which are actually concentration camps. Of course, they are located in strategically discreet places, so the visitors or tourists cannot see them. People disliking the regime are sent there, even if their objections only have been expressed verbally, regardless of their age and sex. Unpaid for their labors, they also are badly fed. Refusal to work means physical elimination without due process or a court hearing.

Father was spared this exile in the farm because in the G-2, when asked about his refusal to work, he rightly answered he'd done so all his life, and uselessly since his business had been expropriated in spite of the fact that he had not been a Batista follower; on the contrary, he explained, had contributed to the regime's overthrow. Perhaps because he was telling an uncontestable truth, or in respect of his fifty-eight years and faltering health, he was allowed to go free.

In 1960, at the beginning of the Revolution, Fidel Castro said only the properties of people dealing dishonestly would be expropriated. Later he said that nationalization of big foreign companies, such as the electric company, the telephone company, would take place. Finally, he seized the big companies, claiming that their owners didn't have the right to own so much while others lacked the most indispensable necessities. But Castro did not stop there. He wound up stating that all the merchants were thieves, buying merchandise at $10.00 and selling it at $11.00! With such feather bedding as an excuse, he seized all factories, clothing stores, markets, furniture stores, and other enterprises, stripping their owners.

His philosophy "for the people and by the people" was his excuse for terrible robberies. No little kiosk, humble fruit shop, Chinese stall, or fruit and vegetable handcart remained in the streets. Chinese refugees who had fled from communism in faraway Asia were repatriated by Fidel, stripped of a choice for their own lives.

The real thief in Cuba was Castro. All the property seized, homes, cars and yachts, were not given to the people as publicly stated. The magnificent residences were now occupied by Communists and the regime's high officials, and they cruised in luxurious yachts. Again, there were privileged and unprivileged; only this time, the new class had done nothing to earn it. And instead of "for the people and by the people," it was "for Fidel and by Fidel." Thanks to Fidel's perpetual economic idiocy, the poor people suffered more than ever. As the nation plunged into the most abject poverty, bigger and bigger economic sacrifices were demanded from a nation that gradually was lacking even the basic means to live passably. I graduated from the Veterinary School for Animal Genetics from the University, not a lawyer as I'd first dreamed. His ministers were individuals that, at the most, had completed sixth grade in elementary school. It was irrelevant. The relevant thing is they were for the Revolution, and the more ignorant they were, the more fanatical. Castro controlled everything and everyone, down to even what people could say or even think. The dream of freedom was now a nightmarish prison.

CHAPTER VIII: AGUILA 70 (EAGLE 70)

After graduation I began to work at Genetic Dairy Cattle Enterprises, a subsidiary of the Economic Department of the Prime Minister's Office, where I noticed even the Cuban revolutionaries or communists didn't believe in Fidel anymore. They played his game so they could have a car or a Soviet jeep while the rest of the population had to manage in crowded buses.

Just trying to get into the buses was a heroic task. The regime had created the problem by intervening in the bus system, putting unqualified individuals in charge and awkwardly destroying what had already existed. These communist directors, besides enjoying certain privileges, such as special vehicles, clothing, food, and quotas, could steal as much as they wanted.

My enterprise was given 1,343 caballerias, a land measure about 33 1/4 acres each, between the Cuban provinces of Havana and Matanzas, in an area called Tapaste. They nicknamed it Siberia, although it was a fruit farm mainly planted with red mamey trees that take fifteen or twenty years to give fruit. Then the management of the Genetic Dairy Cattle Enterprises, without thinking twice, ordered the fruit trees to be destroyed and the land turned back to pasture. When Commander Curbelo visited the farm and saw what was taking place, he tried stopping the destruction, but was too late. There wasn't a tree left. When he asked who had ordered it, the director of the enterprise appeared, followed by his communist lackey. Commander Fidel Castro had ordered it, he said. Commander Curbelo had no choice but to give the green light to the project. This incident, which I witnessed, was due to

Fidel's whim to transform the farm into a gigantic dairy, labeled Niña Bonita, or Pretty Girl.

Later, in 1970, Fidel himself gave orders to dismantle the dairy and its many innovations—air-conditioned sheds and costly constructions to maintain and acclimate the cattle, along with concrete sheds especially designed for mechanical milking. He wrecked what had cost millions for the purpose of growing sugarcane. His new whim was to obtain ten million tons of sugar, and the farm was located in the proximity of a sugar plantation. Of course, they also blew up all installations, razing to the ground special pastures prepared for valuable cattle imported from Canada, requiring a diet of maize, alfalfa, and pangola, more expensive than regular feed.

Despite their efforts, the bragged-about quota was not reached, and sugarcane was even sown in the Miramar and Vedado gardens. They had rushed to implement one of Fidel's projects, but as with all of Fidel's plans, it was gigantic but impractical. Not counting the aborted 10 million-ton sugar harvest, here are some of his other grandiose plans, and their outcome.

1. The world's largest dam.
2. An enormous coffee plan.
3. The world's biggest zoo.
4. Cuba, the only country without illiterates in the world.

First, the biggest dam in the world, the Paso Seco, was one of the most dismal failures perpetrated by Commander Fidel Castro. It was inspired by the following incident. In the aftermath of a hurricane in Havana, Avenue 100 was inundated, including hospitals located on the thoroughfare. In my opinion, this was due to the awful maintenance of the sewers. The Paso Seco River runs across this area and had overflowed. Fidel, upon visiting the tragic site, suddenly exclaimed, "This calls for the building of the world's biggest dam."

Planning the dam and building it was started immediately, using imported communist technicians. It was proposed that in order to inundate such a central area, the affected inhabitants would be evacuated. The inhabitants of the little village of Paso Seco, located between Havana's city limits and the town of Managua, comprised 500 homes. Residents had built homes in the suburbs because they wanted to shun the city's bustle, preferring a quiet, residential area, until Fidel conceived of the dam.

Five hundred homes were demolished, their residents transferred to Havana against their will, living in residences that were inferior in comfort and cost to the homes they had owned before. They protested that the commission in charge of building the dam did not permit them to transfer the remains of their dead ones, buried in Paso Seco Cemetery. The Commander, as Fidel was known, was in a hurry to complete this project and had no time for sentimentalities. They continued wrecking until they closed the great double-way Avenue 100 crossing zone.

Next, they built enormous columns for the construction of a huge bridge spanning over the dam. When the columns were finished, the order was given to inundate the area. Since it was their first experiment, they deviated and closed the river, and all Paso Seco including the cemetery was flooded along Avenue 100 for a stretch of twenty miles.

This was not all. Fidel, impressed by his handiwork ordered great quantities of assorted fish worth thousands of dollars, mostly from Africa. They were set free in the water, and such convenient warning signs as "Fishing is Forbidden," "No Fishing Allowed in the Dam Area," and "Fish Reproduction Area" were posted.

Technicians, in a hurry to please Castro, had overlooked an important detail: that area was so great that the ground swallowed the water as though it were a sewer. When the prefabricated beams for the gigantic bridge were to be put in place, one of the technicians observed the water did not rise but sank. Thinking the river water was insufficient, they initiated the canalization of two rivers near the dam, but it was useless. Exhaustive investigation gave no clue as to the source of the problem. Technicians now contemplated a more serious problem: how to tell Fidel that after spending many millions, the project was a total failure.

As expected, his reaction was violent. Lucky technicians and engineers in the Dam Commission were sentenced to forced labor in a farm. The others were sent to prison, charged with sabotage and negligence with regards to the people's interests. This was not enough for Castro. He spoke to French engineers in Cuba under contract for the performance of various industrial constructions.

After inspecting the work done, they suggested digging up the site where the water was escaping and filling it with concrete, thus saving the project. Castro believed them. He made them abandon their other projects, devoting themselves to the dam. Incidentally, the Frenchmen were being paid in dollars, not Cuban money. It had no value outside the national boundaries since it was not backed by the gold standard.

Concrete mixers made countless trips to the site, pouring enough concrete in the dam to build another city, but the water continued escaping. Finally, the engineers gave up and their contracts for other projects in Cuba were cancelled. They were expelled to France. In the meantime, fish were dying in the dam for lack of water, and the majestic columns seemed to be saying in stone language to the ruins of the Paso Seco Village, "Now we're drier than ever."

Signs forbidding fishing were changed. Now they read, "Vegetable Plan." Instead of a gigantic dam, a brook remained. Since the economy was in shambles and there was a shortage of food to feed the population, Castro had the new idea of using all the water in a vegetable project. And filling the huge stretch of desolate ground, they proposed building a gigantic park to be named after Lenin, one of the fathers of communism. Never before had Lenin's name been used as such a big joke around the world.

The second project, the gigantic Coffee Plan, was another farce. Before sowing the coffee, Castro pre-sold beans the plant would produce to France and Italy in exchange for agricultural implements and luxurious Alfa Romeo cars. This was a fiasco because the coffee tree requires shade, and the crop was planted where there wasn't any. The plants perished, scorched by the fiery tropical sun. Naturally, the Government had to pay for the cars and implements with the national economy in even worse shape. The patient Cuban people had to suffer due to these castles in the air that Castro was forever creating.

The third plan, the biggest zoo in the world, turned out to be a vast collection of animals let loose in a vast stretch of land. Problems arose when they were brought from the old zoo. Almost all of the animals had died in the former park since it had not been maintained. Replacing exotic animals entailed a considerable monetary investment. The Castro Administration could not afford it, so the grounds stayed empty, although it was ready to receive new animals if times changed for the better.

The fourth plan had the goal to make Cuba the only country in the world without illiterates and was conducted by people who themselves were illiterate. But Castro continued, saying, "Go forward, comrades! Never backward, not even for taking impulse!"

But it was impossible to go backward. Only destruction and ashes remained. And after being through with Cuba, Fidel would do the same to other countries in the American continent and then try to do this to the rest of the world.

"We've a long way to go, comrades!" is what Fidel and his gang of hoodlums seemed to be implying, while American nations, including the United States, were absurdly indifferent to the physical and moral destruction of the Cuban people. They played dangerous Russian roulette, not knowing which of them would be the next hit by the Communist bullet.

Cuba: Russian Roulette of the World

Julio Antonio at 23 years old

I had just gotten off the phone with Sandra, and needed to prepare myself for another meeting. I sorted through the papers on my desk, put a sheaf in a desk drawer and grabbed a folder marked in Spanish with what would translate into English as "Classified, High Command" on it. I carefully concealed it within my portfolio and closed my desk drawer.

I went out into the hallway, carefully checking to make certain that no one was around. In case someone could hear my movements and to give myself cover, I went to the bathroom and washed my hands and face. I returned to my office, again checking to reassure myself that it was clear, quickly grabbed my portfolio, checked my watch, and left.

As I got into my black Russian Volga sedan, I could see a few other cars scattered throughout the parking garage, but no one was about. Reassured, I started the car and left, returning the waves of the guards at the gate. The streets of Havana were festive as I drove towards Chinatown, with Carnival celebrants in costume walking around gaily.

After carefully navigating the slow traffic in the Carnival district, I turned into Chinatown and pulled up on a street and parked. The dingy streets were decorated by Chinese lanterns and signs in either Mandarin or Cantonese. I got out and walked a few hundred meters to over to an antique shop. I entered the quaint store, decorated with Buddhas, bamboo, and other cultural items. Chandee, a long-haired Asian girl of about twenty-one, was at the desk. Her pretty eyes lit up with recognition as she saw me, and we embraced over the counter and greeted each other with a kiss on the cheek.

"Please, get this out quickly, Chandee," I said as I slid my portfolio over to her.

"It's nice to see you, too, Julio Antonio," she said teasingly with a wink, even as she passed the portfolio to another Chinese woman behind the counter. This lady took the contents out of the portfolio, handed that back to me, and concealed the documents in a bag with some small antique trinkets. She then left quickly through the front door.

We walked into the back of the store. As we passed through a decorated curtain, I asked, "How is your father?"

Xiang, her father and a balding fifty-five-year-old Chinese man with a long, thin mustache stepped out of the back area. "I'm old, but well. How's your uncle?"

He smiled at me as we shook hands and clapped each other on the back. "Fine. How are things at your shop?"

"Waiting for the government to take over my business each day, we never know. It will be harder with Chandee leaving."

"It will only be for a while, Father," Chandee started in mild protest, but her father cut her off.

"No. We've already discussed this. You are leaving Cuba permanently. It's too dangerous."

I was distinctly uncomfortable in the middle of this impasse between father and daughter. Chandee turned to me and said, "My father and I have not yet decided yet if I am coming back from Canada."

"It might be best for you to leave," I said, "at least for a while—especially considering what is in that package."

"Oh?" Xiang inquired.

"Pictures and plans, locations for the new missile bases." I explained. "Things are going to get hot again when this news gets passed along."

Chandee, Xiang and I sat down at a small table while Mrs. Xiang, a plump, middle-aged Chinese lady brought us tea. "Imagine my luck," Xiang observed, "fleeing China to escape communism, and it just follows me here."

"Here you are, Julio Antonio," Mrs. Xiang said as she set out the tea. "Hot tea lifts the spirits."

Xiang looked a little annoyed at the interruption, so I made it a point to comment politely. "Thank you." I sipped the tea. "Mmm. Tilo tea. Good for the nerves." I smiled at Xiang as Mrs. Xiang shuffled out.

At that moment, Yein, Xiang's youngest daughter of about seventeen, burst in and interrupted the tea gathering. "G-2! G-2 outside! They are covering the exits!"

We could hear the sound of pounding feet outside and knew there was precious little time. Mrs. Xiang handed Chandee a travel bag. "Here. Go. It's already packed for you."

Chandee nodded and hugged her mother. At the same time, Xiang was moving a cabinet with a display of fine China dishes. Concealed behind it was a passage, and he motioned for Chandee and me to go through. "Hurry. They won't find anything in our shop. Go! Go!"

I patted him on the shoulder and led the way into the darkness. The corridor was dimly lit by light bulbs hanging from flimsy wires. Cobwebs hung from the ceiling, and discarded junk lined the walls. We walked as quickly as we could through the narrow corridor while avoiding the debris.

We exited the dark corridor and found ourselves in the back warehouse of a textile business. Many Chinese workers were there, laboring hard with ratty sewing machines. With more room to move, we started to run. A few of the workers looked up, but most of them ignored us and kept sewing. We came to a door in the back of the building and opened it.

We came out of the door into a meat packing plant. Sides of meat hung from the ceiling among tables with Chinese men cutting and packing the meat. Once more, only a few actually looked up at us while most ignored us as we quietly rushed toward a back door.

Out on the street, we quickly walked toward my car, which was parked a short distance from the antique shop. As we approached the car, one of the G-2 agents returned to their grey Volga outside the store. We ducked down behind my car as the agent picked up his car radio. "Yes. We have the store surrounded. We are searching it from top to bottom. If they have anything to hide...."

While he was engaged, I managed to get into my car, unlock the passenger door to allow Chandee to slip inside. Once she was secure, I casually started the engine and quietly pulled past the G-2 car, while Chandee ducked to keep her head down.

The day had turned overcast, and I pulled the car off onto a side street. People walked the street, minding their own business as I parked the car and opened the door for Chandee. We walked up to a dirty apartment building with a door buzzer. The name next to the button was written in one of the Chinese languages. Chandee pressed it and a voice answered in Mandarin.

Chandee replied with, "It's me." The door opened, and we entered the building. We walked to a specific apartment. Chandee was about to knock when she hesitated and turned to me impulsively. "Julio Antonio, we may never see each other again." She took my hands into hers as her eyes welled with tears.

"This is Castro's world," I said. "Divided families, lost friends. Pain and misery. You have to be strong."

"I pray this nightmare will end soon." She looked down for a moment, and then looked back up to me. Before I could react, she quickly gave me a deep kiss. "You have brought a light into my heart in the middle of all this evil. Thank you."

"Don't worry," I reassured her, "your family will get out of here and join you soon."

We embraced, and she quickly turned to knock softly on the door. I walked away sadly as a chubby, middle-aged Chinese couple answered the door and took Chandee into an embrace.

I later learned, much to my pain, that the G-2 had arrested my friend Xiang. As part of their interrogation, they had cut off his fingers with a pair of metal shears. In spite of that torment, that brave man said nothing to his questioners. The trail the G-2 was following ended there.

Dec. 24, 1970, Christmas Day in Cuba

I never will forget for the rest of my life my last Christmas Day in Cuba; it remains, to this day, a very vivid memory in my mind. After my diligence, I found a way to pull a few strings through my contacts and obtain a few pounds of rice, black beans, a rack of pork ribs, and a loaf of bread. In Cuba, this was considered contraband. Everything was considered contraband, unless it was bought through the markets controlled by the government as part of your ration book. Anything not listed in your ration book was therefore contraband, and black marketeering was punishable by ten years in prison. Even though all the markets had been confiscated by the government, they all had long lines due to the shortage of produce on the shelves. Frequently, people had to go home at the end of the day to return the next day in the hopes of finding their basic groceries. Additionally, you were assigned to a specific market; one could not go across town to try a different one.

I drove myself to my uncle's house, in the hopes of having a modest celebration with the things I had obtained. When I reached his house, my aunt began to prepare the ribs. She had to go to extremes to conceal the smell of the cooking meat from the neighbors. She used sugar, enclosed the ribs in a metal container with lime juice sprinkled over the metal top, and closed all the doors and windows. In Cuba, it has long been a tradition for families to roast a small pig as part of the Christmas celebration, and then invite friends and family to come and partake of the special meal. The new regime, however, silently attempted to change this tradition. Castro and his cronies kept this change quiet because they didn't want to expose to foreign visitors how miserable the conditions in which the Cuban people really were living under this dictatorship.

The Christmas holiday had been classified by the government as a religious and therefore contra-revolutionary act. If any informants with the C.D.R. were to report any smell of roasting pork or other suspicious behavior, my aunt and uncle risked the possibility of the G-2 and the secret police coming to the house and arresting the people for questioning. If any evidence was found that the household was violating the government's mandate, we could face imprisonment for a long time—not for celebrating Christmas, but for the contraband involved in pursuing the celebration of the holiday.

When we were ready to sit down to eat, my aunt was going back and forth to the kitchen, and she saw the patrol for the C.D.R. coming to our door through the kitchen window. She ran to the table to grab the pot with the pork ribs, disappearing through the door to the patio, even though she had been burning potpourri and cleaners to avoid any lingering smell in the air.

We opened the door and greeted the C.D.R. people. They gave us the excuse that they needed to search to see how many children under the age of six were living in the house. This was ridiculous, since the entire neighborhood knew there were no children here; it was simply a reason to have these people gain entry to the premises. After the patrol left, we still controlled ourselves, and did not sit down at the table to eat until midnight, almost three hours later. That was the only way to be certain they wouldn't smell anything, return, and catch us with the meat on the table. My aunt went to the patio and retrieved the meat from under some ground cover at the bottom of the coconut tree. For fear of additional smells escaping our control, rather than heat up the meat, we ate it cold with the white rice, black beans and a piece of bread. That was how we celebrated my last Christmas in Cuba.

Leaving my office in Rancho Boyeros the next day, I bumped into my old friend, Kinqui. Someone had told him that I worked there, and he had decided to wait for me at the entrance. He was afraid to be recognized, possibly doing me harm. I protested, but he assured me we could take advantage of the position I held, fighting the regime in many ways. I had a Soviet jeep assigned to me recently, with the logo CCP (standing for Centro Control Pecuario[3] in Spanish, though many mistook that to mean the Soviet CCCP) as did other veterinarians who went into the field. Kinqui's face twisted when I asked about how he had been able to escape La Cabaña.

"Buddy, don't know how to begin to tell you. La Cabaña is a place to go crazy...do you know we did forced labor and hardly received anything to eat? And, if we protested, the monthly family visits were forbidden. My poor mother had a heart failure and almost died. She's still sick. I tried to behave myself in La Cabaña. I didn't want her to have more grief. For good conduct, I was allowed to work in a farm here in Wajay. I work from six in the morning to six in the afternoon…. You can see how much those bastards squeeze us!" I observed him closely. A portion of his right ear was missing. He touched it and said, "Do you know who did it? Che Guevara, that son of a bitch!"

"But how did it happen?" I asked, not quite recovered from the shock.

---

[3] In English, this would roughly translate to the Central Control of Livestock

"Well, we were in the prison patio and one by one they stripped us and searched our cells. They repeated the so-called requisition. With their bayonets the soldiers forced us to walk back and forth and they hit us every time it pleased them. They also smashed everything they found in the cells. Armando, my cellmate, was sick and refused to strip down, his body shivering with fever. Then Che got there and the soldiers, to show off in front of him, tried to strip Armando by force. Armando got so mad that he grabbed the rifle of one of the soldiers. Then Che pulled out his gun and shot Armando at close range, warning him to let go of the rifle or he'd kill him. Realizing he was in a disadvantageous position, without time to even cock or fire the arm, Armando dropped it. And this bastard, Che, went to him, gun in hand, picked up the rifle and gave it to the soldier. Then he hit Armando in the head with his gun. Can you believe it? Armando fell to the ground without losing consciousness and yelled at him with all his might, calling him a bastard and a coward."

"But what did you have to do with this episode?" I asked.

"Because, after Che kicked him in the mouth with the tip of his boot, I couldn't restrain myself. Naked as I was, I got out of formation and ran to Che, shouting at him, 'You, coward, degenerate, this man is sick!' Before I could reach him with my hands, a soldier hit me on the head with his rifle butt, and Che approached me, scolding the soldier.

"'This is not done, comrade,' he said. 'One has to be reasonable with the inmates,' and he stretched his hand to help me. 'Come on, get up and tell me what you were planning to do.'

"Impulsively, I raised myself a bit and spat on his face. Then Che hit me in full face with his gun, and in a daze, I got up again, feeling the blood running down my face. Two or three soldiers held me, but I continued shouting. 'Cowards, murderers!'

"It was at this moment Che took out the bayonet of one of the rifles and in front of the others mutilated my ear. Naturally, I passed out. According to the other prisoners he threw the piece of flesh to them. I was sent to cut sugarcane."

When Kinqui finished his account, his face was red and his hands made fists, in a symbolic, destructive gesture.

"Take it easy, Kinqui," I told him, "Che was already executed in Bolivia, and the rest of these assassins will end up the same way. Someday this system will fall and many will have to render accounts—to God and to men. The important thing is to reorganize our forces, okay? We'll talk about it tomorrow evening."

That same day, I went to Varadero to meet some friends. Taking many precautions, we had organized the group Aguila 70, taking our name from the majestic eagle. It was mostly integrated by professional young men, recently graduated from the communist universities, as well as Cisneros and Pablo. The only one over fifty was our friend, the Professor, an intellectual who was also gifted with the unbelievable courage, intelligence, and willpower to solve many of our problems.

That evening in beautiful Varadero Beach, communist soldiers were searching the highway. I stopped the jeep, but they signaled me to continue. Making a quick turn to the left, I passed vehicles that were being searched, and one of the soldiers, the youngest, smiled at me. I said mockingly, "Good night, comrade!"

At my destination, everybody was anxiously waiting. The Professor asked me about the delay. "I thought something was wrong...Did you bring the equipment?" I told him it was in the jeep, and I described the search I had just witnessed. In his opinion, they had let me pass because I was driving a Soviet jeep. "Didn't I tell you that jeep was going to be of service to you?" he remarked.

We sat around a table and the Professor took some papers out of his briefcase. The picture was out of sight, as someone in the group said. They showed the powerful Russian torpedo boats and the little bridge where they were moored. They were the best in the island and very expensive. Therefore, they were only available in conspicuous places and important posts, to impress the tourists and diplomatic personalities visiting Cuba. These torpedo boats represented military power, with its usual psychological impact. In the western and eastern coasts, only small fishing boats were utilized for watching and almost all the people engaged in this activity belonged to the Cuban Intelligence Service. Those who refused to do it were considered "not clear" and after a few days were sent to work on land in other occupations.

The boats had, therefore, the double function of fishing for both fish and men—the brave ones who dared to leave or enter Cuba secretly, escaping from communist terror or coming to fight it. The fishermen were equipped with modern phonic devices used to notify the navy post if something was awry or if people were trying to leave the country. If they caught these would-be emigrants, they delivered them to the authorities.

Our purpose that evening was to destroy the torpedo boats moored at the G-2 pier, as nicknamed by the Varadero residents. Explaining through these photos, the Professor showed us how to reach our objective without being seen. We marked in a small map of the area the buoys serving as our markers.

Besides myself, the men in the group were Cisneros, a gigantic, congenial black man; Pablo, a medium-sized but extremely strong man; and Mario, a nervous type, but as daring and brave as anyone could be. We climbed into the jeep and the Professor put on a heavy coat, as it was cold.

On arriving to our destination, Mario said, "Hey, look, they are shooting star shells."

After checking the time on his wristwatch, the Professor told us not to be alarmed. At that time the star shells were routine, just to make a fuss. "Try to be precise and quick," he said. "I know the explosives will not blow up until midnight, but it will be better to be home before that. How much time do you need?" he asked me.

"Perhaps an hour and if you don't find us here when you return, come back every twenty minutes. Don't stay still very long; it's dangerous."

The Professor unloaded the underwater fishing equipment and sped away. From mangroves near the beach, we walked to the reefs. Soon we saw the first buoy that would lead us. We took off our clothes and put on the equipment. There were nine explosives in all, two for the others, and three for me. To relieve the tension, Mario made a joke at Cisneros' expense. "You're lucky, Cisneros. Who the heck is going to see you in the dark?"

"Go ahead, make fun of me," said the good natured man, "but don't ask me to rub your legs underwater because you have cramps. Don't ask for help."

"The best help you can give is to shut your trap if the coast guard vessel passes by," retorted Mario. "You seem to carry a neon light in your mouth when you laugh."

Hardly had Mario finished the joke when we heard a motor and lay down on the ground. A boat passed by, its potent searchlights illuminating everything. It stopped for a few moments before turning around and coming towards us. Its motor never stopped, and the reflection of its lights passed above us over and over. After minutes that seemed hours, we overheard somebody saying, "It can't be. What you saw were the shadows of the trees."

"I would have sworn there were some men in this area," said another voice.

I crouched down even farther, although it would be difficult for them to see us. We were dressed in black, and the night was very dark. Besides, the unevenness of the ground kept us outside the range of the searchlight. After a while the noise of the motor diminished to nothing. We all rose up at the same time. Cisneros insisted we had been seen.

"You're wrong," said Pablo, "if they'd seen us, they wouldn't have left."

"Let's not waste any more time and just do what we have to do. It's dangerous to be here any longer," I insisted.

We plunged in the cold waters of Varadero, so pleasant in summer. After a long swim, I stuck my head out so that I could see through the lower part of my mask the course we were following. The buoy was a few meters away. About 100 meters from the pier, I pulled off my mask. This we would do frequently to orient ourselves. I saw car lights above the pier. We stopped to deliberate, forming a round table in the water, a quarter of a yard between each of us. There was unusual traffic above. A motorboat passed so near us we heard its crew. I took off my snorkel and asked my companions if we should wait a little longer, but they let me decide.

"Okay," I explained, "it was not in our plans, but if we wait for the cars to depart, we will have less time to get away."

Equipment included a respiration tube, mask, a pair of flippers, a knife, and a belt made of lead from discarded accumulators. We made them by melting the lead and shaping it upwards, according to everyone's weight. Naturally, it was painted black, even the mask's metal ring, so its glare wouldn't give us away. Mario had stolen the black garments from the university theatre group. The students used them for doing gymnasium. Their double use to us would be to keep us warm under the water and make us invisible. It was a perfect camouflage. We couldn't have real underwater fishing suits because the government had declared this sport dangerous for national security. It was impossible to acquire this kind of equipment.

When we were a few meters from the pier we realized the guards were listening to a song on the radio, "La Vaca Matilda," or "The Cow Named Matilda." It was actually a Communist jingle to advertise how to preserve the cattle's pastures. Radio and TV stations did not broadcast commercials, so they had to fill those empty spots with anything, including the silly song the guards were listening to.

We accomplished our mission, and after placing some cigarette cases on each one of the boat hulls, we took depth and a few minutes later swam towards the buoy and then reached the beach, at twenty minutes to 11:00. Our plan had come through perfectly. We changed back into our clothes behind a rock where we had left our regular clothes in a plastic bag, protecting them from the night dew along with our equipment. Later on, we hurried through the mangroves and lay down on the wet grass behind some bushes by the highway.

Ten minutes later a car pulled nearer, but it didn't make the agreed-upon sign and continued on its course. The next car changed lights and stopped near us. We ran to the car, looking at both sides of the road to be sure nobody was seeing us, and got into the vehicle as fast as we could.

"Let's go home to celebrate," said the Professor. "It will be interesting to watch what the people do."

The first explosion occurred at ten minutes after midnight, followed by others, until the smoke column grew huge. Sirens sounded from military vehicles and then ambulances passed by, and at 2:30 in the morning, the bustle still had not stopped. We had dealt a hard blow to Castro communism. Eight of their best torpedo boats had been blown to pieces. The group dispersed after setting up the next meeting for the following weekend and assigning missions to each one of us. At three in the morning, I left for Havana.

Very early, Kinqui visited me at my house. Because our date was for the evening, I questioned his presence there at that hour. As usual, he made light of everything. "It's nothing; I didn't feel like going to work"

"Are you kidding?" I said, knowing well nobody could be absent from work on such a flimsy excuse.

"Listen, partner, the only way out is to take advantage of a communist's weak point. The guy responsible in the farm is a communist. Once in a while I present him with a pig's leg, and when I miss work, he writes down I was there. I watch his back, and he watches mine. Do you understand?"

"And how do you manage to present him with pig legs when there's shortage of everything?"

"I have my ways. Near here, between Wajay and El Chico there is a pig farm. The pigs are imported from Canada by Fidel Castro, and they don't notice when I steal one."

"Really, Kinqui, you're incorrigible," I said, "but I do have to go to work. I don't have a gimmick as you have. Do you want to come along? Today we're going to test the fat of the milk of the F-1."

"What does F-1 mean?"

"It's another stroke of genius of the Castro regime—crossing Holstein cattle with the Cebu or Creole. The results are calamitous, because the Cebu is a nervous breed and does not give too much milk. Of course, Fidel is convinced that after the fourth or fifth crossing we shall obtain cattle that will give abundant milk and won't be as susceptible to sickness as the Holstein. Well, by then, about four years from now, the specimen won't be F-1 anymore, but F-5 or F-6. Actually, it takes about ten years to know if the experiment works."

"Yes, these people's plans are so grandiose and so long term that they are never fulfilled. They disappear as by magic. Now you see it, now you don't."

We went to Arroyo Arenas, where Fidel had his Ninas Bonitas dairies. As Kinqui had observed, everything in communist Cuba had to be grandiose. These cows, the "pretty girls," didn't lack anything. The installations had cost millions of dollars—stalls provided with milking machines, air conditioned so the cattle from Canada wouldn't suffer in the Cuban heat, individual electric plants for each of these plans, and drinking water facilities—while in the capital there was not enough water for the people. Medicines regularly imported from Canada in huge orders placed with the Roger labs and the same medicines were not always available at the children's hospital (for example, vitamin K, anti-hemorrhage, all kinds of antibiotics, penicillin, tetracycline, chloraphenicol, and others). After all, children did not represent any benefit for Castro, economically; on the contrary, more births meant more difficulty in providing food for the people.

This problem was neatly solved. Large hospitals, such as Hospital Nacional, Clinico-Quirurgico, and Calixto Garcia, performed free abortions for the women requesting it, whether they were single or married, with government approval. They also practiced tube-binding and placed contraceptive coils on request.

Conversely, in order to accelerate cattle reproduction, artificial insemination was practiced in the cattle ranches. All the dairy production was mainly converted into cheese and other products to be sold abroad. Beef sold for an excellent price in the world market. They called it "red gold." The beef proceeds, of course, continued making Castro and his piranha rich, providing them with the sweet life and continued replenishment of their savings in Swiss bank accounts.

By the door of the genetic enterprise where I worked, a guard stood with a rifle and a small shelter to protect him from the weather. He said hello to me and opened the gates. In a very soft voice, Kinqui asked me, "Why the hell do these people have to have a military guard in a milk research enterprise? This is the result of the psychological military brainwashing. They are completely in power, so that the people don't try to do anything."

I answered, "I'll let you know why they do this. They're manufacturing here the most expensive, most sophisticated cheeses you have ever seen, heard of, or tasted. Brie, cheese with fruit stuffed inside of it— they make it for exporting only, and they're very concerned that the regular people here don't notice what we're doing. You know, the milk is extremely rationed, only a single liter for babies per day, from birth until they're seven years old. After that, they never see milk again in their lives until they get over eighty. In the meantime, we produce vast quantities of these expensive cheeses so we can continue exporting revolutions around the world."

Kinqui couldn't contain himself. "What unscrupulous dictators these people are!"

After I finished putting my test samples of the milk from the animals into test tubes, I numbered them with a small tape according to the animal from which the sample was taken. We took the samples to a lab in the center of Havana to analyze the proteins and fat. We returned to my office to drop off the reports from the previous analysis. Some of these animals came back positive for mastitis, which could have spread streptococci bacteria and developed into severe diarrhea and vomiting in people with a weaker immune system.

If the enterprise could not turn the product over for industrial use, they sold it to the public or sent it to the cafeteria and restaurants for customers' consumption. Many times, I had to repress my indignation for this callousness.

One day after work, Kinqui and I went to the National Airport to see Sandra, my girlfriend, colleague, and co-fighter, who worked for the Rancho Boyeros Institute after she had left the Naval Academy. Due to an injury, she had been relocated there to work with aquatic animals in a special division that worked with dolphins. On our way there, I gave Kinqui details about what happened the night before in Varadero, the purpose of our secret organization, and asked him to join us. He accepted.

Sandra greeted me with a kiss on the cheek.

"You remember our old friend, Kinqui?" I asked her.

"Oh, my God, yes!" she exclaimed, greeting him warmly. "We were kids together!"

Not only was Sandra even more beautiful, with big eyes and a slender body, she was affectionate and kind. She had lived alone in a very comfortable place ever since she was a University student.

"Don't worry about anything," I said to her when we sat in her living room. "We've known Kinqui for a long time, and he's going to work with us. You know he'd never do anything to harm us."

"My only concern," said Sandra "is that he be cautious, having been a political prisoner and all that. Probably he's watched all the time."

"That's nothing," maintained Kinqui. "I've been accustomed to evading and confusing the communists all my life."

I pulled out my briefcase papers marked with red and blue dots pointing to strategic places in the airport blueprint and where the planes were stored. "Sandra," I said, "here's our map. Each bomb must be placed where it's marked red and blue. Study it well and then burn the papers. Also, tell me at what time you want them to explode. If you succeed in putting them in the planes marked with the red dots, Castro won't be able to send supplies to the communist guerillas around the world; bombs placed at the blue dots will collapse the building completely. The map has been prepared toward that end."

Kinqui objected. "What are you planning to do at the airport, my friends? Do you realize how many lives will be lost?"

"And do you know how many lives are lost every day in the communist prisons, you who were there?" said Sandra, looking at him solemnly. "Do you know how many children die unattended and without medicine in the hospitals and how many pregnant women suffer from anemia for lack of adequate nourishment? Yes, in the name of all the young men that are executed by the firing squad, we're going to blow up the airport! The world will know Cuba is not resigned to being enslaved."

"Remember, Kinqui, this is war! A war against Castro and his gang of criminals!" I added.

"You're right," said Kinqui, "forgive me."

"There's nothing to forgive," I told him. "It only shows you're still compassionate, in spite of the hatred that could be expected from you, having endured prison."

"When do we strike, Julio Antonio?" asked Sandra.

"Next week. Fidel is going to speak at the graduation of several pilots. That day we'll carry out our plan. I hope it's the last time he speaks, but it depends on whether we succeed. That's why we have chosen your group. You and other pretty girls will pass in front of the soldiers that are always watching the places where Fidel appears. You'll flirt a little with them and then, bang! The bearded one and his henchmen will blow up."

"We'll do as you say, Boss. You'll be proud of me and the rest," said Sandra, kissing me.

At eleven thirty that evening we were standing in front of a fishing boat in Puerto Esperanza, on another mission. I asked one of the caretakers where we could find Captain Marrero.

"He isn't here," the man said, "but do you see that little green house?" He pointed to a chalet located one block away. "That's his house. Surely he must be there."

We found Marrero sprawled on a hammock in the porch. At first when he heard the jeep, he hesitated, but then he saw me and his face broke into a smile.

"What's the matter?" I shouted at him. "Don't you recognize me? Are you getting old?"

"Oh no, not at all, I'm just beginning to live! I waited for you but then I decided to lie down on the hammock. I love to sleep outside!"

Marrero was a strong, medium size man of about forty-five years, always dressed in white. His pleasant face sported a long, well-groomed beard. He grabbed a flashlight and a small bag near him.

"And who is this?" he asked gesturing toward Kinqui.

"He's my friend Kinqui! When I can't come, he'll take my place. He's completely reliable."

"Fine, let's walk to the beach," he said. Walking along the sea's edge we climbed up a mound and some steep rocks. "These cliffs are dangerous. They cut like knives," Marrero remarked.

He didn't have to say it. We had cut ourselves already. Marrero took two oars out of a cave and jumped into a small boat in which we joined him. He started to row. "Do you see that light?" Marrero asked Kinqui who had never been in that place. "We're going there," he said, pointing to a far point. "So, you'll have a chance to row...that's Cayo Arenas."

Before reaching the Cayo, we'd taken off our shirts. Rowing had made us sweat profusely, as if we were immersed in a Turkish bath, in spite of the dawn's cool breeze. We entered the Cayo through an inlet shaped like a channel, and we anchored the boat. Following Captain Marrero, we saw him kneel by some coconut tree trunks pulling out a plastic bag. "Here are goodies for everyone. This time they left more than we expected."

We returned to the boat, and after leaving the inlet, Marrero let go of the oars and raised his head to listen to a distant noise. Then he took the oars again and rowed back into the inlet, saying, "It sounds like a small patrol motorboat. Let's hide out in the boat, just in case."

The three of us lay down in the boat and threw several dry branches on top. We had time for no more. Then we ran to the nearby bushes and dropped on the grass, staring at the dark waters. The motor boat finally appeared, with its identifying spotlight shedding light on the rocks and mangrove swamp. It stopped, the motor turned over again, and it slowly entered the inlet where we'd left our boat. The men stopped near us, and although it was totally black, we could see their movements from our hiding place.

One of them jumped ashore and said loudly, "Look, it's a small boat!" He pushed back the bushes camouflaging it. From the motor boat, another soldier aimed the spotlight at the little boat. "There's oars in it," he said.

Another soldier got off the motorboat. He carried a tommy gun in his right hand and a powerful flashlight in his left. Searching the surroundings, one of his boots stepped on my outstretched hand. It felt like a crab bite. Holding back the pain, I laid deadly still, with my face against the earth.

After ten or fifteen minutes of searching, they changed their mind and two of them walked to the small reef while the third started the motor boat and brought it a short distance from our vessel. They placed it in such a way that it was invisible, especially with the potent spotlight turned off. Stepping ashore, he went to some nearby bushes and not finding them too convenient, moved to others that were thicker, thus remaining an obstacle in front of our boat, lying in wait for us. He turned his back to us.

"I'm going to split his head," I said, but before going ahead with it, I consulted Marrero. He also thought with this attack we'd be burning the place, but after their surprising intrusion, we were immobilized. Fortunately, Marrero knew how to pilot a motor boat.

Kinqui insisted on doing the attack. He looked for an adequate rock while Marrero gave him his knife. It began to rain, and by a flashing light we saw Kinqui approach a soldier. Then we heard an agonizing scream and shot, followed by an ever louder scream. We ran to help Kinqui, who fortunately, had not been the victim.

"I didn't hit him hard enough," said Kinqui, "And he made the mistake of turning around to shoot me. I had to kill him."

"Are you wounded?" asked Marrero.

"No, he only had time to shoot in the air. He was stunned after I hit him with the rock."

The soldier was lying facedown. I felt for his pulse; he was dead. We decided to leave and head out of the inlet immediately.

I took the tommy gun that had belonged to the dead man and gave Kinqui the bag containing the explosives. While Marrero looked for controls to start the motorboat, I fired at our boat. When it was flooded with water we ran to the motorboat and got away quickly, all the time hearing the soldiers firing. At last we were out of their range.

We arrived at Marrero's chalet at 10:00 a.m., and he prepared oyster cocktails for us before our departure for Havana. I dropped Kinqui off at his home and went directly to my work. There was a surprise in store for me. A political conference was being held, presided over by Captain Henry Villegas Tamayo, alias "Pompo," an ex-fighter in the Sierra Maestra and Che's aborted Bolivian campaign.

Pompo told us in detail the purpose of this adventure. It was designed to spread revolution to the other South American countries with Bolivia as the continent's second base of operations. This country had been chosen for communist infiltration because its geographical situation made it an ideal area. Since it lacked oceans, after taking up power and communizing their own nation, the communist Bolivians would have to fight with their neighbors, who eventually would close their borders to them. In such an event they would have to find an outlet to the sea, in order to transport their products.

He also explained the amount of money in dollars, Bolivian pesos, and other foreign currency the adventure had required. Frankly, it was unbelievable to hear this from the mouth of one of the participants. While the Cuban people lacked the most necessary resources, millions of dollars were wasted in stupid and shameful infiltrations of sister nations, just to export Russian communism to all the Americas.

After this lecture, I worked in my office until midnight and then left for Sandra's house. She was awake, leaning on pillows scattered throughout the floor, her head buried in the seat of an armchair. She responded to my kisses and embraces with sobs, which alarmed me.

"What is it, my love?"

"It's that I never know if you will come back or not. And to think that they could kill you, and I, who love you so much, might never know it."

I kissed her, soothing her and promising she would go with me to Varadero the next day.

Her eyes lit up. "Really? Will you take me?"

We went to sleep. The next day was Saturday. I ate breakfast in a hurry. I had time to appreciate the morning's splendor and Sandra's beauty, even with her rumpled housecoat and messy hair.

"Don't make me wait. Be ready at noon," I whispered as I took her in my arms.

At the lab, I picked up some test results and transferred them to models used to compute in old IBM machines. Afterwards, I went to Kinqui's house and honked the horn of my jeep to wake him. He came out still buttoning his shirt. We picked up Sandra, and the three of us left for Varadero.

After an hour's drive, we stopped at a cafeteria, not too sure we would get to eat. Sometimes, food was available, but the long waiting line discouraged people. This place, on the contrary, was desolate—a bad sign. Sure enough, all there was to be had was watery melon juice served in small size cups, at fifty cents per cup. As Castro always says: "All for the people and by the people!"

In Varadero, communists had finished searching the week before. It was a good thing because inside the jeep we carried ten explosive loads and a .38 caliber pistol. Already the team was waiting for me at the house, and the Professor was pleasantly surprised to see Sandra.

I had introduced Kinqui and asked for Mario, the only one who had not yet arrived. My question seemed to worry the

Professor. "Something very unpleasant has happened in connection with Mario. Tell us what you saw, Cisneros."

He passed his hand over his face and started to tell. "I saw Mario in Havana, in Calle 23, with two other men, one of whom I'm convinced is from the G-2. I remember that face. They were getting out of the Havana Libre Hotel, excitedly gesturing. One of the men grabbed Mario by the shirt collar pushing him. I was amazed, because Mario is not a man to let anybody rough him around unless—"

"True," I agreed, interrupting. "Did he see you?"

"No, I was on the other side of the street, at Radio Centro, buying tickets so my wife and child could go to the movies that evening without having to stand in line. As for Mario and the other men, they must have agreed on something because they all left in a car."

"Are you sure it was Mario?" Pablo insisted.

"You can bet your life it was him."

Pablo suggested that perhaps Mario had been detained, but Cisneros disagreed. "No, he was arguing, but in a friendly way. In the end, one of them gave him a friendly slap on his back. I'm sure they came to an agreement."

At that precise moment there was a knock at the door. The Professor was going to get up when Pablo stopped him and he himself went to open it. I warned my friends. "If it's Mario, don't say a word of what we've discussed, do you understand? If it's what I suspect, we must act with care, as if nothing happened."

Mario entered, greeting us with a nervous smile, immediately asking, "Well what's new? Did the material we expected arrive?"

Cisneros answered. "No, nothing arrived yet."

Then the Professor said he wanted to speak to me about foreign contacts. "Naturally, the action in the airport will have to be canceled," Pablo suggested.

"Perhaps not," said the Professor, slowly reflecting. "Maybe I can solve the explosives problem. However, we will have to cancel all the operations for the time being. I'd really like to know why the boys didn't leave us the explosives this time. I wonder what happened to them. Anyway, stay calm and don't keep anything in your homes that can implicate you. You can't be too cautious."

"Probably they're delayed, that's all," ventured Mario. "Some last-minute difficulty we've yet to find out."

"Yes, Mario," I said, "and it's precisely the nature of that difficulty we've got to find out."

Sandra and Kinqui climbed into the jeep with me. We made several detours hoping to confuse any possible tail. I parked in an alley. My buddies tried to appease my fears. As for Sandra, she always had thought Mario was a good boy.

"It would be too bad if he's an informer," she commented.

"I'm almost sure he is," I said, although I'd never suspected it before. "The bad part is that he knows our airport contacts because on one occasion he accompanied me on a trip to Santa Clara, and he returned alone, to let the Professor know we needed him in that city. I also told him to communicate with the Santa Clara people so they could reserve an immediate return trip for the Professor. It's ridiculous to make reservations fifteen or twenty days ahead but you know how awful the service is. That's how he met the other group. It was my mistake, I admit it. I feel responsible for what may happen to you. In any case we shall watch him. Soon we'll know."

After twenty minutes, we returned to the house and found the Professor sitting on the porch. We all got in, and before I could say anything, he told us, "If Mario belongs to the security forces, we are in danger. But if we act intelligently, the situation will not be that serious. I don't believe the G-2 is planning to immediately arrest us, or we'd already be in jail. I have a feeling they want more information. Perhaps something Mario doesn't know yet...names of contacts to obtain explosives...places where they come from. Just in case, I'm going to mark on the map how to get out of the country. If something suddenly happens, I don't want you to stay in Cuba at the mercy of these communists. You are one of the most vulnerable because of your government job."

"Come on, Professor, we are all implicated, even Kinqui, who has just met Mario," I protested.

"I agree," he said, "but while the others go to prison, you'll be shot."

"What about you, Professor?"

"I'm an old man, and they can execute me if they want. But you are young. If they can prove it, you'll have to leave Cuba."

The doorbell rang and Kinqui went to the door. By the angry faces of Pablo and Cisneros, we suspected the worst.

"Mario is a traitor!" Cisneros exclaimed. "I knew I wasn't mistaken! Pablo and I saw him. The same man was waiting for him at the pizzeria, and Mario gave him all the details about what was said here. When the man left, he remained, waiting to be served."

"Then you can identify this individual, can you?" I asked.

"Sure, I know him well! He was the one who questioned me at the G-2 when Playa Giron erupted," he answered.

"Then let's go find Mario," I said.

The Professor held my arm, asking me in a low voice what I intended to do.

"I intend to make the louse talk. Wait for me. And you, Pablo, come with me."

"Forgive me, but I think you shouldn't," said the Professor. "I'll bring him over myself."

"But why you, Professor?" I asked him, confused.

"Very simple: because you are all supposed to be en route to Havana or going that way. He will be surprised to see you, and he may decide not to come. With me, he'll come, and then we can all ask him."

When he left, Sandra stood by the glass window watching him. I went to her, and nostalgically we admired the lovely blue water and the fine, clean, pure white sand. She pressed my hand. "If we ever have to separate, think of how much I have loved you and will tomorrow," she said. We embraced.

Our companions sat around a table in the library, sick with worry about the incident. Sandra, for whom Mario was almost an unknown person, asked me sadly what I intended to do with him. "Whatever it is, it won't be decided by me alone. It affects all. Now, what do you think a traitor deserves?"

Her compassion dominated her. "I know, but he's so young..."

To cut off this conversation, I sat with her on the sofa and occupied myself in cleaning my pistol. I had hardly begun when we heard the sound of an approaching motor car and went to the library to tell the others. "They're here! Now be quiet and let's give the Professor time to bring him to this room."

I hid the gun under my shirt, as we heard the voices of the Professor and Mario from closer and closer.

There are no words to describe Mario's astonishment when he saw us there. He barely managed to say, with obvious concern, "Hey, what are you guys doing here?"

Cisneros accused him first. "We are here, Mario, to ask you how you could have sunk so low as to become a dirty informer."

Mario looked at us one by one, still incredulous, waiting to hear any minute the laughs, and the end of a bad joke. But as we kept our accusing attitude, he tried to draw out his gun. At that moment, the Professor, who entered the door behind Mario, pointed his pistol at the back of Mario's neck and said, "Drop that gun, you coward!"

When Mario did, Pablo picked up the gun, and holding Mario by the collar of his shirt forced him to sit down in a chair. "What do we do with this traitor?" he asked me.

"I believe we must give him the opportunity to explain his behavior. Come on, Mario, begin your story; we don't have much time to waste on you."

We all sat, except the Professor who remained standing by Mario aiming his gun at him. "I know I have done something bad, but I had no other alternative. They would have shot me if I didn't."

"And how did it start, Mario? Since when?" I asked.

He broke down crying, which made me very angry.

"You should have acted like a man to the end! So, you had the nerve to betray your friends and now you cannot face the consequences? Finish your story. We don't have any more time to waste," I repeated.

"Well," continued Mario, "two weeks ago they arrested me and took me to the G-2 in Villa Marista."

"Where did they detain you?" asked the Professor.

"When I was leaving my work two men approached me and asked my name. I asked why, but one of them took out his State Security card and made me go with them. After keeping me for six hours in a cell they took me to an office where there were two officers. They read the charges but asked me to work for them, under the promise to destroy the evidence against me and set me free if I accepted."

Pablo asked him if he felt any remorse when he accepted the Security men's proposition. Mario hid his face in his hands and leaned forward in the chair.

"Yes, I did. In fact, when I furnished my first information, at the Habana Libre, I refused to do it again. I was ready to die. But I became scared and let them persuade me to continue. They are strong. Don't kid yourself. They have pictures of all of you and are aware of every step you take. They haven't arrested you because they want to catch the connection that is bringing the explosives."

Fear was written on his face. Mario continued, looking at all of us as though trying to convince us he didn't have any choice. We didn't either. "If you can't lick them, join them," he said. "Otherwise, they'll wind up shooting all of us."

I got up and signaled Pablo and Cisneros, who immediately jumped Mario, hand tying him. "Please don't!" he begged. "Remember, we've been friends for years."

"Yes, Mario," I interjected. "It's a pity you didn't think of that before. Now Kinqui, gag him and take him to my jeep. Here are the keys. Pablo and Cisneros will go with you. As soon as you've completed your mission, go to the Railway Station and buy six second-class tickets for San Luis, Oriente. Then go back to Sandra's. It's the only house they're not watching. But be careful they don't follow you."

When they'd gone out through the back door, the Professor said, "Julio Antonio, you have to leave Cuba immediately. As soon as they discover Mario's absence, and the fact that we know, they'll come to arrest us."

"We all have to leave Cuba immediately," I argued. "Either we all go or we all stay."

After agreeing, the Professor spent the next twenty minutes gathering documents he considered important. The others he destroyed. The three of us were almost ready to leave when Sandra saw an Alfa Romeo through the library window. This was the usual patrol car from the G-2. It was coming in the direction of our house.

"They are coming for us!" she shouted.

I drew back the curtains and verified she was right. "There's no time to waste," I said, giving my gun to Sandra. "Shoot the tires so they can't follow us. If you have to kill the guards, do it!"

We escaped through the back door and climbed into the Professor's old Jaguar. He sat by my side and Sandra sat in the back. We watched the car approaching and we had to pass it in order to leave. There was only one highway leading to the chalet.

They saw us leaving. Soon they had blocked us with their car and then stepped out. I repeated my instructions to Sandra and the Professor to shoot the car's tires. I increased the Jaguar's speed. Two of the communist guards lay face down on the road while the other two did the same in the ditches, shooting at our car, and perforating the windshield. The Professor shot two of the car's tires.

Almost on the verge of colliding with the Alfa Romeo, I hit the car's brakes and turned to the left. As the car slid to the right, it struck the other vehicle. The impact moved it out of the way. The guards lying on the highway were pressed between the two cars.

I turned to the right, continuing to drive while the other two guards started to shoot at us. In his efforts to eliminate the guard to his right, the Professor leaned out too much, was hit and fell on his seat, his face covered with blood. I tried to raise him up but heard so many shots that I decided to leave that place at full speed. Sandra kept shooting through the back glass while the other guard, standing in the middle of the road continued firing at us. The Alfa Romeo became a bonfire with flames shooting into the air.

When we had gained some distance, Sandra leaned down to examine the Professor. "His pulse is weak, he's unconscious," she said, in answer to my unspoken question. "He has lost a great deal of blood. The bullet grazed his head and it's embedded in the frontal area." Sandra took off her blouse, tore it, and improvised a bandage on the wounded man's head. I could do nothing but drive.

Then I saw a Soviet Urals motorcycle at the side of the cafeteria located on the right side of the freeway. I turned the car to the right and drove into the bushes. When I thought it was safe, I stopped the car.

Sandra questioned this action.

"Don't be alarmed," I said. "We're going to change vehicles. In this one, we won't reach Havana without being arrested."

The Jaguar was destroyed. I went to the cafeteria, walking close to the vegetation so they couldn't see me from inside. When I was by the motorcycle, I climbed on top of it and pulled off the ignition wires, connecting them. When the indicating light turned on, I stepped on the starter pedal and fled.

I met the others in a few seconds and propped the Professor in the sidecar between Sandra and me. I found a portfolio and threw it into the bushes. I also found a brown fur collared jacket, a helmet, and goggles, which Sandra put on. If they were looking for a woman and two men, they would never recognize us. I helped her to climb into the back seat.

We traveled at a regular speed, trying to appear as normal as possible. Naturally, we passed several patrol cars from the Security and Police. The Professor, looking pale, was starting to regain consciousness. He even tried to talk, but we didn't let him. He remained quiet, leaning his head against the back seat.

At the Havana gateway, after having crossed the tunnel under the harbor, we saw soldiers dismounting two trucks, seemingly there to search the cars. Standing in the traffic boxes, they stopped all vehicles. I felt relieved to have been able to evade them. We continued without any more incidents towards Rancho Boyeros and Sandra's home.

Kinqui opened the door. He warned the others, who had their guns aimed at the door.

I told him to open the garage door quickly because of the Professor's weakened condition and refused to give any more details for the time being. We put him to bed and ministered to his wound.

While Kinqui and I transferred the Professor from the motorcycle, Sandra sterilized surgical instruments as I had instructed her. The wounded Professor was later placed on the kitchen table, in front of my buddies. I succeeded in extracting the bullet from his head. Once it was done, I left him to Sandra's care and started to leave, against protests from Kinqui who didn't want me to go back to work.

"The Security must be waiting for you. They'll arrest you. In any case, I'll go with you."

"No pal, you stay here. And if I don't come back, you know what you have to do. As for you two, Pablo and Cisneros, good luck. Trust Kinqui if I cannot make it. He knows the plan to follow," I repeated several times. "Now don't get mushy," I added, seeing the sorrowful look my companions gave me.

Sandra gave me the chain and cross she always wore, saying, "Don't put it away, no matter what happens. It will protect you."

At the lab I found a cryptic note from the director demanding to see me urgently, but nothing else. The job that should have been assigned to me that day wasn't there. The staff had no response when I asked. Feeling apprehensive, I presented myself at the office, where the personnel director had even a bigger surprise for me.

"Oh, finally you're here...Give me the keys to your jeep. I think they've got a good job for you today."

I handed him the keys and went to see the director, who greeted me cordially. Another surprise. I was already prepared for the worst.

"We want you to do an urgent revision in a Pinar del Rio dairy. Fidel is planning to inspect it with some Canadian veterinarians visiting Cuba. The animals not passing your inspection will immediately be sent to another dairy." He gave me a long list with the numbers of the cattle at the dairy about to be visited by the Canadians.

"Use my Volga and be careful. The motor has just been repaired," he added, to my complete relief. Obviously, the Security forces had not told them anything yet.

I took my leave. Before I went to my new mission the next day, I prepared myself and my plans. At Sandra's, everybody was gloomy, but not because of the Professor's health; that was improving. He was in the bedroom, still sleeping under the effects of the anesthesia from his surgery.

"I just know all our people have been arrested," explained Kinqui, "and the airport has been militarized. Mario told them. They must be looking for us. We have to leave the island."

"You're right," I said. "But first we've got to take the Professor to a safe place, and I have a few important things to do."

I said goodbye to my friends and drove in my Volga to the Coppelia Ice Cream Parlor. When I arrived, I could see the line was so long that it would take a couple of hours to get through it, even though it was still early in the morning. I spotted my contact, already seated and with an ice cream order for myself and a drink for him. He was a nondescript black man, tall and skinny in his thirties, today dressed in a plain blue work outfit. His codename was Chopin; I never called him by his real name. He greeted me with his usual smile. His white teeth always reminded me of the ivory keys of a grand piano. He sat at our table, reading a newspaper and drinking the Cuban coffee in front of him.

I was happy to meet with him, as I had already obtained a package for him and was about to make contact anyway. As I slid into my seat, I casually slipped an envelope over to him. Equally casually, he slid it off the table and into his bag. He glanced at me over the paper. He gave me a small roll of papers bound with a rubber band. "This is the electrical schematic for the microphones on the podium," he told me. As I tucked it away inside my shirt, he continued, "Julio Antonio, you have to leave Cuba right away."

This confirmed a fear that had been growing in my mind recently, as I had noticed the increasing air of suspicion in the office. Piñeiro, especially, wasn't fond of me and seemed to be watching me ever more closely.

"What has happened?" I asked him.

"I'm sorry, but the information was released to the U.N. about Castro's troop movements in Africa. The information could only have come from your office."

"I made it clear that information should not be released publicly!" I exclaimed quietly, struggling to contain my anger. "They're certain to find me out now!"

My contact nodded. "I know, damn politicians; there was nothing we could do. Even as we speak, people from your office are being taken in for questioning. If you don't leave in the next twenty-four hours—forty-eight hours tops—they will find you and kill you."

I put my head in my hands in despair and frustration.

"We have made arrangements to get you out."

"No," I said flatly, thinking of the others who would be implicated by my sudden absence.

"It will be tonight," he said remorselessly.

"No!" I repeated more firmly.

"I'm sorry, Julio Antonio, but it's for your own good."

"You don't understand—there are people who have been close to me. Some of them have been helping me, and Castro's people move from suspicion to certainty very easily. I need to bring them out, as well. Sandra, Kinqui, Cisneros, everyone. I can't leave them behind to face death when I can save them, as well. I need your word that they will be protected as you are protecting me."

"We thought you might feel that way, and the arrangements include them. It will be more dangerous with the greater numbers; but if you want to live, you and your associates will have to leave within the next forty-eight hours. It will take the communist red tape that long to move against you. If you take longer, you guys could be in great danger."

It was July of 1971. The preparations for the 26th of July celebrations were under way for the anniversary of the Revolution the next day. This event was held in the Plaza of the Revolution, where Fidel Castro had delivered many speeches. As part of the usual celebrations, Castro was to make a speech. This one was supposed to be the last one he made. I arrived at the Hotel Havana Libre in the Vedado downtown district of Havana, where we were planning our mission. We had decided to take advantage of the situation to make what would prove to be one of the most elaborate attempts on the life of Fidel Castro. Even with only forty-eight hours left in the country, I wanted to take my last shot at this regime that had hurt so many.

Dressed in my military uniform, I was meeting my friend Olerio, who was dressed in the uniform of the Civil Guard. We were both tense, as what we were about to do involved a great degree of risk. Failure or detection wouldn't provide any avenue of escape; it would mean instant death by summary execution. Olerio crossed himself as he said, "This plan must not fail! Lord, please end the suffering of the people."

"Let us pray it will be Castro's last speech," I said. I pulled out the Caridad del Cobre that had been given to me by Yaneba and the crucifix given to me by Sandra from beneath my shirt and kissed them.

"Amen," concluded Olerio. He hesitated. "You have my papers?"

"Right here," I replied as I handed them to him.

He smiled as he rolled them up and tucked them away. "He always adjusts those microphones before he speaks."

"Good luck to you," I said. He got up, and we shook hands before embracing. We left the hotel, heading in separate directions.

Hours later, the final preparations for the speech were being made, and people had already begun to arrive, filing in and finding seats, although the VIP seats on the podium were still empty.

Olerio had now switched to a workman's outfit, wearing a hard hat, utility vest, and large tool belt. He had joined two other workers in setting up the sound system for the speech. He looked around carefully to make sure no one was watching and then slipped unseen beneath the podium.

There was plenty of room to work underneath the podium, and light trickling in from various holes in the platform construction gave him ample visibility to work. He grabbed the wires coming down from above. He worked fast, in case any motion by the microphones above would betray the presence of someone working with the wires. He pulled out some wire strippers from the belt and started to strip away the insulation on the cables leading to the microphones. He took out a voltmeter and set it to measure the amperage and applied the testers to the wires, holding the wires carefully to avoid touching the exposed copper. He looked at the reading and nodded in satisfaction.

In the meantime, the VIPs had begun to arrive. I entered with two other high-ranking military personnel and took a seat, looking around casually to make sure all was well. I saw Olerio's two friends by the podium were still in place, keeping watch to make sure Olerio was able to work undisturbed.

Piñeiro walked in with two of his subordinates in his immaculate uniform. He signaled to his men to take up positions around the podium, sniffed at the air, and looked around. Seeing me, he nodded slightly, and I replied with a nod of my own. Almost as if he felt something was amiss, he strode toward the podium, looking out at the crowd. Suddenly, he turned toward the podium. Holding my breath, I tried to see what he was looking at, but his back blocked my view. What I learned later was that he had noticed a slight movement with the microphones. Going over to get a closer look, he noticed a gnat flying around one of the microphones. When it landed, it was vaporized into a puff of smoke by the current, surprising him.

I tried to maintain an appearance of calm by engaging in casual talk with another officer, but I couldn't help but keep looking over towards the G-2 agent. Piñeiro moved closer to the microphone, careful not to touch it as he gave it a minute inspection. After watching a third gnat get vaporized, Piñeiro knew something was terribly wrong and went into action. He put his hand on his pistol, gestured to two of his guards to follow him, and then ran down the stairs. I quickly excused myself from the conversation and ran down after them.

Not knowing what was about to happen, I placed my hand on my own pistol. When I reached the ground, I saw Piñeiro and his men looking for a way under the platform. They found a way in, and I hesitated, wondering what I should do. I could feel the sweat pouring down my face, knowing that Olerio had no place to hide under there. Just as I decided to brave it and proceed forward, my worst fears were confirmed by the sound of a single pistol shot. I broke into a run.

When I burst in, I saw Piñeiro standing over the corpse of Olerio. My friend was lying in a pool of blood with part of his skull missing. Piñeiro whirled at my intrusion. "What are you doing here?" he demanded of me.

"I...I heard something," I stammered. "I knew something was wrong when I saw you leave the podium, and I thought I should come and see if I could help you." As I was talking, I heard two shots and a scream as the guards executed the two men who had been helping Olerio.

"This son of a bitch tried to kill Fidel!" Piñeiro said angrily as he kicked the body of my friend, and I was just barely able to restrain myself from wincing. He was completely irrational; I was worried that in this state he might shoot anyone he even suspected might be involved in this. He looked at me suspiciously. "How did you get here so quickly?"

"When I saw you go down the stairs, I thought something was wrong, Commandante," I repeated with strong conviction. I knew my life hung in the balance if I couldn't convince him of my innocence and sincere intentions.

He took a few steps and got right up into my face. "Or, maybe...maybe...." He hesitated. "No. It couldn't be." He shook his head and patted my shoulder.

A few more soldiers burst in just then, led by a young captain. "Commandante Piñeiro! Is everyone all right?"

"Yes," Piñeiro replied, "we have it under control." He spat on Olerio's corpse. "Take this traitor dog out of here!"

"Yes, Commandante!" the captain said crisply. He turned to a pair of soldiers. "Get some canvas."

"And get a technician to fix this," Piñeiro added, gesturing to the wires.

"Should we tell Commandante Fidel about this?" the captain inquired.

"No!" Piñeiro replied reflexively. He paused as he thought about it further. "No, don't bother the Commandante en Jefe with this trash."

I watched him as he bent over the wires to examine Olerio's handiwork, and then slipped out as the soldiers came back with the canvas tarp for the body, and the electrician came in to effect the repairs. Like all the other attempts on Castro's life, this one had failed, and I needed to get away from the incriminating scene. I had to return to my pose, however briefly, as an ardent supporter and admirer of Fidel's. When Piñeiro came out, just in time for the speech, he resumed his usual position just behind Castro. As I enthusiastically applauded the speech, I couldn't help but notice the suspicious look thrown in my direction from Piñeiro.

After Castro finished his speech, I slipped away, called my uncle to arrange a meeting with my contact at his house, and went over there. After I explained the situation, my trainer and mentor in intelligence, the General, gave me a can of shoe polish full of microfilm, carefully sealed. He gave me a codename told me to give only to that contact and no one else after I escaped. "Not even your closest friends can know about this," he said. He gave me a map. "Follow this exactly, as this will not only let you know which houses are safe and which to avoid, but also help you avoid the mines in the minefield. If you get caught, be sure you don't get caught with this. This is classified intelligence information."

"Don't worry about it," I said. "No one will know."

He added, "He is in charge of naval intelligence at the U.S. base."

I hugged my uncle and the General, and they wished me good luck. They looked at me compassionately, because they knew the odds were high that this would be the last time they would ever see me.

CHAPTER IX: THE ESCAPE

We initiated preparations for our escape. "Listen, Kinqui," I said to my friend, "We need you to perform one of your marvelous animal-stealing tricks for us."

"Very well, Doctor. Where is the fattest and healthiest specimen?" he asked, already enjoying his prank.

"Take the 'instruments' and I'll tell you where," I replied.

While Kinqui went to look for knives and other implements, Cisneros returned from the kitchen with items already in hand.

"Cisneros, you're always ready for thefts," kidded Pablo.

We agreed that Pablo would stay with Sandra to help take care of the Professor. Meanwhile we went by freeway to the farm Novia del Mediodia, renowned for its excellent Cebu cattle. The field was deserted and the cattle were roaming loose through the huge paddock. When we got out of the freeway, we quickly advanced up a slope so the farmhands couldn't see us. Cisneros was the first to dismount, rope in hand, ready to lasso a good specimen. We crawled under the barbed wire fence, and Cisneros, without further preliminaries, threw the rope and, incredibly lucky, caught a small, handsome bull. "I got it, I got it!" he happily yelled, trying to catch our eyes.

"Be careful!" shouted Kinqui, noticing the trapped animal was starting to run wildly. "Listen Cisneros, let it go or you will get killed."

Cisneros obeyed too late and fell into a puddle. When we rescued him, he was covered with mud and excrement. The bull had dragged him through ruts formed by the water overflow from the drinking trough and the animal's hoofs. Kinqui fell to his knees with laughter. Cisneros, at first furious, ended up joining in the general merriment.

Soon Kinqui caught the bull, and in less than an hour, we had carved and boned it completely. Then we put it inside nylon bags and took it to the Volga. Kinqui continued teasing Cisneros, comparing him to John Wayne and other film cowboys.

"Quit it, man," he said, pretending to be annoyed.

Our next move was to have Kinqui take the Professor to Captain Marrero, accompanied by Sandra, thus dispelling suspicions.

Pablo and Cisneros were to accomplish the part of our plan having to do with the Alfa Romeos. I would go to pick up a fellow recently released from political prison. He would be our guide.

According to the Professor, he was an experienced underwater swimmer and knew the area from where we could escape.

"Tomorrow evening we depart for Oriente," I said.

"With that fellow you're going to bring here?" asked Kinqui. "Is he to be trusted?"

"I vouch for him," I answered.

Sandra prepared a good dinner of roast beef and baked plantains. The latter had been taken from a farm by Cisneros.

The Professor's condition had improved. After dinner, in private conversation with him, I told him my intention to leave him at Marrero's until he was completely well. He agreed.

"Your guide is a fine man," he said. "He has been a political prisoner for years. Still, learn well the topography and other details, in case you have problems with him. He's somewhat traumatized by his years in prison and although he is brave, sometimes he hesitates. And as you can understand, the least hesitation can cost somebody's life.

"I ask you to be patient with him and not to say a word of this to the others," the Professor continued. "Of course, I don't anticipate anything happening, but if the situation becomes serious and you have to eliminate him, do it. The important thing is that the documents now in your possession arrive at their destination. You must renew the contact with our people there. This man's name is Joaquin. Tell him you are Aguila Azul; that's the password. You'll pick him up at Amistad Street in Old Havana, at ten o'clock tonight."

I said good-bye to the Professor and told him to take good care of himself. He pressed my hands and said emotionally, "Take care, my boy. May God bless you."

Before leaving, I gave final directions to the others. "Sandra, Kinqui, take the Professor to Marrero's house in Puerto Esperanza and tell him not to let the old man out of the house, under any circumstance. This is a very special job, and any mistake can cost us death by firing squad. You are to return here immediately, do you understand? You should be here no later than four o'clock in the morning."

Then I asked Cisneros and Pablo about the explosives.

"We got them," they told me.

"Fine, now take the motorcycle with the sidecar, and remember, it's stolen. As soon as you finish your mission, dump it and return here by bus—no later than midnight, when the patrol cars go out. They might stop you and ask for the motorcycle license and registration."

We helped Sandra seat the Professor in the car. When they were gone, Cisneros and Pablo sped away on the motorcycle. "What about us?" asked Kinqui.

"We take the bus," I said.

"Oh no, that's what you think. I have a better idea. Wait for me ten minutes. I'll be back."

Kinqui, always resourceful, quickly reappeared, driving a Ford station wagon. "I found it around the corner," he said.

He'd stolen a vehicle from Fleet Operations, a department in charge of grouping all the vehicles of heavy load and transportation under the state control. Its owners, private individuals, had thus become state employees. Though they had ownership, they had to justify the gasoline they received, according to assigned trips. From the money earned on each trip, they had to contribute a portion to the state, and they couldn't drive the car for personal use.

We parked the station wagon on Amistad Street, away from the address the Professor had given us. The building at that address was in ruins. After climbing stairs and standing in front of the designated door, I had second thoughts, remembering the odd things our friend had told us about this Joaquin. Kinqui offered to go through the side window while I knocked at the door.

After repeated and increasingly loud knocks, someone unfastened a door-latch and opened the decrepit door. In the room was an individual about thirty-five years old, of medium weight and height. "Who sent you?" he asked.

"I was sent by the Professor," I replied.

"OK, come in." He let me in and slammed the door shut after I entered, then aimed a pistol at me. "Who are you?"

Undisturbed, I sat down in the rundown sofa and said, "Aguila Azul."

The man answered, "Joaquin." He apologized for his mistrust. "They're looking for me, and one never knows. However, you'll have to answer some questions."

"You are the one who will have to answer questions" I said. Kinqui, who had sneaked into the house through the window, was pointing his gun at the man's back. "By the way," I said while browsing through a big book I'd found at the end table, "Stop pointing your gun at me."

"Why?" the man insisted.

"Because he says so!" answered Kinqui, coming closer to Joaquin, until he dropped his gun.

"Sit down," I commanded Joaquin. "This is Kinqui. We're a group of fighters and have to leave Cuba unexpectedly. According to the Professor, you're in a similar situation, more or less, and you know the place from where we intend to escape. You're also supposed to be a good underwater swimmer. So, if you agree, you can go with us and be our guide. The thing is to help each other. Do you understand? One thing is for sure: you have to decide it right now. Time is short."

Joaquin hesitated briefly. "Yes, but I've promised a friend to take him with me when I escape."

"Then I'm sorry," I said. "There are too many people in our plan, and we came to see you because the Professor has been wounded."

I got up and Kinqui shook hands with him. Still holding Kinqui's hand, Joaquin looked at me and suddenly changed his mind. "I'll go with you. Wait for me. I'm going to gather some papers. I also have four tommy guns with four hundred bullets. What do I do with all this?"

"Get a sack and put everything into it. We'll carry it to the station wagon."

Minutes later, we went down the rotten staircase, trying not to make too much noise when our feet touched the squeaky steps. "Be careful with that old woman sitting over there," Joaquin warned us when we got to the door. "She's from the Neighbors Committee."

The woman, sitting at the entrance of the building next door was heavy-set, in her forties, and fanning herself while not missing any detail around her. Seeing this, I told Kinqui to bring the station wagon to the door, while we waited inside of the building. Joaquin became immediately restless. "She may get your license number, or she may wonder what three men are doing, carrying a sack at this time of the evening."

"Don't worry," I said. "This station wagon is stolen. We'll get rid of it right away."

When Kinqui returned, we started to load the vehicle with the heavy sack and a suitcase containing Joaquin's personal effects, his fishing gear, and his papers. The woman got up and came towards us. Kinqui was the first to see her.

"Hey, Julio Antonio, the woman is coming to us."

"Don't say anything, Joaquin," I warned. "You leave this matter to me."

I climbed into the wagon through one door while I motioned him to open the other side and get in.

At that moment, the informer shouted, "Just a minute, comrades. Wait a minute."

"What do you want?" I asked her, without getting out of the station wagon.

"Can you identify yourselves?"

I opened the door and got out. "Sure, comrade, but who are you?"

"I'm in charge of the C.D.R. vigilance."

I in turn pulled out my I.D., which she hardly could see in the dark, and told her, "I am an inspector in the offices of the Prime Minister, and we are checking the living conditions in this building."

"Oh, I see, excuse me. But you know..."

"That's all right. You're doing your job. Good evening, comrade." I turned to Kinqui. "Move on, Lieutenant."

And we sped away from there.

Kinqui complained that he had been a lieutenant for too long. Joaquin didn't understand our mutual kidding, but he made an effort to smile and be agreeable. "Truly, boys, you're brave."

"No, we're not," I disagreed. "We're cunning. That's a lesson we have learned from people: always treat them courteously—if hypocritically. What would you gain by confrontation and defiance? Ten years in prison."

Joaquin had just received his first lesson on how to cope with the communists. Throughout his years in prison, he had been a rebel on hunger strikes, refusing to be rehabilitated.

This had earned him insults, mistreatment, stays in punishment cells, and endless grief still stamped on his face. Although he had not been practical, we couldn't help admiring him. He had served his term without bowing down to the assassins, although his sacrifice had been useless. Those who accepted rehabilitation were allowed to leave prison. Freed, feigning remorse, he could attempt to fight again. Many of his prison mates had done so. On the other hand, when the non-rehabilitated left prison, they became human wrecks from the many tortures they had endured. Joaquin was a typical victim with shattered nerves destroyed by endless questionings.

Author's I.D. as Medical Inspector, Genetic Researcher of Dairy Production, Dept. of the Prime Minister's Office

Joaquin didn't know that, out of necessity, we had learned the communist phraseology in our daily street work. In a pinch, we could pass as one of them, and we knew how to exploit this to an advantage. There was such confusion and fear regarding the G-2 apparatus that everyone suspected everyone else, and nobody knew who was who—even among secret police ranks. It was not unusual for two untidy looking fellows to approach an individual, show him their G-2 identification cards, and arrest him. The agents would take him to headquarters in Villas Maristas in any kind of vehicle, even an old and dilapidated one. That is how Castro maintained psychological control and fear in the people.

Arriving at Rancho Boyeros I noticed two cars parked near our house, facing opposite directions, each with one man inside. I felt apprehensive—much more so when I was able to see the cars better.

"Don't stop, go on, go on!" I warned Kinqui, who, instead of complying, looked at me in surprise.

"Go on, I say, damn it, don't stop for anything!"

Through the back view mirror, I saw one of the men, in the car parked in opposite direction to ours, put his head out of the window, to see us better. But he didn't start the car. At the airport entrance, I told Kinqui, never taking my eyes off the mirror, "Let's leave the station wagon here, in the parking lot. If I am not mistaken, they have the house under surveillance and are waiting to arrest all of us at one time."

Joaquin became agitated. "We'd better throw these arms in a ditch. They were mostly taken from guards in the streets. Stop right now. I'm going to dump this sack right here!"

"We don't have to throw away those arms," I assured him. "Maybe we're worrying for nothing. In any case this station wagon is not our property, and we're going to abandon it once we don't need it anymore."

We returned from the lot and sat down a half a block from the airport, in a small, circular lot, where we could watch. After twenty minutes, the two cars were still parked in the same place. There were many people, despite the late hour. Buses ran infrequently, and people crowded the bus stops at all hours.

Kinqui remarked, "I wish we knew if they were waiting for us. Naturally, if the house is being watched, they'll arrest Pablo and Cisneros, who will be the first to arrive, don't you think?"

"I've been thinking the same thing," I said. "But maybe we're torturing ourselves for nothing. We still have one hour. They won't come back until midnight."

Suddenly, I had what I thought was a good idea. "Kinqui, there's a simple way to find out if the house is being watched or not, but for this we need paper, string, and newspapers, as if for wrapping a package."

"I'll get them," he volunteered, sharing my enthusiasm even before I told him the plan. He hurried up to get the things I needed.

I told Joaquin to keep watching. "Don't move from here under any circumstance, and tell Kinqui to wait for me here when he returns. I have something to do."

I drove to the nearby airport, trying to find some things I would need. After I parked, I decided to use the airport bathroom.

As I walked in, I saw a line of families who were lucky enough to be able to leave Cuba legally and permanently. Down the line walked military officers with baskets. These were to take every last piece of jewelry and valuables from anyone leaving. They could leave with their clothes, but not their jewelry. These would go instead to Castro's regime. I shook my head and entered the bathroom.

As I was washing my hands, an older man came in. I recognized him immediately.

"Dr. Noriega!" I said in surprise.

He looked at me for a moment, then recognized me.

"Julio Antonio! All grown up!"

We hugged. He told me that his family was leaving and that he had come here to flush his gold Mason ring down the drain rather than letting the communists have it.

"That is a shame," I answered.

"I don't think I can do it. I'll have to put it in the basket."

Then he took out a card and quickly wrote something. "Here. This is my address in Miami. It seems Adolf Hitler has been resurrected in Cuba."

He walked back out to the terminal. As I left, I saw him sadly place the ring in the basket of valuables, as his wife, crying, dropped in her wedding ring. One of the G-2 agents took the basket, eyeing the ring. I sighed and walked out.

I walked through the vacant lots located a block away and picked up a 30-inch-long piece of dried trunk with a transversal twig about five or six inches long. I wrapped it up with dirty papers and went back to my buddies. Kinqui had brought several paper bags from a nearby bakery, obtained through clever persuasion.

"Where did you get such a long rope?" I asked.

"It was very easy. It's the rope they had tied between columns in the bakery, so the citizens know where to line up."

His eyes glinted with the mischief that never left him, even in danger. "Tomorrow they won't know."

The three of us went to the vacant lot to prepare the package. I explained my plan as I revealed the items I had retrieved from the airport.

While this was happening, Pablo and Cisneros were situating the explosives in Rancho Boyeros, in the Endiste, an enterprise devoted by the government to the importation of Alfa Romeos and agricultural equipment, as well as general transportation vehicles. The Endiste occupied a vast stretch of land in Rancho Boyeros Avenue and 100 Street. It contained equipment valued at millions of dollars. My buddies had been forced to climb a huge fence built by the communists encircling the place, ostensibly erected to defeat saboteurs. Every time one of them passed by, they stopped working. Pablo had been behind a tractor, and Cisneros had taken care of connecting the detonators and explosives.

When we finished the package, I asked who would take it to the house. I felt the package, and so did Kinqui.

"You have outdone yourself, Julio Antonio!" said Kinqui. "It looks like a machine gun. Some surprise is in store for them when they open that! What do you say, Joaquin?"

Joaquin smiled faintly. "It's a good idea," was his only comment.

On our way to the bus stop Kinqui said, "Listen, I know who can take the package there. Wait for me right here."

"What are you going to do?" I asked.

"I'm going to look for the boy who was sweeping the porch at the bakery."

"But if he's working, he's not going to leave the place right now, is he?"

"Well, he doesn't work there, exactly. He's a little slow, mentally. He goes there to help a little, in exchange for baked desserts and bread, that's all."

"All right," I said, "but take him with you to the other side of the street. That way when they ask him where he was given the package, he'll point out in opposite direction to ours. Then come back as soon as possible. Do you have any money?"

"Yes, I have some," said Kinqui after searching his pocket.

"That kid is brave," said Joaquin after Kinqui left.

"A kid he is not, but brave, yes—as are the others you'll meet later."

Kinqui came back after a while. "Look carefully. You'll laugh."

I complied. The men parked in the two cars could not see us, but we could watch all their movements. In one of the cars, the fellow smoked continuously. All of a sudden, the boy, about twelve or thirteen, appeared. He was tall, and according to Kinqui, ate voraciously. He probably didn't have any food at home, and his parents let him fend for himself.

The boy crossed the street and stopped in front of the garden's iron gate looking in all directions. He carried the package in his right hand and rested it on his shoulder. The men in the cars raised themselves up to watch him, but the boy didn't go into the house. Instead, he turned around and crossed the street again, and from there he looked around again, uneasily, betraying his guilt. Finally, he returned towards the house and this time, very decidedly opened the gate, entered the porch and rang the doorbell. Surprised, two men we had not noticed before simultaneously came from one side of the house, aiming guns at him. One of the men took the package and opened it. He grimaced and dropped the package which splattered on the ground, "What is... this is shit!"

We looked at each other, starting to laugh. "Now we know. Let's go," I said to my companions.

Kinqui couldn't stop laughing until Joaquin reprimanded him.

"Listen, buddy, you're something else. What is going to happen to the boy?"

"Don't worry about him, Joaquin," I said. "Don't forget he's abnormal. When they realize it, they'll let him go."

Before boarding the station wagon, we surveyed the surroundings. All was still quiet, so we drove up Rancho Boyeros Avenue. We had twenty minutes to intercept Cisneros and Pablo before they arrived at the house. Passing the house, we saw the four men questioning the little boy inside one of the cars. Two of the men were outside the car and two were inside, and the doors towards the street were open.

A mile past the place, more or less, I told Kinqui, "Stay here and if you see them, stop them. I know this is very unlikely to happen, as they have orders to abandon the motorcycle."

Joaquin broke his silence again. "It's going to be difficult to intercept them before they arrive at the house. If they take the bus, the stop for the airport route is precisely in front of the house, and if those men see somebody there, they'll detain them before we can warn them."

On crossing Fontanar, a residential suburb located in that area, we saw a big flame and cloud of smoke to the right of the avenue. As we approached it, we could see a car burning.

"It's an Alfa Romeo," Joaquin shouted. "It must have caught fire!"

I slowed down. It was an Alfa Romeo all right—a green one. Amazingly, nobody was around, although the fire had just begun. We proceeded. Half a kilometer ahead, in front of the countryside restaurant Rio Cristal, stood two men on the other side of the avenue in the light of the bus stop stall.

It was Pablo and Cisneros.

While an alarmed Joaquin asked all kind of questions, I turned the station wagon around and jumped over the division of the double way, blowing the horn. Pablo and Cisneros instinctively put their hands to their waists to pull out their guns, but on seeing us, they smiled joyfully. The bus was stopping at that moment, and Cisneros said in mockery what actually was a solemn truth. "Listen, we escaped by a hair's breadth."

Hounded by the noise of the fire truck sirens we sped away from Rio Cristal. Death had ventured close. Fortunately, we had snatched its prey. Still dazzled by so many successive events in just one night, we neglected to introduce Joaquin to the other two.

As we passed the burning car, I asked who had done it. I suspected Pablo.

"I did," answered Cisneros.

"Why here, in the middle of this avenue?" I scolded. "What an irresponsible thing to do."

"I know," said Cisneros, "but the other operation failed and it annoyed us. This Alfa Romeo apparently had a breakdown, and since Alfa Romeos are the cars used by the communist big shots, we burned it with gasoline from the motorcycle."

"What about the motorcycle?" Joaquin asked, entering the conversation with his new friends.

"We threw it down the ravine, towards the river, in Rio Cristal," said Pablo. "I feel sorry, because the operation failed on my account."

Cisneros contradicted him. "No, Pablo, it only failed because one of the guards caught you trying to jump over the fence on our way out. Almost all the explosives had been placed. We saved our skin because he was fast enough, and we had time to escape in the motorcycle."

"Yes, and in the course of your escape you had time to accomplish minor missions," I remarked, "such as burning an Alfa Romeo stalled in the avenue. What you don't know is that you saved your lives thanks to that little delay. In front of the house there are two cars of the G-2 waiting for any of us."

As we drove, I filled them in on our portion of the night's adventures. As we approached the house, I made some recommendations. "Observe the two cars parked in front but in opposite directions. Don't make any gestures when we pass in front of them. Better yet, turn your head to the other side. They might suspect five men in a car."

"What about Sandra?" asked Cisneros. "Isn't she in danger?"

"It's ok," I replied. "We have time to intercept her in Artemisa when she returns from her trip. Then we'll stay overnight in a farm I know of until tomorrow morning when we leave Havana."

The two cars were parked in the same place when we passed by the house.

Cisneros had a very special reason for concern. "I bet they ate all the meat we had there."

"You really are gluttonous, Cisneros," said Pablo, who then asked about the underwater fishing equipment.

"It's in the trunk of the Volga," I answered, "together with the rest of the gear, including bottles to carry water for our trip."

Still within the sight of the house, two men got into one of the cars and followed us. I accelerated the old station wagon and with the other car almost behind us, we entered the small town of Santiago de Las Vegas. Near the city limits, they caught up and signaled us, this time blowing the siren close to where the roadway ended. Past that point was a curvy, narrow, and deteriorated two-way highway. When we stopped, the car attempted to pass us.

"Hold on!" I said. I turned the steering wheel so I would hit the car with the back of the station wagon to force it off the road.

"We must do something," said Kinqui, with his pistol in his hand. "They'll catch up with us again."

"Don't shoot!" I commanded. "Wait until we get to Rincon. There's a four-way junction there, and they may take the wrong one. If not, we'll to give these communists a dose of their own medicine."

We raced through Rincon, and at the end of the town we saw through the rearview mirror that the G-2's 1959 Ford was coming in our direction.

"At the first curve, I'll stop as if the station wagon had gotten out of the highway," I warned them. "Kinqui, leave that door open. I will take care of the one that approaches me and you take care of the other one. I'm going to stay inside the station wagon."

At the first curve, I drove the vehicle off the highway and put on the brakes. All my companions got out quickly while the car ignition and headlights remained on. The left side was leaning over the ditch, and with the left door open, it gave the impression of an accident.

Before the men arrived, I drew out my gun and inserted a bullet in the chamber. Then I leaned over the wheel to wait. The car stopped a few yards away from the station wagon, and without approaching us, the Security men ordered us to come out of the vehicle with our hands up. The only response was the sound of crickets and harvest bugs.

One of the men came nearer. He stuck his head through the window and flooded me with light from his flashlight. Then he shouted to his companions. "Hey, here's one that's unconscious!"

As soon as he opened the door, I shot him. As he fell, he fired a shot that hit the station wagon ceiling. This was followed by other shots of unknown origin, because Cisneros was at that moment killing the second occupant of the patrol while the man I'd shot was trying to escape.

We got away from there in a hurry and traveled a long time in silence. At last, Joaquin recovered enough to say. "Really, kids, either you are completely crazy or you're about the bravest people I've ever known."

No one answered. Kinqui leaned back on his seat and tried to sleep. Cisneros and Pablo did the same, leaning against each other. They didn't feel like talking, not having quite accepted the idea of Joaquin accompanying us in our escape. He had been a legend, a leader in the prison where he'd spent ten years, not only for his hunger strikes and escape attempts, but because of his intelligence and bravery. Unfortunately, our friend Mario's betrayal had made us distrustful.

Realizing Joaquin was beginning to feel this coldness towards him, I directed a conversation at him. "Is it true you were only twenty-two years old when they put you in prison?"

"That's right," he said. "I was just a kid. I lost my youth in prison. Look at me, almost bald and wrinkled after the tortures I had to endure. And what's worse, for a cause that isn't ours anymore. It's now at the power level between Russia and the United States. And we can't do anything, because our hands are tied. We have no arms. No explosives. We can't combat these people."

"I don't agree with you," I said. "First, this is our problem, not the United States'. They did not put Fidel here to rule us. So, we have to find a way to wipe him and his gang out without waiting for anybody's help. We shouldn't care who was or wasn't a Batista follower. To fight Castro-communism, all we need are people who are not communists and want to return freedom and civil rights to Cuba. Everything else is unimportant."

"I hope you're right," said Joaquin after brief hesitation, "but I believe we cannot do anything, and all sacrifice is useless without the help of the United States."

We stopped there. At half past midnight, we came to Artemisa and parked the station wagon at the entrance of the city in front of a farm located on the highway leading to Havana. Cisneros and Pablo went to the other side of the highway and we stayed by the station wagon. We watched every time a car approached, waiting to see Sandra's Volga. It took her three hours to appear. At our shouts and signals she slowed down and asked, distrustfully, "What do you want? Who is it?"

"It's us, Sandra!" Kinqui yelled.

Right away she pulled the car by the side of the road and asked for me. I approached her, carrying a heavy box containing ammunition.

"I'm here all right, honey. Your Julio Antonio is here. Please open the trunk." Once I had deposited the box, I turned to Sandra, who was stunned by the sight of Cisneros bearing the tommy guns. "Let's go. I'll explain everything in the car. Was everything all right with the Professor?"

"Yes, fine," she said. She gave me the car keys, but Kinqui asked for them.

Pablo, Cisneros and Joaquin climbed into the back seat while Sandra and I sat in the front with Kinqui.

"Where to, boss?" asked Kinqui. "Where are we going to spend the night?"

"In a fine place, you'll see," I said, "I'll guide you."

When we passed Artemisa and were driving along the highway to Pinar del Rio I told Kinqui to turn to his right. We entered a place that was lush with vegetation. Twenty-five minutes later their curiosity was peaking.

"Do we still have a long way to go, boss?"

"Not too long," I answered.

Sandra, leaning against my shoulder and silently smiled while Pablo remarked on the strategic location of the place, a verdant valley sheltered against the mountains and certainly a safe place. As for Cisneros, he had one thing in mind. "I hope there's plenty of food where we're going."

Kinqui asked Joaquin what they did in prison to gluttonous inmates.

"We had none. Everybody got so little that we were always pining for food. In fact, at one time I almost died when I ate poisonous mushrooms. I was sick with vomiting and diarrhea for three days."

"Do you hear that, Cisneros? One has to pay for being a glutton."

"Quit it, man, don't bug me. I'm not the only one who likes to gobble up all the food in sight."

Finally, we were in front of an enormous iron gate, which I opened and closed after we were all inside. I pointed out the various living quarters of the well-appointed old wooden house. Kinqui parked the car in the barn and I lifted a board in the small steps at the entrance.

"Here's the key, no problem," I said. That was the place where Don Manuel, the owner and an old friend of my father, kept it.

Sandra was delighted with the house. Just like a proper homemaker, she entreated, "Please don't break anything or make it dirty."

As Cisneros asked about beds, I told him they were in the back and he would do well to rest. "We have a busy day ahead of us," I said.

It was almost dawn. I had rested for a while by Sandra's side, but since she immediately fell asleep, I gently kissed her goodnight and covered her with a blanket. Then I returned to the living room to talk to the others about the next day's schedule.

"Well, Kinqui, among other things, we have to bury the tommy guns and the ammunition in a safe place and look for any meat we can find on the farm. Otherwise we have to go get it. We're going to need it for the trip. We also have to prepare bundles of water and food to be carried by each of us."

"I'll take care of the tommy guns," volunteered Kinqui. Joaquin went with us to search the farm, but the only thing we found was an old cow that was about eight months pregnant. Although I insisted that we look for another animal, at the end we had no choice but sacrifice it.

We finished this operation at 9:00 in the morning, and on our way to the house we cut off two bunches of plantains. Joaquin said something about going back later to extract honey from hives he had seen there that, according to him, had enough honey for an army. Such an offer made every mouth water, especially Cisneros'. They teased him, "Not for you. You haven't lifted a finger," said Kinqui. "Remember the communist slogan: No work, no food."

"Yes," Cisneros retorted, "but what they don't say is that, here in Cuba, those who work don't eat, either!"

First, we helped Sandra in the kitchen and then prepared the packages. This included adjusting of all the underwater equipment and making small tridents to defend ourselves from the fish at the bottom of the sea, since we couldn't carry our rifles. For this we used tacks and nails and small wood pieces. Kinqui prepared magnificent depth belts, and we decided on the clothes everyone would wear. Kinqui, Pablo and Cisneros would put on Cuban farmer clothes and palm leaf hats. Joaquin and I would wear olive green khaki trousers and white or khaki shirts. Sandra would dress as a communist miliciana. The idea was to look as a team from the Communist Security.

Our reasoning was simple. Whenever the communists went into the country chasing anticommunist countrymen, they dressed in this fashion. The heroic ones were never captured by the army or the G-2. Before the national and world press, the Cuban counter-revolutionaries were always arrested by farmers and members of a militia. The farmers photographed in the publications were soldiers from the regular communist army and the Security, disguised as militia. The idea, in short, was to convince the world opinion that the Cuban people were for the revolution and defended it.

Kinqui and I decided the meat ration for each person, knowing that during our trip we wouldn't have the opportunity to eat. The little towns had no food available. We laughed at Cisneros and his big appetite. "Where is he?" I asked.

"He is after the honey with Joaquin."

"Oh, yes?" said Pablo mischievously. "If you've never seen a deviled black man, you'll see him today. What does Cisneros know about extracting honeycombs from hives? I bet he hasn't seen a bee in his entire life—he's a city boy."

He was right. At that very moment, Cisneros appeared with a bucket of honey in his hand. His face was deformed. Joaquin rushed to explain. "This happened to Cisneros because he didn't listen to me. I warned him not to take his head out of the nylon."

With his eyes lost in his inflated face, he went to ask Sandra to pull out the stings from his face, feeling too miserable to answer Kinqui's teasing. After Sandra treated him by applying an antibiotic used in veterinary medicine for inflammation of the udders of cows with mastitis, we sat down to enjoy a dinner of beefsteaks and mashed green plantains plus the precariously captured honey.

After this banquet, we prepared the meat rations—about twenty steaks each—and put them into nylon bags, since we had to leave the other meat behind at the house.

Each package also contained a pair of flippers, a mask and snorkel, a lead belt prepared according to each person's weight, and a knife for underwater use. There were clothes, a palm leaf hat, and a gallon and a half of water, and a bottle of wine to give us warmth and energy before diving into the cold sea water. We each also carried a compass, a flashlight, bottles of mosquito repellant, small containers of medicine, and other essential items for our escape, which would entail walking many kilometers and swimming a great number of miles.

Finally, we were gathered in the living room, ready to leave, the packages already in the car, when Joaquin said something that we assumed was a joke. "Gentlemen, I think we could make the packages lighter. Just think of all the countryside we have to cross."

"What would you eliminate from your package, for instance?" asked Kinqui.

"The water; the bottles weigh too much. When we get thirsty, we'll take water from the rivers. Look at the map. See how many rivers cross that area?"

"We all have seen the map, Joaquin," said Cisneros. "But what does not appear on the map is that the two banks of those rivers are packed with military units. If you get near one to drink because you're thirsty, you won't get out alive, I assure you."

Joaquin made a display of unnecessary courage. "And what is the problem? I will bring water from the rivers as we need it. I know how to fool the communists."

Sandra's intervention was also useless. He couldn't be persuaded. "Well, if you insist on carrying the bottles, that's up to you. I won't include them in my package. I'll go to the river every time I need to drink water."

"Look, Joaquin," I said at last, "here we do what the majority wants, and the majority has decided you won't go to fetch anything from the river and you'll carry your own water from here. If you don't agree, leave the group and do on your own whatever pleases you. Everything has been planned in a certain way and you're not going to make us change our plans. Nobody is going to wreck our escape by making foolish mistakes."

At departure time, we all got up from our seats except Joaquin. However, I was relieved when, while descending the little steps in front of the chalet, I heard him at my back, talking to Cisneros about bee stings.

The dark night announced a storm, perfect for our purposes, and before taking the road we gave a last look to the place shrouded in darkness, a symbol of the dimness that had fallen upon our dear Cuba. We kept silent, well aware that one of the surprise searches they frequently made in all the highways would be sufficient to upset our escape and end our lives. And yet, we felt calm, in spite of a shortness of arms and the impending dangers.

After some time driving on the road to Artemisa, I fell asleep. Suddenly, I woke up, shaken by Sandra who was saying. "Listen, I think they're doing a search."

She was right. There were several patrol cars at the entrance of the town. They stopped us, naturally, and one of them came to the window and asked Kinqui for his license. Perhaps because I had been awakened so abruptly or because I knew the now bewildered Kinqui didn't have a driver's license, my preservation instinct made me react violently. I addressed the guard swearing an obscenity. "What the hell is the matter now, man?" I felt Sandra's fingers nailed to my thighs as hooks. She was horrified to think what would follow to this explosion.

"How do you dare to show me such disrespect?" asked the policeman.

"Disrespect, you say? Well, let me tell you. I want you to know I work in the Prime Minister's Offices, and we're on a special mission—an urgent inspection in the Pinar del Rio province. We're too tired to have to put up with your antics."

The man was not to be easily scared. "I have nothing to say. Follow me to the police station. You are all under arrest!"

On our way to the station I had time to measure the enormity of what had happened and my mistake in addressing an officer in that manner. I could see my companions, petrified by fear, holding their breath and expecting the worst to happen. The police station was nothing but a small house by the highway. There, the offended policeman told the story to the desk lieutenant while another policeman searched our car and announced in loud voice, "Look, they're carrying underwater fishing equipment and flippers!"

He got the keys from Kinqui and was about to open the trunk when I addressed him again, this time with great authority and firmness. "Obviously you don't know who we are. We carry that equipment because of our mission. And you know very well who is allowed to carry them," I added, all intent in making them believe we were agents for the G-2.

Their attitude changed right away. The lieutenant condescended to reason with me. "Comrade, I don't know why you were so rude with this other comrade when he stopped you in the highway. Honestly, you showed the attitude of an enemy of the revolution."

"Watch your language!" I said, pretending to be insulted. "You don't know who you're talking to. I work in the offices of the Prime Minister, and I came here to carry out an important job entrusted to me by Fidel. As for being an enemy of the revolution, don't you make any mistake, comrade. Get it into your head that we're true revolutionaries!"

"Yes, but anyhow we've got to make a report, since the driver is not carrying his license." said the officer. Of course, I didn't want any report on file because the G-2 could use it to trace our operations.

I, who had assumed all responsibility and had the lives of my companions in my hands, resolved to stake all I had. It was simply a matter of bragging even more. "You do what you want, but you'd better watch out. And remember, when you fall under my jurisdiction with a problem, I'll treat you the same way you're treating me here tonight while I'm under yours. I'll pay you back in your own coin."

"But why would you do that? I am only doing my duty," said a much more mellowed lieutenant.

"Yes, but you exceed yourself in your authority, at least with us."

"I don't persecute anybody, believe me," he added, conciliatorily. "You have the wrong opinion about me, comrade."

I gave him an ultimatum. "Let's solve this at once. What is the telephone number of the G-2 in this town?"

He had no choice but look for the phone number. I asked permission to use the paid telephone in front of the porch of the station and simulated dialing. I then engaged in an excited conversation, gesticulating a lot while I talked to the air. In the corner of my eye I saw the policemen holding a little conference. As a result of this, when I went back inside, the lieutenant told me, "Listen, buddy, let's try to settle this without having to waste another minute. We're all revolutionaries and we don't want to hinder your work. Excuse any misunderstanding. You are at liberty to leave when you want."

"Now you're talking business. If at any time you have a problem, see me at the Office of the Prime Minister."

We wound up getting so friendly that the lieutenant and the other guards came to the street to wish us a good trip.

A new incident, unfortunately, was still ahead for us.

Entering Havana City limits, we noticed unusual traffic in the Arroyo Arenas hamlet. Kinqui slowed down, and at the junction, a guard in uniform signaled us to stop. He was waving a small red flag. Our driver stopped ten meters from the individual. Luckily, it was only a military unit in motion. A huge sledge was towing Soviet war tanks and several jeeps loaded with antiaircraft machine guns.

We patiently watched the slow passing of the war caravan, a spectacle now common in Cuba to constantly remind people that the communists had the power. For this reason, there was constant traffic of military troops and units in the interior and in Havana. Commonly viewed were small air-to-air rockets, Soviet war tanks, small tanks—or amphibians, as the Castro people call them—cannons, and many more artifacts. Continuing our journey, we felt free to make comments.

Cisneros was unable to understand how Castro's government could go on acquiring military arms and vehicles from Russia when the population was starving.

"And what do they care if the people starve?" Sandra said. "The elite don't lack for food or anything they need. They can continue buying arms because they know guns keep the people fearful. So much so, they don't dare to mount an attack. That's how they maintain their oppression and tyranny."

We arrived at the railway terminal located in Old Havana— an area that showed the signs of many years of total neglect.

We unloaded the packages and divided ourselves into two groups so we wouldn't be too conspicuous. In one group went Pablo, Sandra, and Joaquin, and in the other group went, Kinqui, Cisneros, and I. We agreed not to speak to one another or even sit in the same vicinity. If someone was detained or if one of the groups were identified and arrested, the other would continue with the scheduled plan. As I found out later, this was much easier said than done.

We sat in separate benches to wait for the train's departure. From our seats we heard the "all aboard" announcement through the loudspeaker. When we got up, two men approached Sandra and took her by the arm. One of them showed her an I.D. and escorted her to the other end of the station. Cisneros asked me if there was anything we could do. Kinqui didn't say anything.

I impulsively headed in their direction, but Kinqui walked even faster to intercept me. His hands were two clamps on my shoulders. "What in the world are you doing? Do you want the rest of us to get arrested?" He pointed to Joaquin and Pablo who hadn't moved from their bench.

"We've got to do something. We can't let them take her away like that." I said in anguish.

Joaquin and Pablo remained seated. Kinqui walked away, saying, "Wait for me here, I'll be back in a minute." He searched inside his bundles and pulled out an object, which he put in one of his pockets.

The two men who had detained Sandra were joined by two others who had been watching at the station's entrance. Our companion behaved bravely. Mindful of our safety, not once did she look around or even resist.

I was immersed in painful thoughts when a tremendous explosion brought me back to reality. Screams were heard and confusion reigned. A cloud of smoke enveloped the building's left wing. From the door, Kinqui beckoned to me.

"Hurry up, they've left Sandra alone in that jeep," he said when I was near.

Sandra let me embrace her. One of her hands was handcuffed to the inside rail of the jeep. She pleaded with us. "Please go back, save yourselves! I'll manage to get out of this one." Again, I tried to hug her, but she gently pushed me off and begged Kinqui, "Take him away, quick! Come to your senses! They'll be back in a moment and if they find you here, you'll be doomed."

Kinqui almost dragged me away. When I looked back, Sandra's face was bathed in tears. "Let's hurry to the train," Kinqui urged. "I placed a grenade in the restroom, and soon the arrests will begin."

Cisneros came back whispering, "Don't look back, but I think one of the fellows is watching us." Then he bent down to pick up his bundles and Kinqui and I did the same. While walking to the arrival platform, he told us the rest of the story. "They put her in a G-2 car. There are two more outside. It seems they had her photo and that's why they arrested her, but Sandra denied it was her. When I noticed a suspicious man at the door, I decided to turn back."

"Yes, and he's following us," confirmed Kinqui.

I made an instant decision. "Well, leave the packages by the platform, and let's get off at different points at the other side of the train. If he follows any of us, that person will take care of him. Afterwards we shall meet here. Come on, there's no time to lose. The train is leaving in ten minutes."

We walked along a cement hall flanked at both sides by trains ready to depart for different destinations. People carrying their bundles walked back and forth, trying to identify the cart or seat assigned to them. Kinqui walked down the steps and turned to the left, where several trains were entering and leaving the station. I stopped near a wagon, and after a few minutes without seeing anybody following me, I went to the spot where Kinqui had disappeared.

The evening was humid, and soon it started to rain. I went through a few wagons without bumping into Kinqui, but in one of them I heard voices and saw a man pointing at Kinqui with his gun. They were close enough, but in the dark evening I had not noticed them. Kinqui was telling him, "Shoot, coward, and kill me, because if you don't, I'll kill you! Yes, you'll have to kill me. I'm not going anywhere with you."

Just as the man was ready to shoot, I approached his back. Unfortunately, I stepped into something and it made a noise. He turned abruptly to shoot at me, but from the next wagon a hand emerged, pushing him and making him lose his footing. The man fell into the train rails at the precise moment a train was leaving the station. He pressed the trigger anyway, but the shot was followed by a cry of terror. The train had smashed him between its wheels. The saving hand had been Cisneros'.

The black man dropped from his hiding place between the two wagons and, despite the fact the train was already moving, we had time to grab the packages and board one of the cars. The last to climb was Cisneros, with our help. As the train whistled and sped off, we leaned against the wagon walls, momentarily exhausted and drenched in rain water. The streaks of electricity lighting the sky dramatized the importance of what had just happened.

After realizing the wagon that we had taken was not the one allotted to us, we went looking for ours. One of the cars was occupied by soldiers, apparently on furlough. Joaquin and Pablo were already sitting in our car. The empty seat that should have been for Sandra made me grieve so visibly that Kinqui tried to comfort me. "Remember, as a woman, she'll have better chances. She won't receive as hard a sentence as we would."

His compassion prompted him to lie. Communists do not make gender distinctions. The Guanajay Prison for Women was crowded with brave Cuban women who had fought communism. In fact, the government had to build two more prison sites they called "Farms for Women's Political Rehabilitation."

Taking that same long trip across the island was an army lieutenant sitting near us who continuously sang the praises of Russia, where he had been studying for three years. The lieutenant, who had come to visit the family, bragged about his participation in the execution of many traitors. He was referring to the execution of brave young men who for the most part had not been tried by ordinary courts but by the so-called Revolutionary Courts. The army officers played the part of judges, prosecutors, and defenders. These trials always ended up with a ten-to-thirty-year sentence or capital punishment.

Disgusted by the lieutenant's conversation, I went to the wagon partition to breathe some air. The new day was going to be as rainy and stormy as the day before. All of a sudden, the train stopped and I almost lost my balance. Already my group was joining me through the hail with the news that the train was derailed and we had to wait for it to be fixed. We got off and so did the other group, but they sat apart on a fallen tree trunk. We only exchanged glances.

It took two hours for the train to be repaired, although this would not be the last time it would jump the track. The last derailment happened at 10:00 in the evening. Consequently, instead of arriving at Oriente at noon we arrived there at almost midnight.

We got off at a tiny railroad station in a small town from where we would take the local train to our final destination. We could have traveled all the way on the central train, but our plan was to make this stop, arriving at our destination in a local second-class train. The express trains from Havana attracted attention. They carried people unknown to the inhabitants of that place. None of us had been there except Joaquin.

After buying our tickets, we sat on a bench at the station while Joaquin and Pablo went to the window to buy their tickets, then sat on the floor near us. This was the first mistake made by the other group, and it could have been fatal.

At 2:00 in the morning everybody slept at the station some on the floor, others leaning on the walls or over the benches. I could not fall asleep. I was worried by the proximity of Pablo and Joaquin surrounded by bundles. The five gave the impression of traveling together, precisely what we wanted to avoid. All at once, two jeeps loaded with soldiers arrived and immediately began to search the bundles and make arrests. Some individuals dealt with items that were scarce and resold them for profit or took them to their families in the cities, both of which was forbidden by the regime.

Believing I was asleep, a soldier shook me. "Hey, you, wake up. Whose packages are these?"

I quickly got up and declared them mine. The soldiers grabbed them and inquired what was inside them.

"Some used clothes for relatives living here, condensed milk cans, and a few trifles."

The soldier looked me up and down with my khaki pants, olive green as his, tall military boots, military belt, and white undershirt. To my right on the bench was a briefcase similar to those used by the G-2. Then he glanced at Kinqui and Cisneros sleeping by my side.

"Are these citizens traveling with you, comrade?"

"Yes, they are with me."

He changed his hostile attitude, took two steps and asked about Joaquin and Pablo sleeping by their bundles on the floor.

"I don't know them," I said, shaking Joaquin's arm and saying. "Wake up comrade they want to talk to you."

Still half asleep, Joaquin raised his head. "What is it, what is it?"

"Nothing, the comrade is doing a search and he wants to talk to you," I answered, indicating the soldier to him. The soldier took one of Joaquin's packages and checked its weight. He also asked about the contents.

"It has clothes, dirty laundry, shoes, and a few other things. I'm returning from a trip to the capital." He had adopted an innocent air and was rubbing his eyes as though he had been soundly asleep.

The soldier released the package and repeated this procedure with the others near us. In some cases, he would touch somebody with the tip of his boot and say, "Come on, get up, this is a search!" A few yards away from us, he arrested a black man who was carrying a coffee bag. He shoved him to make him walk to the jeep.

Another guard picked up one of Joaquin's packages. Intrigued by its weight, he addressed him roughly. "Hey, you, open that package immediately!"

Luckily, before Joaquin could say anything, the other soldier shouted to his companions, "Hey, let's go, I already searched those!"

The guard gave Joaquin an indignant look and let the package go. Before it could hit the floor breaking the water bottles, Joaquin rushed to grab his package.

With Pablo and Kinqui already awake, I scolded Pablo and Joaquin for having sat so close to us. All agreed and apologized, except Joaquin who had another opinion. "It would have happened anyway," he said. Then, under my reproachful eyes, he bent down to gather his packages and walked with Pablo to the other end of the station.

"This fellow is going to cause us trouble," confided Kinqui. "I don't know why, but I wish we had never met him."

We went to the other side to wait for our train. Cisneros, unaware of the incident continued sleeping, sprawled on the bench he had all to himself. It was five thirty in the morning.

Finally, we heard the train whistle and saw a distant light that grew bigger every second.

"Fetch Cisneros!" I told Kinqui, looking at him with joy.

When the two got near us, I was the first in line and that meant we could actually sit during our journey. There were some grumbles from the line, but no one dared to pull out the newcomer, Cisneros, six feet tall and weighing 250 pounds.

It was almost light when the train started to move. It was a small, old, second-rate train, even dirtier and more dilapidated than the one we'd taken from Havana. The group had gotten seats. Joaquin and Pablo were standing, holding onto a bar that ran along the ceiling of the train, from one end of the wagon to the other. The day began with mist and rain.

"I think we are arriving," whispered Kinqui in my ear. This was confirmed by the conductor's announcement.

"We're already in Guantanamo!" laughed Cisneros, feeling happy and nervous at the same time.

I corrected him, in a hush. "No, it's now that we begin our journey."

The train stopped at a small station where the name Guantanamo appeared written on a sign in black on a white background. Guantanamo, a picturesque little town, had been badly neglected, totally forgotten. The streets were in such pot holed conditions they looked as though they'd never been paved.

We grabbed our packages and tried to get off the train, pushing our way through the crowd. Joaquin and Pablo followed us close behind. Three communist soldiers guarded the only exit to the street. Cisneros suggested we go to the restrooms located to the right and leave our packages there until we decided our next stop.

The guards were already searching packages and luggage. A big group of people crowded the place, waiting their turn. We followed Cisneros' advice and went to the latrines. Pablo and Joaquin did the same. We had not counted on this inconvenience, having been under the impression that they did not periodically search the trains, on account of the number of people traveling in them. Now, evidently, they had a good reason for searching the train and they were not concerned with any loss of time.

In the restroom, many people were washing their faces and grooming themselves in front of an extended mirror above the washstands. I took a careful look at the place and noticed that at the right of the last latrine there was a small window, above the two partitions separating one latrine from the other. I told my people to wait for me, and I left. Since I was carrying no package and my clothes qualified me as a reliable fellow in the eyes of the communists, I was not searched at the door.

I walked around the station and verified that the small window in the restroom opened to a side of the station where bushes grew. It was invisible from the street. A few meters from there was a taxi-cab station, and a line of people waiting in front of it.

I rejoined the others and explained my plan. We agreed that Cisneros would hide in the last latrine and throw the packages through the window, and we would pick these up outside. Afterwards, we got out and mixed with the public. Joaquin occupied a place in the line for taxis, and Pablo stood watch to give Kinqui and me a chance to pick up the packages Cisneros handed to us.

Suddenly, Pablo began to whistle our signal. We hid in the bushes. Cisneros did not notice it and tried to pass the final package that fell to the ground with a noise of broken glass. I raised my head and saw a soldier walking along the side of the taxicab station without noticing us. Pablo whistled back to let us know everything was all right.

The bottle containing repellent had broken and the liquid had dampened the cardboard box. Quickly we transferred the rest to another box and buried the discarded one. Each carrying two boxes, we went to the taxicab station and after an hour's wait got a taxi. The driver, a talkative fellow, asked us a lot of questions. He seemed to be a good person, but in our predicament, we had to be cautious. We tried to fend him off. However, we came to a point in our conversation when he said something that sounded like a trap.

"I can see you are good people, real patriots."

From the back seat I answered, "I don't know what you call 'good people,' but we're on a special mission for the government. Is there anything else you want to know?" I asked defiantly.

The driver became worried. "Oh no, nothing at all. I haven't asked you anything important, have I?" He turned to Pablo and Cisneros sitting by him in the front seat. They didn't answer, and the conversation stopped.

In the outskirts of town, I told him to stop. I paid him, and the man drove off through a lonely slope.

"I think we've passed the place," observed Joaquin.

"Don't you think I know it?" I answered. "My intention was to put that man in the wrong track, in case he works for the government, and somebody asks him where we got off. Now we have to go back half a kilometer."

"Do you mean to the junction we left behind, to the right?"

"That's right; now let's proceed. We can change clothes here."

A few minutes later, we were dressed as peasants and the two heavy boxes had been converted into two bags, one for each group. The bags were of rough sailcloth similar to those used by farmers to transport their goods.

It started to rain again, making the transit through muddy roads more difficult. We felt cold, and our clothes were soaked in rain water. Then we saw a two-horse cart coming by. When it was passing us, the farmer stopped as if he wanted to give us a ride. He even asked, "Hey, friends, are you going far?"

Kinqui thanked him, declining. The man said goodbye and continued his way, and five minutes later, the same thing happened with another cart. I proposed to take the next one, provided that Joaquin didn't say a word. We would be in charge of engaging in friendly talk with its driver, to put him off, or in any case, we could justify ourselves by saying we were on an expedition ordered by the Department of Hydraulic Resources of the government, specifically to mark the wells in that area. Joaquin would be on the alert to let us know when we arrived at the exact spot where we had to deviate.

The next cart showed up soon afterward. The good-natured farmer told us the reason for those other two carts. They were woodcutters looking for wood to manufacture coal. We gave the agreed explanation when he inquired about our presence there. I volunteered that our jeep had broken in town and we had decided to do some work that day, continuing on foot.

The farmer recommended we be cautious. Some forests had been mined by the government so no one could reach the coast and escape from the country. Two farmers and their horses had blown into pieces not too long ago, he told us. Sadly, they had not been escaping; they had simply entered the fields adjacent to the coast in search of a lost bull.

"Don't worry, my friend, I'm an engineer and we have brought maps of the zone." At the sight of a hamlet three hundred meters afar, I quickly reacted. "Leave us right here, good man, and thanks a lot."

After the farmer drove off, Joaquin, very displeased, asked me why we had stopped there.

"Because we have been trusting in you who almost delivered us to the lions!" I retorted. "We already passed the place marked on the map and this hamlet is precisely the one we're not supposed to cross under any circumstances, because two guys from the Communist Security live there. Now the priority is to get away from here as fast as we can."

Joaquin didn't say a word.

Getting away from the hamlet, we lost our direction, again because of Joaquin. He declared he had not seen any road to the left, which was the one we should take, and this confused me. And yet, I was positive there was such a road and our absent-minded guide had passed it up. In the middle of an argument, a farmer on horse came near. Without consulting anyone, Joaquin made him stop and asked him, "Say, friend, do you know if there is a road to the left, two or three kilometers from here, leading to the Guaso River?"

After thinking, the man answered, taking a good look at us. "No, the way to the river is to the right, only half a kilometer from here."

We couldn't very well tell Joaquin, in front of this stranger, how imprudent it was of him to have asked. Then I recognized by its color, within a short distance, the friendly house the Professor had told me about when we were making our plans for escape. I said I was going to ask for water, and Cisneros went along while Joaquin kept talking to the farmer.

At the house, a tiny old lady greeted us kindly. I asked for water for the two of us and she went to get it. When she returned with two tin cups of water, I looked at her in the eyes and posed the first difficult question to her. "Lady, could you tell us if the man on a horse talking to my friends over there is a communist?"

She hesitated. "I don't know, my son."

"You know him, don't you?" She nodded, and I understood she wouldn't betray me if I identified myself. However, her face showed distrust and fear. "Lady, I come from Havana. I'm here by recommendation of 'The Professor.'"

The woman made the sign of the cross when she heard the password. "Oh, my son, that man on horse is the worst communist informer in the area; everybody hates him. You have no idea how many have been killed and arrested through him!"

Cisneros protested loudly of Joaquin's irresponsibility. "Damn it, why did he have to stop a man he didn't know? How stupid of him!"

"Well, Cisneros," I said, "let's assume the fellow would have stopped to ask anyway. The worse is that Joaquin has been posing questions to him. Lady, is the road to Guaso River nearby?"

"Yes, my son, three kilometers from here, to the left. Follow it and soon you'll find the railroad tracks."

I grabbed her hands, worn out by hard work, and gratefully said, "Thanks for everything, grandmother!"

"May God bless you, my sons."

When we approached the horseman, Joaquin was asking the man. "Say, do you think we could go across this place, as a shortcut? Through here?"

"Forget about it! All these fields are mined. Many people and animals die here every day crossing those fences." He pointed to the fences the communists had built up around various coasts and beaches, with red signs saying in white letters: No Trespassing Military Zone.

I interrupted Joaquin with deliberate arrogance, to impress the stranger. "Listen, Joaquin, you know very well these military zones are marked! It's here, on the map. Why do you ask silly questions to the comrade?"

Cuba: Russian Roulette of the World

Map of Guantanamo Bay, Similar to Escape Map

Joaquin didn't catch on. In fact, he said something even more compromising. "Yes, but, anyway, this gentleman is from this area and perhaps he knows of a shortcut to reach the river."

The words "gentleman" and "sir" were taboo for the communists. They identified someone as bourgeois and consequently an enemy of the regime. Joaquin had been in prison so long he was ignorant of this detail.

I cut him off even more abruptly. "Listen, Joaquin, I'm the engineer and the one who carries the work plan, so quit talking nonsense. In the first place, we're not going to the river but to some houses near the river, to mark wells. Maybe you don't know the direction but I do. That's why I've brought the maps I was given in the military command of this area. Thanks a lot, comrade," I said to the stranger, "excuse us for having taken up your time."

Hardly had we put some distance between ourselves and the man when Joaquin asked, "Are you sure you know the direction?"

"Keep your mouth shut. The man is riding behind us," said Cisneros, frankly angry.

I revealed the farmer's identity to Pablo and Kinqui, telling them to behave naturally. Joaquin paled and swallowed hard while we accused him with our eyes. Perhaps his long stay in the communist prison had affected him psychologically, but he seemed to be intermittently taking on the persona of one who was in charge. At any rate, his habit of making decisions without consulting us was a source of problems.

The informer followed us on his horse slowly, never losing sight of us. If he had alerted the authorities, we would be surrounded by the army within a few hours. The other alternative was to cross through the mined fields—true suicide. Undoubtedly, the fellow suspected us. When Joaquin stopped him, he was going in the opposite direction from ours. Now he trailed behind us, intent upon verifying our destination and whether our bags really contained engineering equipment. If we took the direction towards the coast and did not pull out any instruments, he would notify the authorities.

The day was misty, despite the sun. Advancing through the muddy road was quite a task. Finally, the time to make a decision about our immediate plans arrived. We were nearing the spot where we had to divert.

"We have to eliminate the damned informer," Cisneros suggested.

"Yes, but the problem is where to leave the body so they cannot find him in several days," said Pablo. "We have no time or anything to bury him with."

Joaquin took a step ahead of us. "Don't worry, I'll take care of him, and afterwards I'll dispose of his corpse. I'll throw him into the river, that's all."

"You're exasperating, Joaquin," I said. "How many times do I have to tell you we cannot go to the river because it is full of military units! What is wrong with you, man?"

He insisted on his stubborn heroism. "That's no problem. You wait for me at the coast and I go alone. I'm strong and can swim through the river up to its mouth and meet you there."

"In that case, if you are so strong, it's time you carry the bag, for a change," argued Cisneros. "You've been dumping that obligation on me since we left town on the excuse that you have to go ahead guiding. Some guiding....."

I proposed a solution. "Gentlemen, if we have to liquidate the informer, the best thing we can do after turning that curve in the road is to ambush him on both sides. He cannot see any of us when he reaches the curve. The nearest one to the ambush will dispose of him with a knife. If he fails, the second man will attempt it, and so on. He has no way out."

Although there were other volunteers, we accepted Cisneros's offer to be the first one. He claimed to have said it first, besides being the largest in the group. The road was rather a ditch at whose sides stood mud walls worked loose by the rains. We hid and waited in ambush, leaving a distance of four or five meters between us.

After patiently waiting, the hateful fellow stopped his horse, briefly hesitated, and tried to go back. He didn't have the time. Cisneros's knife reached him. He fell. When we ran to them, Cisneros was feeling the pulse of the man laying down face in the mud. He was dead.

Joaquin and Pablo mounted the corpse over the horse and tied him to the saddle. On our way to the railroad tracks, we secretly rejoiced thinking the town would be glad we had disposed of the repulsive informer.

The new road was very narrow and was flanked by vegetation and tall trees. Half a kilometer ahead we found the tracks. We were once more on course, thanks to the helpful old lady. We left the lifeless body across the rails so the train would run over it. Then we took the horse's harness and saddle off and let him loose. Now we were entering the danger zone where we absolutely could not be seen; it would be known we were trying to escape.

Two hours later, Joaquin suddenly jumped to the ground, warning of the presence of a guard. We imitated him, as it was dangerous to be seen in that area. I dragged myself towards him and asked where he'd seen it.

"Over there, near the railroad track," he said, while the others joined us and asked for details. After a quarter of an hour I told him to look again. Joaquin crawled behind a big stone as his parapet and returned to confirm that the guard had continued to the same site. When I went to see for myself, I saw something that could hardly be identified as a person, much less a soldier.

I watched for ten minutes and the thing didn't move. I returned to the others and said, "I don't believe it's a person that Joaquin saw, but I'm going to continue ahead with him while you stay here. If there's any danger, I'll whistle for you to join us."

When, with infinite precaution we approached the guard, we discovered instead it was a sign post used by the railroad. Joaquin's wild imagination had cost us precious time. He muttered some excuses, avoiding my eyes. Kinqui broke up the tension with one of his comical outbursts. "By golly, I've never seen a stiffer guard! I bet the Captain told him to stand in attention and hasn't remembered him since!"

We had to laugh. Especially when Cisneros topped this joke by getting near the post and declaring he was going to urinate on the guard for having made him lie on the ground.

At the junction of that railroad line with others, Kinqui said, "Here's where we have to deviate in order to get ourselves in the forest. From now on our march will be more difficult and dangerous."

We made a stop to eat. The sun was shining stronger and we felt warmer. After eating, we refreshed our feet in the water in the small creek and proceeded uneventfully for several hours. At 7:30 in the evening we stopped on a hill and watched a huge bay below sparkling with lights and beacons. All of them, except Joaquin, hugged me. Our goal was almost there. We had arrived.

The map indicated we were three miles from our objective, but our troubles with Joaquin were far from over. Now he proposed to circle around. "You see that mango tree? Everywhere you see a mango tree is a house, which has peasants, and each peasant has a dog which will bark at us, and we'll be discovered."

"What?" asked Pablo, as amazed as the rest by this proposal.

Joaquin raised his hand and with somber gesture, "We'll be discovered and get arrested."

Cisneros lost patience. "You're a coward! That's what's the matter with you! All I see is a tree. It's too dark to know whether or not it's a mango, let alone any house or dogs! Is this all in your mind or what?" And as he stepped forward to attack Joaquin, I intervened.

"Gentlemen, please, we cannot lose our heads now that we are almost there. All we have to do is to consult the majority." Kinqui's opinion was to make a small detour in order to avoid the farmer's houses. The rest was up to me. The detour proved to be costly. Again, we lost our course and ended up in the side of an inaccessible cliff. We retraced our steps and went on in our journey, but instead of being on the beach around 11:30 in the evening, at 2:00 a.m. we still were trying to reach the coast by skirting the huge reefs. Our clothes and boots were torn to shreds and the brambles had bruised even our faces. In certain areas of the practically uninhabitable spot covered by marabou we were forced to crawl over thorns and shrubs.

Suddenly, the earth trembled as a leaf shaken by the wind and we heard an agonizing scream. I fell on the ground by the jolt and after a while we were looking for each other and asking what had happened.

"I think it's a mine!" shouted Pablo.

"Then don't move," I said. "If it's a mine, surely there are many more!"

With a flashlight I followed the scent of burnt flesh and soon found Cisneros' body, completely smashed, dismembered by the explosion. We shivered, dismayed by the loss of our faithful companion whose wholesome joy of living had given us the strength to continue in our escape. With extreme sorrow at the loss of our close friend, we covered him with bushes and branches and went on in a single line, doubling our precautions and stepping on exactly the same spot where the one ahead of us had just trod. We weren't able to leave that inferno of mines, marabous and thorns until four in the morning.

Under intermittent rains and strong winds, we lay down to rest or even try to sleep, partially sheltered by a luxuriant tree. At six we got up, completely drenched. Kinqui had to climb to a tree to orient us, since our compass was all but destroyed by water and hard use. We set our course and proceeded, deadly tired. We already lacked water, and as the day advanced and the sun shone stronger, our thirst became unbearable. Fortunately, on crossing a vast plain, Kinqui discovered a thin stream of water that was sweet and sour. With remnants of sailcloth we improvised a container to drink of the dirty water.

At 5:00, bearded and raggedy, we crossed a brook enlarged by the rains. Its normal quiet currents were now so violent that we had to use our underwater fishing equipment. On the other side of the brook, we sat under a tree and filled our bottles with this delicious water, which we drank to our heart's content. In spite of our fatigue, we felt joyous when Kinqui and I first saw the ocean hardly a kilometer away. We didn't waste any time gathering our bags and continuing our march with renewed enthusiasm.

When we went into the mangroves, I noticed Joaquin getting too far from us and heading to the right, a spot with less vegetation and where he could easily be seen. He complied when I called his attention to it, but after a while he was doing it again. Pablo remarked to me, "I think Joaquin is going crazy. When we were crossing the marabou forest, he took his shirt off and hurled himself down on the ground to warn me he'd seen a shadow. At first, I did the same, but after a while I didn't pay any attention to him."

"Joaquin was tortured in prison," I said, "but he's an excellent person, and a brave man. He endured a lot without giving way."

Later, when we momentarily got separated from the group, I heard a "Halt!" to my right. I threw myself down on the grass behind a mound, and from there I signaled danger to Pablo and Kinqui who also threw themselves down.

"I saw you," the voice said. "Get out of there quickly."

I saw Joaquin to my right, also behind a mound. I asked him by signals what the matter was.

"It's an armed guard!" he answered in a whisper. "Do you think we should start running?"

The voice ordered him to get out. I told Joaquin to comply, but he was afraid.

"Get out of there, don't be afraid," I hissed. "If we try to escape, they'll shoot us in the back."

Joaquin obeyed.

"What are you doing here?" the guard demanded.

Before Joaquin could answer, I stepped out and addressed him with authority.

"And what are you doing here? Where is your military unit and the rest of your companions?"

The dumbfounded guard didn't know how to answer. He was suddenly surrounded by Pablo and Kinqui. I took two steps toward him and grabbed my knife, as did the others.

"What's the matter, are you a military man or not?"

He lowered the rifle, which moments before had been aimed at Joaquin.

"Yes, of course, my unit is near," he said, pointing to his right. "Another comrade and I were catching crabs, and we were already leaving."

"Listen, have you seen some strange activity in this area?"

"No, comrade, everything is quiet. You go on. We're already leaving." He called the other guard who was already coming from the coast, unarmed, with a sack on his shoulder, and went off without ever turning his back to us. He turned left, the direction his unit was supposed to be. As soon as he disappeared, we started an accelerated march.

"Do you think he'll denounce us?" asked Kinqui.

"I don't believe so. But anyway, we ought to reach the mangroves as soon as possible. Surely, they're not going to look for us through those swamps at night, and tomorrow we'll be very far from here."

We sank up to our thighs in the swamp, holding on to branches to keep our balance. We took turns in carrying the bags. The heaviest was the one containing the diving leads.

At 6:00 we reached the coast and sat, exhausted, on sticks and dry trunks the sea had deposited on some high reefs. At night, in spite of the repellent we were doused with, the gnats and mosquitoes attacked us. Every time we touched our faces, our hands had blood. Thus, we waited until the high tide.

After eating our last ration of steak, we drank some wine and put on our underwater fishing equipment. Kinqui announced he couldn't find his snorkel. We searched the bags in vain. Finally, Joaquin came out with his first not only acceptable but brilliant idea: cut off a piece of each snorkel, tie them together, and give it to Kinqui. Naturally, this was not an easy task, but we managed. At the end of the added pieces we made a hole and formed a nozzle.

The snag was that Kinqui had to introduce his tube almost to his throat and swim very little, to save energy. It was decided he would go in the rear, towed by the rest. At 11:30 in the evening another problem arose. Helicopters flew over us, lighting up everything with their potent spotlights.

"I think the guards gave the alarm," said Kinqui, while Pablo observed one of the helicopters quickly approaching us.

"Let's sink deeper in the swamp and keep the bags above our heads," I said. The helicopter flew over us without seeing us, although the helicopters kept shedding light on the dark sky and two torpedo boats were going back and forth to light up the coast. At midnight the tide was completely up. The boats started to send up night flares to illuminate the area.

"I'm going to the water," I told my companions. "Hurry up. There's no time to waste!"

Held by the mangroves, I slipped gently into the icy waters, followed by Pablo. Joaquin was taking his time putting on his equipment while Kinqui was urging him on. We didn't count on having to put up with one more of Joaquin's peculiarities, but at the last crucial moment, standing on the rocks, he declared, "Boys, we'd better postpone it for tomorrow so we can better size up the situation. Nobody can expect to pass undetected under that spotlight. We would be killed." He pointed to the light on his right.

Kinqui answered, "I don't know if they would shoot at us, but if you don't jump in the water right now, I'll drown you."

Pablo seconded. "What the hell is the matter with you? Are you crazy? We've been in the water for ten minutes waiting for you and we're frozen. Jump!"

At last, at 12:15 with all of us in the water, we stretched the rope that would join us. Joaquin, the best swimmer and an experienced underwater fisher was at the head of the convoy, followed by me, Pablo, and Kinqui. Thus, we initiated a ten-hour trip, in waters so cold that we shivered, constantly feeling the fishes and the sharks jumping around us. Ten hours submerged in water, human submarines looking for freedom.

In spite of the dangers we faced and the anxiety for the completion of our escape, we witnessed a spectacle that would require another Jules Verne to describe it. The bottom of the sea is simply phantasmagoric, like watching a city a night sprinkled by luminous signs. In its depths, everything shines: the fish traveling in groups; the seaweed, clinging to everything that swims; sunken pieces of iron and wood; remains of wrecked ships; everything, especially the bottom of the Atlantic, has a breathtaking beauty. In Cuba, the marine fauna is unique as a blooming field, with its perforated leaves called borbonis, or sea bush, and its coral life formations.

At the bottom of the sea there is a tiny and graceful fish that, as a puppy, clings to the boats and all that sails, to spare himself the effort to swim. He only swims by himself when it's a question of eating or mating. They are completely harmless, but when they clung to our thighs and belly to be towed, they felt unpleasantly cold, like frogs. It was useless to scare them away with our tridents. After doing a few turns without getting too far from us, they were on us again.

Guantanamo Bay is kept dirty. The communist government throws all the refuse there from the preserves and sausage factories, shrimp cold storage, and other origins, in order to constantly attract sharks, a latent threat for those planning to escape. The Cuban and the American sides are merely divided by an inlet. Needless to say, the Cuban waters and the others intermingle. The Sunday TV program *Sector 40* is a psychological program to terrorize the population and discourage any attempt to escape through Guantanamo. Numerous incidents of fugitives torn to shreds by the reefs or devoured by the sharks and giant crocodiles are exposed in detail. As soon as we began our escape in a moonless and starless night, the sky turned darker and darker until it rained. Once in a while, I pulled off my mask and watched the light of the two beacons through which we had to cross. It was the border. We had been swimming for hours and were close to its powerful spotlights when I noticed the rope joining me with Joaquin slacked. He took off his snorkel to whisper, covering my back with his arm. "Listen let's get near the little key to the right. I don't think we can pass under those spotlights without being detected."

The others came closer and we made a circle. "How do you have the nerve to stop me for this?" I said, angry as hell. "This isn't the moment to think, much less speak! The only option is to go ahead. If we're killed, that's a chance we have to take!"

Pablo pointed to the right. Twenty meters away from us, there was a little light. The key Joaquin suggested was one where we could make a stop. The light was a lit cigarette of a guard standing in a torpedo boat, smoking while he marched from one side of the vessel to the other. The evidence silenced Joaquin. We dived, and continued swimming.

Twenty minutes later from the ocean's depth came a huge fish that I determined was a shark based on its diameter, all the objects being phosphorescent under water. As it came from the right I tried to swim to the left, and this scared it. When it in turn evaded my unknown human form and I swam in the opposite direction, it hit my right leg with its tail. The impact made me twist in pain. Immediately, the huge fish dived to the bottom and brushed past Pablo and Kinqui's bellies, without hurting them. They confirmed it was a shark, a great white.

Great White Shark

My companions came to my assistance. Joaquin rubbed my leg. We continued swimming but my right leg became increasingly numb and swollen. I detached the flipper from my right foot and swam with my left leg, aided by my arms. The underwater swimmer is not ever supposed to use his arms; it exhausts him quickly. However, I didn't want to be towed; it would mean a delay. We had to cross the border before the tide turned against us, in which case sea currents would push us back towards communist waters. The following night might not be as dark and, therefore, not as favorable.

A few yards from the powerful beacon, we contracted our muscles, descending to the bottom. We reappeared almost in the center of its light. Believing the more potent house light to the left belonged to the communists, we resurfaced too close to the right, towards the other beacon, passing a few meters in front of the communist guards reclining on the piers. Some slept while others listened to Radio Habana. It was tuned so loud we could hear it. This turn could have been fatal.

Again, we dived to the bottom, resurfacing, this time in the dark of the night, our great ally. We swam away from the lights for many hours. Finally, I decided to take a look, with my head slightly above the water. Through the glass I observed the sun was high. At my left was a huge tank, apparently an explosive storage container, with a facsimile of the U.S. flag on it. I stopped swimming and twice pulled hard on the rope connecting me to the group. This was our emergency signal. Everybody came to the surface. We hugged each other when we saw the American flag.

"We're in free land!" we said joyously, putting on our snorkels and advancing towards the place. Not until we removed our gear did my companions notice my swollen leg. I told them not to worry. We had more important things to think about.

"Come on, let's go!" I said, but still I stumbled when I stood up. Supported by Pablo and Kinqui, I joined my companions on our march. Joaquin, meanwhile, was returning from his inspection of the area with an unhappy expression on his face. Kinqui asked him if he was okay.

"I'm all right, but we have to swim another three miles before we arrive. This is only a trench that begins here," and he pointed to the spot where we had emerged from the sea, "and ends up over there."

We walked through the narrow key and, on reaching the other end, lay on the sand, exhausted, hungry and thirsty. For three days we had been eating small portions of meat which were now gone. We also drank seawater after we consumed the water we'd brought with us. The seawater had given us stomach cramps. Joaquin and Kinqui climbed on top of the tank, there signaling the ships leaving the harbor.

It was 10:30 in the morning, I guessed, since my Soviet-made "waterproof" watch had become a fish bowl. After several hours, the sun was unbearable. In the harbor, emptied of ships, none had noticed us or our signals. As we continued looking, we saw the faraway houses where people lived, and sharks jumping like sardines around the key, now much more dangerous since they seldom attack at night, preferring to attack by day.

In spite of the risk involved, Kinqui insisted on going ahead to get help. Of course, he was less fatigued than the rest of us. Afraid of the sharks, I attempted to dissuade him but to no avail. He put on the equipment and jumped into the sea. I made an effort to get up and watch Kinqui's snorkel until it disappeared. Restless, I walked to the edge of the rocks trying to locate him. Finally, I fell down by Pablo and Joaquin, who lay semi-conscious. I was not able to get up again.

Everything swirled around me until I lost consciousness. After what was probably several hours, I heard the distant sound of a siren, like the one used by the communist police. When I opened my eyes, I saw a shadow becoming increasingly clearer until I happily discerned it was Kinqui jumping to the sea from a small patrol boat carrying the American flag. Helping us to our feet he said, "Come on, stand up, we are free men!"

The men in the boat asked if they should come closer to the rocks. We shouted it wouldn't be necessary. Using our last drop of strength, we swam toward the boat climbing on board by our own effort. The marines gave us blankets and a young American officer let us drink water from the canteen he held with hands trembling with emotion.

A true miracle had led us to the heart of Guantanamo base without being spotted by anyone, including their own men. Although such had not been our purpose, our perfect plan had even deceived the security system of the American base. We were almost three miles inside the base. The officer weighed our feat with all the difficulties involved: the hardships, obstacles, persecutions, risk to our own lives, mine fields, swamps, and almost inaccessible sharp rocks capable of smashing anyone falling upon them. We had been swimming without wet suits for twelve hours, submerged in the cold October waters. We were the first fugitives who had been able to get there. "You deserve a medal, boys," he said.

There was a closed station wagon waiting for us on land. They also suggested we cover ourselves with blankets so the Cuban employees on base wouldn't notice us. One of them could be an informer for the G-2, and if he told the communist dictatorship of our presence there, our immediate return would be demanded. The international regulations and codes forbade the granting of asylum on the base.

We traveled for a long time, unaware of our destination, only conscious that the road was extremely bumpy. At the end of our ride we were received by people that belonged to intelligence, as they identified themselves to us.

After a brief rest and a long interview, they informed us we would immediately leave for Florida by military plane. The next day we were taken to the airport, with added precautions. One of the intelligence officers was giving us instructions and explaining the reason for each of these steps. Hidden on the floor of a small bus covered with sailcloth we arrived at the airport. The intelligence officer addressed the passengers already occupying their seats, mostly officers returning to the United States on furlough with their families.

"Ladies and gentlemen, these young men are Cuban professionals who have been bravely fighting the communist system that unfortunately has been implanted in Cuba. Being in constant danger, they have been forced to leave their country. Now they are going to our country with you, and I must ask you to show them the greatest courtesy. At the same time, be as discreet as possible concerning their escape. Have a nice trip!"

The young officer, obviously moved, shook hands with us. The officers occupying the front seats with their wives got up to let us have their seats. When the plane took off and we saw from above and perhaps for the last time, the blue sky and green palm trees, we looked at each other sadly. One of the officers leaned over the back of my seat and said, "It's a pity you can't go back to your homeland, isn't it?"

I looked at him for a few seconds and then turned to Joaquin, Pablo and Kinqui, in search of a common answer. "Yes, it's sad. But we shall return! Isn't it true, fellows?"

"Of course, we will!" was their unanimous answer.

This optimistic, confident exclamation was followed by sorrowful silence. Our beloved Cuba was turning into a tiny light point, as blurred as our uncertain future.

Marxist Paradise on Earth

"Marxism is like a rosebush with no roses; only thorns. It is the hope that someday, on one glorious day in the future, a rose will bloom. Yet this bush will never bloom, and only more and more thorns will appear. Though touted as the redemption of mankind, this ideology leads only to despair. Ambitious men inevitably will seize control and in the name of progress take away freedom of achievement and choice. The end of Marxism is this: the worker becomes a slave to the elite, no better than where he started. I do not wish to live in this kind of world. I would say to you if you do choose this path, plan a way to escape, because most who journey toward this false paradise end up with no way to return. They really can't take you to live in the Paradise as they promise, only to live in the absolute Inferno for the rest of your miserable life."

– Dr. J Antonio del Marmol

CHAPTER X: FREEDOM AND SORROW

October 4, 1971 3:00 PM
Vedado district, Havana Cuba, Castro's office

Fidel Castro pounded his desk and kicked the walls. He was fuming with anger. He strode back and forth in front of Piñeiro, Ramiro, Raul, and some of his other officers. All the men looked worried as he waved his lit cigar in the air and yelled. Piñeiro sat on a chair with his feet up watching Castro rant and rave. Piñeiro knew this was not a joke, but he felt confident about the news he was about to reveal.

"Did del Marmol actually get away?" Castro asked.

"Well, there is a strong possibility that he is dead," Piñeiro answered. "We found his briefcase, and it was covered with bullet holes. We have already arrested his brother-in-law, Canen, and I am confident we will make him talk. But I am pretty sure, my Commander, the Little Traitor is dead. However, if he did manage to escape, he is most likely mortally wounded."

Castro replied, "Well, if he did manage to escape, we are in deep shit and we have a big fucking problem." He raised his head and looked worried. His face was drawn, showing his anger. Then he said, "Let's prepare our story just in case he survived. Let's call the Organization of Estates Americans, the United Nations Organizations, and the North American Press, and we will tell them what their governments have done to help him...let's call him a killer...to escape from justice. Call our special agents in Miami and give them the order to find him and kill him and anybody who is with him. We cannot take any chances. He knows too much!" He pounded on his desk and said, "Okay, let's go. There is no time to waste!"

All the officers nodded and left the room, relieved that the Castro's tirade was over—at least for now. In a few minutes, the Cuban television released the news at a press conference of the escape exaggerating tremendously how many people had been killed and that del Marmol and his accomplices were the number one enemies of the Revolution. Their priority was to capture me—alive, if possible. I had ten years of espionage and damage to Castro to pay for, in their eyes.

A few hours later, the headlines in the American newspapers read, "Murderers escape Cuba. U.S. government protects them in Guantánamo Navy Base. The criminals are expected to land in Miami in the next few hours."

At the same time, while we were still on the plane just leaving the base, a Cuban spy in Miami wearing a white suit and dark glasses, was standing across the street from the Pelicano Restaurant meeting with another spy and giving him pictures of me and my friends, Kinqui, Pablo, and Joaquin. He leaned back against the wall while watching the street, the cars, and people walking by. With a confident smile, he told the other man, "Don't worry. We will get him and his friends before they even get to eat their first Cuban sandwich on Calle Ocho in Miami."

Around the terminal at the airport runway at Fort Lauderdale, Florida, a huge crowd of press and news people from all over were waiting. News trucks and vans lined the road outside. There was a feeding frenzy with reporters running around trying to interview anybody they could find. But nobody knew anything.

Next to the terminal and slightly out of sight, a man in a suit stood watching the crowd. He was an American, about 45 and slightly heavy. He lit a cigarette as he watched the crowd, occasionally glancing skyward. This was O'Brien, a U.S. Intelligence man. He walked over to a pay phone and made a call. "Hey, word of this flight has leaked out and every news crew from California to Moscow is here . . . What . . ? I can't make it there on time. . . . Who? General who? OK. OK. I'm on my way."

He hung up and sped quickly to the main office of the International Command Staff Building at Fort Lauderdale. O'Brien walked inside the front door and over to the receptionist. "Hi. General Samson, please." He handed a business card to the young noncommissioned officer, who then called the general. He said to O'Brien, "You may go right in, agent."

O'Brien walked into the office and shook the general's hand. "Nice to meet you, sir. I really appreciate the ride from your guys. There's no way I could get down there in time otherwise."

"Not a problem," the general replied. "We're always glad to help you Intel boys out of a jam when we can."

The general picked up the phone and ordered a plane to get ready immediately. A few minutes later, O'Brien was aboard an F-4 Phantom jet fighter on his way to intercept the plane coming from Guantanamo.

The pilot was a tall man with brown eyes and auburn hair. He did not look like a Cuban at all. He told O'Brien that his father was Cuban and his mother was Irish and that he was carried to the United States when he was fifteen years old. He knew all about the suffering of the people in Cuba. He said, "It will be a pleasure to help somebody to get away from Castro's bullshit!"

He began to mumble and sing to himself. O'Brien recognized the song immediately: *"Bésame Mucho."* But the pilot had changed the words a bit to *bésame el culo* which meant "kiss my ass" and he was singing, "Castro...kiss my ass...," and laughing at his own joke. He told O'Brien he and his family had to escape Cuba years ago and were almost killed by the sharks when their raft fell apart in the waters off the coast of Florida.

He continued singing and laughing... *"Bésame, Bésame el culo* Oh Castro, you are a royal son of a bitch! *Bésame, Bésame el culo.*" He seemed to be enjoying very much making fun of Castro.

While he was singing this, he turned the plane upside down and O'Brien said, "Please, please. Would you mind if we fly right side up for the rest of the flight?"

The pilot replied, "No problem, chief, we are going to be landing in a few minutes anyway. This trip is in the bag!"

O'Brien said, "Bag. Yeah. I need the barf bag!"

The pilot said, "What? What did you say?"

O'Brien replied, "Nothing. Keep singing. Don't mind me." But he was holding his stomach with both hands and looked as if he would be sick any minute.

The pilot then told O'Brien that the general had arranged for them to land at an alternate place where they would pick up his package before they reached their destination. In the middle of nowhere and away from the view of the public, the F-4 jet landed and rolled to a stop forty miles from Fort Lauderdale at a little airport that was maintained by the intelligence forces for special operations. There was a rolling ladder, a forklift, a few small trucks, a small ground crew, and a little shed with landing lights for night vision. An air crew quickly rolled out a ladder, and O'Brien crawled out and down to the ground. He waved to the pilot and walked to a waiting car.

The driver of the car was dressed in civilian clothes and looked like he could be an intelligence officer. O'Brien could see his pistol and holster under his coat as he moved around.

He said to O'Brien, "That was a quick flight! How was it?"

O'Brien replied, "Lucky I didn't lose my breakfast."

The driver smiled and said, "Come on O'Brien. They'll be on the ground any minute. Your timing is really close."

"I'm just glad to be on the ground. Let's go."

"I have coffee and donuts in the car," the driver said. "Would you like some?"

"Thanks, I'll have some coffee. Maybe that will settle my stomach."

They waited for only a few minutes and then a small passenger plane landed in the distance. The plane rolled to a stop close to them, and the crew quickly pushed the ladder into place. Four men stepped out. While they were still at the top of the ladder, the crew pushed it away from the plane. The men did not move but hung on tightly. Nobody else got off the plane.

The plane then taxied away, headed for the runway, and took off.

O'Brien motioned to the driver to get closer to them, and he pulled the car up to the bottom of the ladder. O'Brien was laughing as he greeted us. "Did you fly that ladder all the way over here?"

"No," I said. "We had a plane when we left! Now all we have is this ladder. Is this the way you North Americans do things?"

"You never know," said O'Brien. "There must be five hundred people waiting for you in Fort Lauderdale. Another thousand protestors are on their way because you guys are supposed to be criminals and we are protecting you. We just made a little change of plans. My name's O'Brien. Get in right away before we are detected by unfriendly eyes and your picture's all over the newspapers again."

Kinqui, Pablo, Joaquin, and I descended the ladder and got into the car. The driver told us to lie down in the back, covered us with a blanket, and drove away.

O'Brien said warmly, "Welcome to the United States!"

Meanwhile, the press was still scrambling around at Fort Lauderdale Airport trying to find some action. They were all getting frustrated. Finally, in the sky to the south a plane could be seen approaching. One of the newscasters shouted, "That must be the plane coming from Guantanamo Bay!"

The reporters ran toward the chain link fence, pushing each other around trying to get in position to get the best pictures. A TV newscaster motioned to her camera man to start rolling and said to the camera, "As you can see, the plane in question with the criminals escaping from Cuba is coming in from Guantanamo Bay. We'll see who they are and try to interview them as soon as they get off the plane." She signaled her camera man to cut and said, "Shut the camera off until I tell you to roll again." She lowered her microphone and said, "It sure as hell took them long enough! I've got things to do. Come on, get that damned plane over here."

Cuba: Russian Roulette of the World

As the plane taxied closer the press gathered like vultures over a kill. The plane taxied to a stop and the mobile staircase was shoved into place. The door opened and marines, sailors, and officers began to pour out, filing down the staircase. At the bottom of the staircase the press crowded around waiting anxiously.

The lady newscaster told her camera man, "Roll the camera!" and she started talking again. "Any second now, we should see who they are. Just to give you a little background, we received word that some notorious criminals escaped from Cuba into the American base and the Cuban government has demanded their immediate return. The Cuban Interior Minister said the United States was under obligation by international treaty to return the criminals to Cuba. We will bring you the latest information as soon as we have more."

She waved to the camera man to follow her and she began to climb the stairway up into the plane. She was so determined that she practically pushed the last Marines who were coming down the stairway out of her way saying, "Excuse me, excuse me!"

She rushed to the top of the stairs followed by the other reporters demanding to look inside the plane. One of the attendants allowed her, the camera man, and another reporter to go inside. There was no one left in the plane. It was empty. She rounded on the attendant and said, "Hey, what's going on? Where are those criminals you are bringing that escaped from Cuba?"

The crewman just shrugged and said, "I don't know what you're talking about. We're not coming from Alcatraz. You must have the wrong plane lady. We bring Navy personnel. We don't transport criminals. Whoever gave you that information... get your money back. They took you for a ride."

The newscaster ignored the crewman. She saw the pilot and co-pilot coming out of the cockpit. "Where are the criminals from Cuba?" she demanded.

The pilot looked at her in wonder and he said, "What the hell are you talking about?"

She said, "You know what I'm talking about. The Cubans. The criminals. They're supposed to be on this plane."

The pilot replied, "I don't know where you got that information but I can assure you it was all wrong. I hope you didn't pay too much for it."

The co-pilot laughed. The newscaster glared at him. The pilot nudged the co-pilot and they walked away.

She walked to the door and yelled out to the rest of the crowd. "We've been skunked. There isn't anybody left on this plane. Damn!"

Her source's information had always been good in the past. *What a waste of time and money*, she thought. She walked down the stairs, handed her mike to one of her crew, and stormed away.

The pilot and co-pilot were in a hangar watching the crowd. The co-pilot said, "Can you believe her? So much for national security."

The pilot responded, "All those people are the same. All they care about is money and sensational news even if they have to create it! That's how they survive. They're like parasites feeding on other people's suffering."

O'Brien's driver transported us from the small airport to a federal building in Miami. We went to an immigration office in order to be processed and admitted as legal immigrants. It looked like an intelligence office. We were interviewed by an officer named Steffan, a man in his forties with white hair at his temples. He asked us a lot of suspicious questions. I didn't trust him.

We arrived a few hours later, and O'Brien drove us to a house in the suburbs of Little Havana. It was not luxurious, but it was well maintained.

"This is a secure house," he told us, giving us the keys. "You'll be safe here until we relocate you to someplace else."

He showed us how everything in the house worked. "When you get hungry, there's a Cuban restaurant called El Pelicano a block from here. It has excellent food, and you don't have to pay; just sign for your meals. The owner, Alfredo, is a good Cuban freedom fighter and he will be delighted to feed you guys every day. He'll take good care of you. We've already arranged to take care of all your expenses. I'll call you guys later."

"Thank you," I said. "What else do you take care of?"

O'Brien smiled and said, "You'll find out more as we go along. You're in good hands. We can do everything and anything."

I smiled. "Even walk on water?"

O'Brien smiled back. "Sometimes. But you never know. Why don't you guys go get some dinner?" He waved goodbye to us and left.

So Kinqui, Pablo, Joaquin, and I decided to do just that. We headed for the restaurant El Pelicano that he had recommended. We were all sitting at a table near the front of the restaurant reading the menus when the owner waved to us. Alfredo was a typical Cuban-looking fellow. He was fair skinned and hazel eyes and very dark, curly hair. He was dressed all in white, wearing a typical Cuban guayabera, a long white shirt with large pockets on both sides at the top and bottom. It was embroidered elaborately on both sides, including the El Pelicano logo. His name tag was pinned to the front.

We introduced ourselves as the ones O'Brien had called ahead about.

He greeted us enthusiastically. "Oh yes, you are the heroes who just escaped from Cuba!" Then he put his hands over his mouth. "Oops, I'm sorry. You have to be careful what you say here in Miami. There are too many Castro spies here. Don't order anything. I am going to bring you the special of the house. It is called the carousel. It has everything: pork chops, chicken, sea food and beef!"

With a smile, he went to the kitchen, and a waitress brought us drinks and set up a table for us. Within a while, Alfredo appeared with delicious and exquisite Cuban food, and we ate like kings.

A few weeks later, we went back to El Pelicano to eat more exquisite Cuban food. We greeted Alfredo, and asked him for the specialty of the house, the carousel. Before the food was ready, Alfredo approached us and said, "You have a telephone call in the back. Come with me."

I got up and followed him through a narrow, dark hallway and through the kitchen door to the phone. Across the street from the restaurant, a man stood on the corner wearing a white suit and dark glasses. It was the same man who had been there earlier talking to another Cuban spy. A car drove up. He approached the car and said, "They are right on schedule. *Las sardinas estan en su lata.*[4]"

The man in the back seat of the car was hidden. He handed a small briefcase to the first man. On his finger was a shiny ring with a Masonic emblem. He said to the man, "Be sure not to miss. We cannot afford a mistake."

The other man smiled, nodded his head, and said, "If this briefcase does not fail, we will not fail!" He took the briefcase, walked across the street to the restaurant and went inside. He sat down at a table next to my friends, nodded and smiled at them and put the briefcase down on the floor. He then ordered lemonade and a Cuban sandwich, and when no one was looking, he discreetly pushed the briefcase with his right foot under our table. He looked very calm while drinking his lemonade and reading the paper.

The carousel had already arrived with some fried macho bananas, and my friends were surprised at the amount of food Alfredo had brought. They began to eat happily. Kinqui called to me loudly, "Come on, Julio Antonio. The food has arrived. It's delicious. Come and eat. Don't let it get cold!"

I looked through the kitchen window and saw them. I waved at them to signal that I heard and would be there soon. As I waved at them, I saw the man in the white suit, and our eyes met briefly. He smiled.

When his sandwich arrived, he paid for his food, and nodding and smiling again at Kinqui, Pablo, and Joaquin, he left. Back in the kitchen, I answered the phone. "Hello?"

---

[4] The sardines are in the can.

A woman's voice was on the line and she said, "This is a message from the Professor. You must leave Miami right now."

I replied, "But, I can't. Who is this?"

The voice said, "You must go. Your life is in danger. The word is out. Castro put a death warrant on you and your friends. You should go to another state far away from Florida as all the Cuban spies will try to kill you. I am a freedom fighter. I am your friend. I have the copy of your picture that they sent to all their spies. Now go, immediately. I will contact you as soon as I can. I have to go now. Do as I say. Trust me, please. Goodbye." And she hung up.

I stood there for a few seconds with the phone still in my ear watching all the Cuban personnel in the kitchen. It seemed to me they were all looking directly at me. I looked at them with trepidation, expecting the worst. Could one of them be the assassin?

Suddenly, while the phone was still in my ear, a huge blast sounded through the restaurant blowing dust, dirt, bottles, and towels into the kitchen. The whole building shook as if an earthquake had struck.

I dropped the phone and dropped to my knees close to the wall. A voice said, "What? What was that?"

A cook with a bloody face said, "It sounded like an explosion!"

I stood up as quickly as I could and ran to the front of the restaurant. The table where my friends and I had been sitting was gone. In the dark dusty cloud, I tripped over something. As I got to my feet again my hand touched the object.

It was a human leg.

It had been severed in the blast and was still bleeding. I instantly pushed it away in horror, and in despair I realized it was probably the leg of one of my friends. I looked in a corner and saw Kinqui lying against a far wall in a pool of blood. Joaquin had a piece of wood piercing his chest. Pablo lay near a wall. His leg was blown off and he was almost dead from loss of blood. His face was covered with blood. I ran to help him, but he just looked at me blankly. Then his eyes rolled to the back of his head and he died.

I ran back to Kinqui hoping to find there was still just a little life left in him. He did not move. I looked at him and saw he had been impaled by a wooden post. He was completely lifeless. I stood up and looked around the room. I put my hands to my head as the impact of what had happened hit me. My three friends were dead. I realized that if it had not been for that phone call, I would have been dead, too.

I stood in silence and in shock. I dropped down to the floor, covered my head with my arms, and as the tears came to my eyes, I wondered what I would do now. I was completely lost in my sorrow. I lay there for a while looking at the stream of blood that was running on the floor from Kinqui's body thinking that as the blood left his body, his young life was leaving forever.

The spy outside with the white suit and the dark glasses was trying to get a look into the restaurant as he took a bite from his Cuban sandwich. He wanted to make sure everyone he had targeted was dead. The smoke was beginning to clear a little bit, and a lady came screaming out of the restaurant. Her face was bloody. Two men, also wearing white guayaberas soaked with blood came out of the restaurant, too. The spy asked the woman, "Is everybody okay in there?"

Horrified, she screamed at him, "Are you crazy? It's not okay! Everybody's dead! There are dead bodies everywhere!"

The man tried to look into the restaurant by leaning in through the shattered windows. He saw three bodies where he had placed the bomb, and he saw another body lying in the corner. He moved in closer to make sure everyone was really dead but a nail from one of the exposed beams tore his suit and cut into his arm. He looked at his arm and saw the blood running out from the cut. He decided the blast would have certainly killed all his targets and he should leave before he got hurt, too.

As he turned to leave, a ceiling beam collapsed and fell onto the floor next to him causing even more dust to spread around the place and making it more difficult to see and to breathe. He began to cough from the dust, put his handkerchief to his mouth, and walked away, dropping the remainder of his Cuban sandwich on the floor.

As the beam collapsed, I raised my head and saw Alfredo coming toward me. He grabbed me by my right arm and helped me up and asked me, "Are you okay? We have to get you out of here through the kitchen."

He pushed broken furniture out of the way, led me through the kitchen to the back of the restaurant, and put me into his car.

"What just happened here?" I gasped. "Right in the middle of the city! In full daylight! Is this a war zone?"

Alfredo stood with blood on his face, shaken to the core. He answered, "Oh, my God! I don't know!"

I said, "All my friends are dead!"

The cook and the busboy came out of the restaurant, and Alfredo said to them, "Call the fire department, the paramedics. Try to save whatever and whoever you can. I will be back as soon as possible."

As Alfredo drove slowly out of the alley and away from the restaurant, I looked back at what was left of the building and mumbled to myself, "This was meant for me. I thought we were safe here. How could I have been so wrong?"

Then I began to realize that I could depend only on myself; I could not trust anyone. But at the same time, I also realized that the woman who had called me on the phone had saved my life. If she had only called me ten minutes earlier, my friends might still be alive.

As we were leaving, we saw a huge crowd gathering in front of the restaurant. Police cars, fire trucks and two ambulances had already arrived.

Alfredo dropped me at the safe house immediately and told me, "Don't open the door for anybody. Don't answer the phone. Don't do anything until O'Brien gets in touch with you. I will call him and tell him what happened. He has a key to this house." He pulled a pistol from his waist and handed it to me. He said, "Do you know how to use this?"

I replied, "Yes, I do."

He said, "Okay, don't hesitate to use it if you need to."

I said, "Thank you."

We said goodbye and he left. I took a shower and was not even dressed completely when I heard the front door open. I grabbed the pistol and pointed it toward the bedroom. O'Brien appeared at the door and said, "Don't shoot. Don't shoot. It's me!"

I said, "Next time you had better whistle or signal or something because from now on I am going to shoot first and ask questions later. I don't want to end up like my friends." I was really pissed and confronted him. "Who the hell knew we were here? You told us we were safe!"

He replied sadly, "I'm really sorry about your friends. I know you are valuable to Castro, but I didn't know you were so valuable that he would risk his reputation and create such a scandal by sending someone to assassinate you and your friends in the center of the city in broad daylight! What do you know that makes him so afraid of you?"

I shook my head and looking disturbed and said, "Let's not talk about it now."

He came close to me and put his arm around my shoulders and said, "Whatever happens, remember I'm your friend."

I looked him straight in the eye and said, "Are you really'?"

He looked at me and said reassuringly, "Yes I am. And I will prove it to you in time."

I shook my head and said, "In time? My father always told me that time is the factor that determines everything in life because people can bullshit you with words, but time will ultimately tell you what the person's values really are!"

He put his head down and then looked up at me and said, "I agree one hundred percent with your old man, but please...trust me and give me some time to prove myself to you."

"This is the second time today someone has asked me for trust. This must be a difficult thing to find here."

"Yes, it is a difficult thing to find. Trust. Now, we have to get out of here."

Cuba: Russian Roulette of the World

"Here?"

"Yes, we have to get you out of Miami," O'Brien said. "This place is not safe for you anymore."

I was furious. "I wish you had figured that out sooner. My three very best friends are dead. Not in Cuba...but here...on free soil!"

"Yes, I can't apologize enough," O'Brien said. "But there is very little we can do about that now. Let's try to keep you alive. I need to take you to Steffan's office so you can be debriefed and get clearance. Let's get the hell out of this state."

I stiffened and stepped back into the room to gather up my stuff and put it into my back pack. "Wait a minute," I said, "my friends just got killed, and now you want me to talk to that moron again. That jerk you call an intelligence officer? I have a very bad feeling about that guy. I don't think he is on our side. He was not debriefing me...he was interrogating me. Of course, I didn't tell him anything. He asked me if I wanted to go to Vietnam. I think he was working for Castro and he wanted to send me to Vietnam to get rid of me."

O'Brien observed my hostility, and he tried to calm me down and comfort me. "Yeah, I know. That guy, Steffan, has a funny attitude."

I replied, "I don't see anything funny about him."

"I don't work with them, and I don't deal with that office very much," he said, trying to justify himself. "Anyway, from now on you and I are a team. You can trust me because we have a mutual friend in Cuba. One in particular: I think you call him the Professor."

I was kind of surprised because I did not expect to hear that. O'Brien noticed my surprise and said, "I couldn't tell you earlier, but now I can. I think when you hear what I have to say, you'll be able to trust me more. Your uncle, the Professor, and I have been working together for many years. Remember, you can only trust your gut feelings. You can only tell Steffan what is necessary to clear you and the rest keep to yourself until you meet the right person. Now, let's get out of here. We've got work to do."

While we were walking to his car in the parking lot, I smiled and said, "I'm glad you told me what you did. I feel better about you now. Thank you for your confidence in me."

We drove for a while and arrived at the Federal Building. We parked in an underground garage and took the elevator up to the floor where Steffan's office was located. O'Brien and I went into the Office of Information. His receptionist called Steffan on the intercom and said, "Agent O'Brien is here with Dr. del Marmol." We heard him on the intercom saying, "Send them in."

We walked into his office. Steffan seemed to dislike Cubans. He had commented before to me that he was sick and tired of Cubans getting a free ride in the United States, pretending to hate Castro and getting so much stuff from our government. Getting much more than he ever got—and for free just because they were anti-communist! They are regarded as heroes. "What about our own boys who are dying in Vietnam! What do they get? A stick in the ass! But you guys get all this shit."

I wondered what is wrong with this guy. I sat down across from him at his desk. He waved to O'Brien briefly with a sour face and looked at me with disdain. He said, "Well, they just confirmed this morning to me that you actually have knowledge of the person in charge of preparing a coup against Castro and the Cuban government."

Pissed off, I leaned back in my chair, turned to my left, and looking at O'Brien I said, "You see, I told you. This is not the kind of question this man is supposed to ask me! This is of no concern to the United States of America. What is this guy trying to do to me? Even if I knew, I could not tell him that."

Steffan made a face and said, "Of course you can, and you will! You bet you will! Even if I have to send you back to Cuba."

O'Brien stood up, reacting to the abusive treatment and raised his voice. "Hey Steffan, lighten up. Even if he doesn't tell you shit, you can't send him back to Cuba! That's bullshit. You don't have the power to do that. I think you're a little out of line. Remember, he's on our side."

Steffan's face turned red as he turned on O'Brien, too, saying "Do me a favor! Get out of my office right now. In here, I do what I want and conduct my interviews the way I want. If you don't like it, get out of my office!"

O'Brien shook his head. He looked at me and said, "You're right! He *is* a royal asshole. Don't let him get to you. I'll wait for you outside." And he walked out of the office.

Steffan stood up, walked after O'Brien, and slammed the door behind him, locking it. He turned back to me and said, "Now listen to me. I am through bullshitting with you. You either tell me who is in charge of the coup to kill Castro and take over in Cuba, or I will report you to my superiors and convince them that you are a Soviet-trained double agent. Believe me, no matter what O'Brien says, I'll send you back to Cuba or at least put you in federal prison with the worst criminals in the country."

I stood up from my chair and looked down at him where he was sitting behind his desk, shook both of my hands in front of his face in mock terror. "Ooh, ooh, you are scaring me so much! Do you know who you are talking to, you moron? If I was able to fool Castro and his most highly trained agents for eleven years, do you think a puppet like you can intimidate me? Forget it." I shook my finger in his face and said, "Fuck you! I have already told you all you have to know. Our debriefing is over, and the names I gave you before, figure out who is the leader!" I walked to the door, unlocked it, went out, and slammed it just as he had done when O'Brien had left.

O'Brien was smiling from ear to ear. "Whoever trained you did a good job. I love the way you handled that asshole! I'm going to report this to my superiors, and I'll make sure you don't have to come back to this guy again."

As we were walking down the hallway Steffan came out of his office hollering, "You have to bring him back tomorrow at the same time, O'Brien."

We both smiled and O'Brien said, "Fuck you, Steffan."

We left the building and O'Brien told me that it would probably take a few weeks for him to arrange for my relocation.

We stopped in a little market and picked up some bread, ham, pickles, juice, and milk so I would have something to eat. He dropped me off at the safe house and told me not to open the door for anyone until he came back in a few days. He said he would telephone me and would let the phone ring once and then he would hang up. He would call back again and let the phone ring once and then hang up. Then, he would call back the third time and let it ring until I answered. This would be our signal. He said goodbye and left.

Nearly eight days later, I was running out of food and going crazy with boredom. I was preparing a sandwich when the phone rang. It rang according to our plan, and the third time it rang, I picked it up. It was O'Brien.

He said, "Are you okay? Is everything alright? Do you still have some food left?"

I answered, "Just barely. I am on my last slice of bread. I have it in my hand with guava jelly on it ready to eat."

He laughed and said, "Throw it away. I'll be there in a few minutes. I'm taking you out for a good meal—at the El Pelicano. I have to talk to you."

I made a sour face and said, "Are you sure that it's safe to go there?"

"Yeah. They're remodeling the restaurant, but it's open for business in the section that's not damaged. Life goes on. Alfredo will be really glad to see you. However, if you want to go someplace else, that's fine with me. But I think you'll be okay there now."

"Well, alright. If you think it's safe. They probably think I'm dead now anyway and will not even be looking for me. Even if they are, that is the last place they would expect me to be."

A few minutes later O'Brien picked me up and we went to the restaurant. Drop cloth covers were hiding the damage and workers were repairing the walls and floor. But tables were set up, people were eating, and just as O'Brien had said, life went on.

Alfredo approached us and after saying hello, he gave me a big hug and said, "I am sorry about your friends, but at least you are okay. It is good to see you." He took our order and went to the kitchen.

I was silent and O'Brien tried to start a conversation. "I know it's been a little tough these last couple of weeks, and I—"

"Tough?" I interrupted. "Is any of this garbage your doing?"

"No. I promise. My job is to help you get a new start and to help you with your fight back in Cuba."

"Then who is this bastard, Steffan?" I said. "What is he trying to do, ruin all the refugees? I feel like I'm back in Cuba!"

"He's supposed to go to Washington tomorrow anyway."

I smiled. "Good. Maybe his plane will crash."

O'Brien looked at me with compassion. "Now don't get hostile," he said. "He's just doing his job. What if you really were a double spy? His job is to make you mad enough to tell the truth."

"O'Brien. If I were a double spy trained by the Russians, I would have known what to do with that bastard."

O'Brien raised his hand for me to stop talking and said, "I know you're telling the truth, but there are Cuban spies all around here. I don't want to draw any attention."

"Too late. That bomb in the restaurant was for me. But, right now, I'm too hungry to talk about that stuff."

O'Brien was taken aback by my casual attitude. After dinner, on our way out of the El Pelicano, Alfredo called out to me. "Dr. del Marmol, phone call! Please, over here."

I said, "Should I bring my friend? I don't want to lose any more."

Alfredo said, "I'll watch the front."

Before O'Brien could do anything, I headed for the kitchen. He tried to follow me but when he got to the door it was locked. He could only pound on the door.

I went to the phone and picked up the receiver. "Hello?"

The same mysterious woman's voice was on the phone. She said, "You must stop talking to Steffan. He is a Cuban spy. He reports directly to G-2 in Havana. Do you understand?"

"Yes."

The voice said, "I am very sorry about the death of our friends. Welcome to the U.S. I will get in touch with you personally soon. You should leave Miami as soon as the authorities allow you. Goodbye." And she hung up.

I hung up too and looked around the kitchen. Nobody was paying any attention to me as they were all working.

I looked around for Alfredo, but he was gone. I walked toward the door leading into the restaurant and pushed it open. O'Brien was waiting in the dining room, somewhat pissed off. He said, "Man, I thought you were heading for a trap. I couldn't get through that door. Are you OK?"

"Fine. Are you?"

"Yeah, sure. Come on, let's get out of here. You never know what's going to happen."

The next day close to lunch time, I was feeling a bit more comfortable, and I decided to walk to the restaurant to get a Cuban sandwich. I said hello to Alfredo and he said to me, "Oh, I am glad to see you. I want to show you something. Follow me."

I followed him back to his office which was a small room behind the kitchen and he said, "I want you to meet someone." He opened the curtains on one side of the office which was connected with the kitchen and a pretty blonde woman with a familiar face came out. "Dr. del Marmol," he said, "I want you to meet a good friend, a great freedom fighter."

The young lady was in her twenties, blue eyed and with a trim figure. I took her hand and kissed it, "Nice to meet you."

She said, "Nice to see you again."

"Have we met before?"

She smiled and replied, "Yes, a long time ago. You probably don't remember me. I was just a little girl."

"Where was that?" I said. "Your voice actually is familiar to me. I think I heard you just recently—not years ago!"

She smiled again and said, "You are right on both counts. You don't remember me, but I remember you very well. You came to say goodbye to me and helped us get our boat launched into the ocean."

I studied her for a moment and then it hit me who she was. I opened my arms to her and she entered into them very emotionally as she remembered her family, who was now all gone. "Oh my God! Yaneba! I remember now. You are Yaneba," I said. "I thought all of you were killed!" I grabbed my medallion and added, "I still have it."

She smiled and pulled out my crucifix. "I have mine, too, and...they were. I am the only one who lived. That is why I made a promise to myself then to fight Castro and his bandidos until the end of my life to help prevent him from bringing his misery and death to the rest of the world."

I shook my head and then I smiled and shook my finger at her and said, "Now I know. You are the one who called me to the phone the day my friends were killed. Thank you very much. You saved my life."

"I tried to call you sooner," she said regretfully, "but the line was busy."

Alfredo put his left hand over his mouth and said, "Oh, my God. I remember. Yes, you are right. I was on the phone for almost forty-five minutes before they arrived to the restaurant. I was placing my weekly order for supplies."

I shook my head again and said, "It was destiny. There's nothing we can do to change it."

Yaneba replied, "At the very least I think you have now learned that you can trust me."

I said, "We are on the same side. Of course I trust you."

She said, "Yes, we surely are." She smiled and added, "Remember my job now is to keep you safe. What a great pleasure it is for me to do so."

I replied, "How did you know where I was?"

She said, "Like I say, that is my job." She took my hand in a lovely, compassionate gesture and said, "I don't think you should walk the streets of Miami looking like Dr. del Marmol. You have exposed yourself too much. Not too long ago they tried to kill you right here in this place. We have to make you look like someone else so your enemies will not recognize you." With a mysterious smile she opened her briefcase and pulled out a false beard and mustache which could be attached to the skin. She also pulled out a rain hat, handed them to me and said, "Try these on and let's see how you look." She pulled up a chair and said, "Sit down. I am going to make you a new face." She also pulled out a plastic nose, attached it to my nose and covered it with thick makeup, making me look Arabian.

Alfredo was watching all this with fascination seeing Yaneba transform me into a person he had never seen before in just a few minutes. When she finished, he put a double mirror in front of my face and said, "Don't you think you look a lot better? No one will recognize you now."

I pulled the mirror away from me a little bit and said, "My God! What did you do to me? I can't believe it!"

She stepped back, looked at me, and said, "Much, much better."

I said, "Yes, I believe it. I don't even recognize myself...but I like my old face better."

Alfredo said, "My God, not even your mother would recognize you now. Yaneba, you are very talented."

Yaneba smiled and said, "Thank you. That is what I have been trained for. Now, we must go. We have a lot to talk about."

I was fascinated not only with her beauty but also with her ability. We said goodbye to Alfredo and walked to her car. Not until we were on the road did I ask her where we were going.

"To my place. I live in Golden Beach. We will have privacy there and I can tell you about what is going on in Miami and in the rest of the world. You are very valuable to us, and my job is to keep you alive."

I said, "Okay, that's fine with me."

We arrived at her oyster-white, Mediterranean-style house on the beach. She pushed a little button in the roof of her car and the gates opened. I looked in fascination, as I had never seen such a thing at a private home. As she drove the car down her driveway, I saw the tile and rocks around the palm trees in beautifully designed circles. The trees were blowing gently in the wind. The only thing that separated the ocean from her house was a small wall made of rocks on the beach. I turned to look at the gates we had just come through and watched them in astonishment as they closed by themselves. She smiled as she noticed me looking at everything in wonder like a kid with a new toy. As I watched the gates close, she said, "This is a new technology."

I just moved my head up and down affirmatively and then I said, "Boy, this is beautiful. This is *your* house?"

She replied, "Yes, and your house, too. If you want, you can move here. You will be much safer. I trust no one in the government. They don't work for principles and ideas; they respond only to dollars. This is the only thing I have left of my family. I have no one in this country."

I replied, "Well, you have me now."

She smiled and said, "Yes, I know. Thank you. That is why I am so happy you are still alive!"

I felt the cold November wind from the ocean as we walked into the front door of her house. We walked into the living room and she said, "What would you like to drink? I have wine, beer, and cold champagne."

I replied, "The third one is my choice. I love cold champagne. Yes, very cold."

"Okay, I will pour a couple of glasses and I'll put the rest of the bottle in the freezer."

"Fantastic!" I said. "I like it like that."

She walked into the kitchen and I sat down on a huge beautiful white sofa with big pillows around. The leather of the sofa was so smooth it felt like you were being held by a warm hand and your body massaged gently with almond cream. As I looked around, I noticed the whole house was decorated in a futuristic manner. There was a huge white bear rug on the floor in front of the fireplace, which was surrounded with black and white marble tile. There was an S-shaped bar with concealed lights showing through, separating the kitchen from the dining room.

As she came back into the living room from the kitchen, she said, "Relax and make yourself comfortable just as if you were in your own home."

I watched her as she walked back into the kitchen. She was wearing tight black leather pants with high black boots and a beautiful beige blouse. Her waist was so tiny she resembled a little Coca-Cola bottle. She looked like a model out of a magazine. Her hips moved slowly from side to side as she walked, and I could not take my eyes off of her. I smiled and shook my head from side to side and told myself, "Oh no, I cannot get involved with this lady. I still remember her as an innocent little girl on the beach in Cuba who had given me a little kiss before she left with her family." I picked up a magazine from the table and thought to myself how quickly time passes and how things change. How could that little girl already have grown up to be such a beautiful woman? Sandra came into my mind and the horrible moment when they arrested her and handcuffed her to the Soviet Jeep. Like a movie in my mind I saw her looking at me. Our eyes met and I saw the tears and frustration in her face as the soldiers took her away. They passed so close to us that she turned her face away to divert their attention from where she was looking in order to protect us. I was so deep in my thoughts that I did not notice that Yaneba was already beside me with two glasses of champagne.

She said, "Come back to this world. I'll give you a penny for your thoughts."

I looked at her again and smiled, but I no longer saw that beautiful woman. I saw the little girl with the innocent face. She was once again on the beach that night leaving Cuba with her family, taking my cross and kissing it with a sad face. I looked at her for a few seconds, but I did not reach for the glass of champagne that she was offering to me. She realized I was still distracted as I kept looking at her but said nothing.

She grabbed my hand and put the glass into it and folded my fingers around it. She said, "How do you explain that I have your smile in my mind all these years? How is this possible? My memory is still clear about that dark night on the beach when you helped us load the boat. How can one person have such a huge emotional effect on you when you only were around him when you were a kid? Some people call that pure love."

She looked at me, still holding my hand in hers. I saw those big blue eyes and long eyelashes moving up and down like the leaves of a palm tree moving in the ocean breeze in an erotic romantic dance under a full moon on a tropical night. I smelled her exquisite perfume, a combination of jasmine and gardenia with citrus and recently cut rainforest wood. It penetrated my senses, and in that moment, I saw her slowly growing up from that little girl into a woman. I was filled with desire.

She slowly released my hand and sat down in a chair still looking at me. I saw inside her peach colored lips through the beautiful refined crystal Bacara glass as she drank the champagne. They opened like the petals of a rose waiting for the rain on a spring night. She was sitting straight in front of me and she continued looking at me as she drank her champagne. Her breathing became more rapid and her nostrils opened and closed faster and faster as if looking for oxygen. Her brain seemed to be demanding more air than was available in the room which appeared to be getting smaller. I looked down at her firm breasts with her fair skin that had been bronzed by the tropical sun, and in my imagination they looked like two ripe peaches full of juice in the tree. With her rapid breathing I imagined them wanting to get out of the tree before they fell to the ground and to be given to someone to alleviate his thirst and hunger. I was staring at her breasts indiscreetly for too long, and she became shy and a little embarrassed. She looked down and she noticed I crossed my legs in order to hide my excitement and desire.

She took a small sip of her champagne and stood up and said, "I am going to make something for us to eat as I am hungry and you probably are, too. I expect you went to the restaurant to have dinner, but we were distracted and got too deep in conversation and your disguise. I did not see you eat anything?"

I smiled and put my right arm on my stomach and said, "Yes, I am a little bit hungry."

She said, "I will prepare some snacks, and then if you don't mind, I am going to change my clothes in order to get more comfortable. Then I will cook dinner for you."

I answered, "I don't mind. We are in your house. I will wait for you."

She went into the kitchen and pulled out some Cuban crackers, opened the refrigerator and got some salami, ham, and cheese. She brought out a tray full of goodies and asked me, "Do you like olives?"

I said, "I love olives...especially if they are stuffed with red bell pepper."

She smiled and said, "My God, we have a lot of things in common." She went back to the refrigerator and came back with a bowl of olives. As she deposited the olives in front of me, I smelled her perfume again. I absorbed the aroma like a smoker who had given up cigarettes and was suddenly surrounded by smoke. Her arm accidentally brushed against mine, and I felt a surge of electricity moving all over my body. I closed my eyes for a few seconds, and I let my imagination float in that beautiful house on the beach with that woman in my arms.

When I opened my eyes, I saw through the window a heavy wind blowing. It was moving the leaves of the palm trees and it started to rain. She walked to the window to close it as a cold breeze started to create a chill in the living room. She bent over the fireplace and started a fire. The light from the fire cast shadows on the walls and the ceiling, making the room even cozier, warmer, and more romantic.

She turned around to see what I was doing. Realizing I was looking at her, she smiled and walked away to her bedroom. In a few minutes she returned. She had changed into white shorts which showed her beautiful legs. They too had been tanned by the tropical sun. She was wearing a short tee shirt which exposed her middle. It only covered her breasts. I could see her flat stomach and her belly button. She went into the kitchen and opened the refrigerator again and put some shrimp on a plate and came back into the living room with me. As she bent in front of me to put the shrimp down on the table, I could see she was not wearing a bra. I could see her breasts completely. Her body was like a beautiful tree with ripe, succulent fruit within reach that you have to restrain yourself to not grab. I got chills in my body and intense sexual desire. I grabbed my glass of champagne and emptied it. Yaneba looked at me and smiled. She took the bottle and refilled my glass.

She said, "You really like champagne, don't you?"

I replied, "Yes, I do, but I cannot drink more than three of four glasses because I am a light weight. I don't like to lose control."

She smiled and said with satisfaction, "Very good. I like a man who knows his limits."

We drank and ate for a little while. She looked at me once in a while and smiled, and I looked at her once in a while and smiled back. We were like little inexperienced kids who did not know what they were doing next. We looked at the fire and the chimney in silence until finally she broke the ice.

"I think it is better that you and I talk about us before we talk about any political things," she said.

Her smile disappeared, and she became serious. She concentrated on her next words. She moved her head from one side to the other and at the same time she said, "I think we are in trouble."

I smiled back at her and said, "I have been in trouble from the day I was born. This is nothing new to me. Tell me, why do you think we are in trouble?"

She smiled a little sarcastically and pointed her index finger at me and said, "You are my trouble."

I replied with surprise, "I am your trouble. Why?"

She took a little sip of her champagne and said, "I don't know why, but I had a crush on you when I was eleven years old, and I have had fantasies about you for years. Now when I actually see you, I like you even more than in my fantasies, and it seems you're attracted to me too. Please tell me if I'm right or wrong."

We looked at each other, and I answered, "Yes, I am extremely attracted to you. You actually fascinate me."

She smiled and said, "You tell me then, is this not a big problem? You and I are supposed to work together, and I am to be responsible for your security. I am to go wherever you go and keep you safe. How can I do my job right if we get involved and

I fall in love with you? I not only will be distracted myself, but I could be putting your life in danger. This is a very serious conflict."

I replied, "We are adults. We can control ourselves. And just because we are attracted to each other and you had an innocent crush on me when you were a little girl, this does not mean we have to get in bed together and have sex."

She reclined in her seat and she took another sip of her champagne and said, "Well, you are a man in control, and you know your limits. I will put myself in your hands because I am not that strong."

I smiled and said, "Until today I have always been in control and knew my limitations. Besides, I am in love with Sandra and she is pregnant and is going to have my baby. Unfortunately, she was arrested in the final moments as we were leaving Cuba. You remember Sandra, don't you?"

As I told her about Sandra, I became emotional and tears came to my eyes. I stood up and went to the kitchen as I did not want her to see me crying. I went to the kitchen sink and washed my face. When I turned away from the sink, she was standing behind me with a towel.

She smiled and said, "Of course, I remember Sandra. How could I ever forget her? She is a very lucky woman to have you. You must love her very much, huh?"

I replied, "Yes, I do, and I am a very lucky man to have her love, as she is a wonderful girl. And I have to be realistic. I may never see my child or her again."

She said, "It hurts when the person you love is not with you."

I could hold the tears no longer and they started to run down my face involuntarily as I bit my lip trying to keep them back. She saw my pain, and she too became emotional and teary eyed.

"Let go," she told me. "It's okay to cry."

She hugged me and comforted me as I cried on her shoulder. I felt her body heat, and I began to feel sexual desire again. I separated from her in a very gentle way. With my fingers I wiped the tears from her eyes that were running down her cheeks. I tried to tried to smile and told her that we should not be depressed. We needed to thank God a million times just for being alive because we had both been through hell and back.

She nodded her head in agreement, and with her hand she touched my head and agreed that we should both be happy, not sad. She asked me how I would feel about going to my house and picking up my things and staying there with her for a while. She felt it would be much safer for me.

I said it would not be too much to pick up my things, but I asked her if she was sure this is what she wanted, as I did not want to impose on her.

She replied, "This will make my work much easier, as you will be close to me and I will be able to watch over you better. Besides, this is a big house. I am by myself here, and you will be company for me. I don't think I could find better company than you. Do you mind?"

I said, "No. Thank you very much. It will be a great pleasure for me to stay here with you. This is a beautiful house, and you are a wonderful person. Who could say no to you?"

She smiled and she said, "Okay, let's go then."

We left her house and drove to mine to pick up the few clothes they had given me at Guantanamo Base. I called O'Brien using the number I had been given by him for emergencies only.

He answered the phone and said, "Yes. Are you okay?"

I said, "I am fine. I just called you because I am not going to be here anymore. I am moving to a more secure place."

O'Brien said, "Are you sure about that? A more secure place than where you are right now?"

I said with conviction, "Yes, I believe it will be better to move from here. Actually, I am moving in with Cuban freedom fighters, and my contact is the same one who called me the day they bombed the restaurant and killed my friends. She is the one who saved my life."

He asked me, "What is the address of the place where you will be staying?"

I said, "I am sorry but I cannot reveal that on this phone right now, but I will give you a phone number and you can call me using the same code we had before. We will keep in contact. This will not change anything between us."

He replied, "Okay, I trust you. Whatever you think is best for your security is fine with me."

I gave him the number and ended the call. Yaneba put her hand on my shoulder and said with a worried expression on her face, "Thank you for your confidence. However, I do not want to meet your friend in intelligence unless it is absolutely necessary." She rubbed her forehead with her fingers and then said, "He is your friend today, but be extremely careful with him because when you least expect it, politics change. What is okay today could be politically incorrect tomorrow. Sometimes they change their minds when you are doing something for them, and you are the one who ends up in deep shit. You could wind up either in a federal prison, the patsy in a huge political scandal. Or they might abandon you in some foreign country where they never acknowledge you were working for them. This is how these people function, but it is good to maintain a relationship with them. It could be beneficial for future operations. You never know, maybe you could work as an ambassador between us to reestablish our relationship and open a new hope and trust. The trust we lost in them many years ago. Who can forget the Bay of Pigs? They left us, pulled the ships out and left us to die. Just remember, be careful with these people. Be extremely careful with these people. You can never hide from them; they see everything."

"Okay," I answered as we left the house. "Thank you very much for your advice. I will remember that."

We arrived at her house and she prepared an excellent Cuban dinner. She made *bistec en cazuela* (beef steak in tomato and bell pepper sauce with olives and raisins), *arroz blanco* (white rice) and *plátanos maduros fritos* (fried ripe plantains). It was nearly midnight when we ate. We talked after dinner until nearly 2:00 in the morning. She showed me the guest room, where I put all my stuff. It was a large and beautiful room. Very luxurious, very different from where I had been staying. The bathroom connected between her master bedroom and my room. She gave me the key to the house and told me that key also opened the gate to the driveway.

She asked me, "Please, if you meet with O'Brien, do not bring him to my house. Believe me, this is a security measure. It may come in handy one day. I do not want him to know where we are."

I said, "Don't worry about it. Things are going to be done the way you want."

She leaned over, kissed my cheek, and wished me a good night's rest. I smelled her exquisite perfume again. After she left, I lay back on the big comfortable bed. The room smelled good, like potpourri flowers. The ceiling in the room had little stars in it. When I turned the lights off, they sparkled gently. Lying back in the bed, I looked at all these little things and realized how different life was in this country from the miseries in Cuba. The ceilings in even the fanciest hotel had peeling, hundred-year-old paint.

So this was what Castro said was so horrible. This was capitalism. I shook my head and, gazing at the little stars, I fell deeply asleep.

The next day morning, Yaneba knocked at the door to my room. I did not answer, as I had completely passed out. She opened the door and in a very friendly voice she said, "Wake up. Wake up. *Bello durmiente* (sleeping beauty). It is already nine-thirty."

She sat down on the edge of my bed and placed a tray with orange juice, toast, and *café con leche* (coffee and milk) and sweet *biscochos* (cookies). I was half asleep, and as I opened my eyes I said, "Oh, my gosh. Breakfast in bed. You are spoiling me too much. Should I expect this every morning?"

She smiled and said, "Oh no. One for you and one for me. In other words, tomorrow I will expect you to bring breakfast in bed to me! And I like my eggs over easy."

"Okay," I said. "No problem. I can do that for you."

"No!" she laughed. "I am just kidding. You don't have to do anything. It is my pleasure to do this for you."

By now I was completely awake and alert. "I would love to do that for you," I said seriously. "I am not a typical Cuban. I don't feel I would be less macho to do that for you. On the contrary, I would feel pleasure to do that for my honey. I know you are not my honey, but I don't care."

She smiled and said, "I see you are a very different breed of Cuban."

We chatted over breakfast, and she told me she wanted to introduce me to different leaders of Cuban political organizations in exile. But she warned me, "Don't believe anything they tell you, and don't let them involve you in any of their organizations because I want you to see for yourself what is going on in Miami. Miami is like a political rural pharmacy where you can find anything except nails."

I smiled and said, "Maybe if you look hard enough, you could find one with nails!"

She smiled and told me, "Yes, you are right about that."

After a few hours Yaneba had taken me to all the offices of the Cuban political organizations. I realized why Castro had been in power so long in Cuba: even after all the years they had spent together in Miami, they still were in disagreement. And they all wanted to be president; no one wanted to be a soldier. I was really disappointed to see the discrepancies between my compatriots. There was not a single person who was supposed to be the leader who spoke respectfully of the leaders of the other groups. Ironically, though, they were all working for the same goal. They should have been all together sharing the same sentiments and feelings. I could only compare this with the many small-town religious groups, which were all supposed to believe in the almighty God but because the friends of the family were members of a different religion, they did not even speak to them.

Yaneba saw my frustration when I tried to talk to them and bring them together and they would not listen to me. They advised me not to get involved in any other group because they were all bad. Each one felt their group was the only good one. After visiting the last group, we went back home.

A few days later, Yaneba said, "Let's go now. I want to introduce you to the man who assigned me to take care of you."

We arrived at a building and parked in the underground parking. We took the elevator to the top floor. We walked down the hallway and entered an office that looked like an accounting office. She said hello to all the workers and then a lady opened a hidden door which was behind a revolving bar. We entered another office where several men sat at desks. At the rear of the room was an office enclosed by glass. The man inside was large—about six feet tall and three hundred pounds. He had dark skin like he'd been in the tropical sun and straight black hair. He introduced himself cordially and said, "Look what we have here! My favorite girl. She is the smartest, the most efficient, and the most dependable woman I know."

Yaneba said, "That's enough, Marcos."

He continued laughingly, "No, no, no. You are not only beautiful, smart, and all those other things, but you are loyal. To me that is the best quality in any human being."

She smiled, slightly embarrassed, and said, "Okay Marcos. Thank you."

Marcos extended his hand towards me and said, "Nice to meet you. I have heard so many good things about you I feel that I already know you."

I said, "Thank you. The pleasure is mine. Thank you again for the warning the other day. Even though my friends lost their lives, you guys saved mine. I am grateful for that."

Marcos turned serious and said, "I am sorry. Really sorry that Yaneba could not warn you a little bit sooner. But believe me, we feel the deaths of your friends like the deaths of our own friends. In other words, we all suffered a great loss."

I answered, nodding my head in agreement, "Yes, it's true. It was a terrible loss."

Just then the office door opened, and three men came in. The man in front was skinny, good looking, tall, middle aged, about six foot two inches, and had curly black hair. He acted a bit cocky and sure of himself. He said hello to Marcos, and as he passed Yaneba he held her arm and said affectionately, "Hello, honey."

She pulled away from him, moved closer to me and with a very serious face she said, "I have a name, Victor, and I am not your honey!"

He grinned abashedly as everybody was looking at him, and he said, "OK, love. Whatever you say, honey!"

Behind him was a younger man, a mulatto with wavy hair and blue eyes. I recognized him as Arturo, one of my old compatriots from Cuba. He pushed Victor out of the way and came to hug me. "Julio Antonio! I never thought I'd see you again!"

I smiled and returned the hug, giving the rude man a sour look.

Marcos tried to alleviate the tension and said to the man, "Victor, come over here. I want to show you something."

While he walked to the desk, I looked to the third man, who was tall, quiet, and unassuming. He had dark, straight hair and thick prescription glasses. He seemed to observe everything with a keen intelligence. "Roberto," he said by way of introduction, and extended his hand to me and then Yaneba.

Victor walked to the desk, where Marcos handed him some photos. As he approached, he said, "The yacht is ready, and my men are ready too. Whenever you want to take that trip, everything is in place."

Yaneba moved even closer to me and held my arm. We looked into each other's eyes. She smiled and appeared to be a little embarrassed. I immediately I realized there must have been a history between her and Victor. I held her arm and whispered in her ear, "Do you want to go? Is everything okay with you?"

She looked at me and smiled with satisfaction because she realized that I had picked up on her unspoken message. She kissed me tenderly on the cheek in front of everyone. That called everyone's attention to us and surprised them, as Yaneba had not been inclined to show attention to anyone in the past.

They thought we had just met and did not know we had known each other since she was a little child in Cuba.

She squeezed my arm and whispered to me, "Don't worry about it. I'm okay. We will leave when you have finished your meeting with Marcos."

Marcos exchanged a few words with Victor and then brought him over to me. He said, "Dr. del Marmol, this is Victor. He is the chief of operations in our organization."

Victor came close and looked at me with resentment. He extended his hand politely but without warmth, and he said, "Oh. You are the new hero in town. It is my pleasure to meet you." At the same time, he looked at Yaneba as if to imply that my heroism was the reason she was being so nice to me.

Before I could answer, Marcos said, "I am the one who assigned Yaneba to be in charge of Dr. del Marmol's security."

Victor looked at me resentfully and said, "Ah-ha! Is she taking good care of you? She is good. You don't have to worry with this kind of protection."

Yaneba looked at him as if she could gladly kill him. I let go of his hand and said coldly, "It's a pleasure."

Victor said then, "I hear you are a great deep-sea scuba diver. We are going to need a professional diver to head up the team in our next operation in a few days. Would you be interested in coming with us to Cuba? Of course, you might be afraid to go back so soon; they might still be looking for you."

I paused, smiled, and looked into Yaneba's eyes. Then I turned to him and said, "I'm pretty sure you could find many scuba divers here who are even more qualified than me to lead your team. I have decided after I saw my friends blown up in pieces a few weeks ago to operate, for now, on my own—responsible only for my own life, not for the lives of others. From this position, I will protect others the best way I can, but not making decisions as to whether they live or die. In answer to your implication that I might be afraid to go back to Cuba...we all have moments or times when we are afraid. The important thing is to be able to control that fear and still be able to walk with that fear on our shoulders—not chained by it—and finish with courage to accomplish what must be done. Believe me, I know what I am talking about because I have lived with that fear for eleven years and have accomplished with pride my missions, and I am here today still alive. Anyway, thank you for your offer. I work solo now. Do you understand?"

He did not say a word. He was speechless. He looked at me as if to say...where the hell did this guy come from? Yaneba looked at me proudly. She smiled and said, "We will all help you in whatever you need. We all respect your decision to work alone. It will be an honor to work with you. There are not too many honorable people left on this earth." And she gave Victor a knowing look. "Is that not true Marcos? I mean, that we will help him in whatever he needs?"

Marcos was standing by us holding a folder in his hand and he was caught by surprise by her question. He paused a moment and then he said, "Of course. How could we deny help to a valiant man like this?" He patted my shoulder. "Anything you need, all you have to do is ask." With that, he pressed my shoulder and said, "Come with me. I want to introduce you to everybody else."

Victor then went to his own desk and began to make phone calls. He did not come with us. Arturo tagged along while Roberto remained with Victor.

Marcos introduced me to everyone, and when we arrived at the last desk, he introduced me to a young, skinny, charismatic Cuban man with perfect white teeth. The young man said to me, "Remember me, Julio Antonio? I'm Hernesto! I knew you when we were kids! I heard what you guys did in Guantanamo, and I think you guys are awesome!"

"Of course, I remember you, my friend," I said as I embraced him.

Marcos smiled and whispered to me, "This is one of the best young men I have here. You can trust him with your life."

I looked at Marcos and nodded my head. "I know his caliber. We used to do things together."

Close to the last desk was a pretty, red-haired Cuban lady who was smiling ear to ear. She looked familiar, but I didn't recognize her. She extended her hand and said, "My name is Elizabeth. I am at your service. Do you remember me? My brother Hernesto and I never thought we'd see you again."

I replied, remembering her from my childhood, "What a beautiful woman you've become." She smiled in response. I said, "My God, Marcos! You have all my childhood friends working for you here."

Marcos replied with a smile, "Great. It will make you feel like you're back home. This young lady, like Yaneba, lost all her family as she tried to escape from Cuba. She and Hernesto were the only survivors. She is extremely loyal and very well trained."

She said, "For me, it will be a pleasure to work with somebody like you who has genuine values. I read your file, whatever was not classified, and your background is really impressive. But the way you guys left Cuba? That earned all of my respect."

I looked in her eyes as she extended her hand to me and said, "I'm really sorry about the cowardly way our friends were killed. You must be very frustrated. I feel that pain right here in my heart." With that she took my hand and held it to her chest and tears came to her eyes.

I felt her empathy, her emotion, and her loyalty, and I knew in that moment that this woman was capable of dying for her beliefs. I said, "Thank you very much. I believe you and Hernesto can be great assets to my research team. I will need a good team who are knowledgeable in many things: explosives, banking, cleaning up after a mess, terminating a potential enemy, investigation, and follow up on international terrorist activities."

Marcos said, "I have no problem with them working with you. Actually, you and I should not see each other after today. Just in case anything goes wrong, we won't damage the others in the organization. Remember, we will be doing things that are illegal under the laws of the United States. Unfortunately, if we don't do these things, we risk losing our freedom. We have to fight fire with fire!"

I nodded in agreement and smiled at Marcos. I put my right arm on Yaneba's left shoulder and said, "Marcos, if it is alright with you, Yaneba can be our courier. I know she is important to your organization, but I trust her completely. I cannot say that about anyone else."

Marcos smiled and replied, "It is not my organization; it is our organization. You are a part of this whether you want to be or not! But if you wish, I can assign her to work directly with your team." He then said jokingly, "I am not a jealous man! I will share my best woman with you!"

We all smiled. Yaneba who had been quiet throughout this whole conversation now said, "Thank you for your confidence, but it does not make any difference which group any of us work with. The important thing is to end the injustice and abuse to human rights that has been going on in Cuba for so many years already. That's the most important thing right now."

Everyone nodded in agreement and she looked at me, smiled, and winked. On the other side of the room, Victor, who was completely isolated from our conversation, pretended to be busy. In that moment, the lady who had initially brought us into the office returned with a tray of Cuban sandwiches, saying, "*A almorzar, a almorzar. Que de todas maneras el mundo se va acabar.*" (To lunch, to lunch because no matter what we do the world is going to end anyway.) The lady came back and forth several times bringing more jars with orange juice and *guarapo* (sugar cane juice). Everybody began to eat.

Marcos came close to me, grabbed a sandwich, excused us from the others and said to me, "I need to speak with you privately."

I grabbed a sandwich, too, and walked with him to the end of the salon to his office. As we passed Victor, who had returned to his desk to eat his sandwich, I noticed him looking at me in an unfriendly way.

Marcos said to me, "Don't pay too much attention to Victor. He is a bit insecure and extremely jealous. We call him Othello. I believe he and Yaneba in the past may have had some kind of relationship. Maybe that is the reason he is not cordial to you.

But when you get to know him, you will find he is not a bad person."

I smiled and answered, "Don't worry. I don't pay too much attention to these kinds of things."

Marcos looked at me with approval and said, "Good. Good. That is the way it should be. You are a different kind of man." He put his hand on my shoulder and patted me a couple of times. Then he said in a sad voice, "I hate to be the bearer of bad news, but I have to tell you something of extreme importance."

As we walked into his office, he closed the door behind us and told me to sit down in front of his desk and then went around the desk and sat in his chair. He put the folder he had been carrying on his desk and told me, "This is about your lady in Cuba, Sandra. I believe she is with one of the big honchos in the G-2 in Havana and she is living like the queen of Sheba. We don't know if he converted her to his ideas or if she is only pretending in order to survive. The truth of the matter is that she is in the circle of the big honchos in the government."

I looked deep into his eyes. My expression changed completely. I put my sandwich down on his desk and with much discontent in my voice I asked him, "Are you sure of this information?"

He nodded and slowly pushed the folder towards me. "I don't want to do this, but I have to."

I took the folder in my hands, opened it and my facial expression turned harsh as I saw several photos of Sandra kissing a guy dressed in civilian clothes on the beach, at restaurants, on the street and dancing at what looked like official gatherings with the same man. She was dressed beautifully, and she looked damned good—which only made me feel worse. A deep pain stabbed me in the chest, and I could not stop the tears from rolling down my cheeks. I immediately wiped my face with my sleeve and tried to recover my dignity, shaking my head.

Marcos, understanding my pain, tried to comfort me. He leaned across the desk and touched my arm with his hand and said, "I'm sorry. But it's my duty to tell you this. I cannot let you be ignorant of what is going on."

I tried to smile but it did not come through as such. I said, "Don't worry about it. I'm glad you told me this. I need to know."

He let go of my arm, reached into the bottom drawer of his desk, and pulled out a bottle of Bacardi Añejo. He poured some into his glass that already had orange juice in it and offered the bottle to me. I shook my head and declined the drink, thanking him.

He sat back in his chair, took a long sip of his drink, and said, "What shit Castro is creating in Cuba. He has separated an entire population of families and is creating pain everywhere. I don't think there is even a tiny place in this world where a Cuban man or woman is not in pain because of the loved ones they have left behind."

I said, "Yes. He is the one that is responsible for all of us leaving Cuba. Before him there was no immigration problem. Cuba was such a wealthy little island no one wanted to leave. Everyone wanted to be there. But it is not only Castro we have to blame. It was our choice in selecting who we associate with. Because the ones closest to us, in whom we put all our trust, can bring us a lot more pain than our enemy...like the pain I am feeling in my chest right now from the deception of being betrayed."

Marcos picked up the bottle and refilled his glass and tried to cheer me up by saying, "Remember, maybe she is only pretending in order to survive."

I grabbed the folder from the table and shook it and said, "She is sure doing a good job pretending. She even convinced me!"

Marcos offered me a drink again before he put the bottle back in the drawer of his desk. My Cuban sandwich was still sitting practically intact on his desk. I had been drinking the orange juice and it was nearly gone and I extended my almost empty glass to him and said, "I never drink hard liquor, but what the hell! Maybe this will help me."

He filled it up and I took a few sips from the glass and I felt the alcohol burning my mouth and throat. A few seconds later I began to feel my legs relaxing and I continued to drink until the glass was empty. Marcos pulled the bottle out again and filled up my glass. He said, "This is good medicine. It cures all diseases; even broken hearts!"

I was already a little tipsy, and I pointed to him with my finger, shook it, and said, "Okay, I trust you. I want to get rid of the pain in my chest."

Marcos refilled the glass and said, "I assure you, when you finish this glass, you won't have any pain anywhere!"

We had been there in his office now for almost half an hour. The other people had finished lunch and had gone back to their respective desks. Yaneba was outside the office. She had been talking to Elizabeth and Hernesto, respectfully killing time so as not to interrupt us. But now it had been so long that she quietly knocked on the door and made a signal through the glass asking permission to come in. Marcos signaled her to come in and simultaneously hid the bottle in the drawer.

I turned around to see who it was. As I swiveled my chair, I looked at her with glassy eyes. The whole room turned with me. She was very observant and noticed that I was not together and that my sandwich was on Marcos' desk practically untouched.

She did not look happy at what she saw and said to Marcos, "I am sorry to interrupt but I have to take Dr. del Marmol to the DMV in order to get his license."

Marcos replied, "That's fine. We are finished. You guys can go."

Yaneba placed her right hand on the left corner of my swivel chair, and I held her by her arm as I spun around and asked her, "You want a drink?"

She looked at me in confusion and then she smelled the alcohol in the glass and on my breath. She said, "No. Please. It's too early for a drink!"

I smiled and said, "Why not?" *¡Hay que beber y templar; pues el mundo se va acabar!* (We have to drink and fuck because the world is going to end no matter what!)

She took the glass from my hand, shot Marcos an accusing glare, and said, "What did you give him to drink, Marcos? He has to take a driving test today. What did you do?"

Marcos said, "Well, he had some pain and I thought a little drink would help him, but I guess he overdid it!"

I interrupted them and said, "Where is the restroom? I think I'm going to be sick."

They both pointed right away to the door in the back on the right side of the office. When I stood up the whole office was reeling around me. I held on to the back of the chair, but it swiveled, and Yaneba had to hold it steady for me. I rushed to the restroom, leaving Yaneba and Marcos in the office.

My stomach was rumbling, and I was sure everyone heard it as I passed by their desks. I was afraid I would not make it in time to the toilet. When I crossed in front of Victor's desk, I smiled. It crossed my mind that if I could not make it to the toilet to throw up, I would do it on his desk...the son of a bitch. He looked at me in an unfriendly way as I smiled, and luckily, I made it to the toilet before I threw up. I don't know how long I was there, but it seemed like forever. I was sweating profusely. I felt my head pounding like a locomotive.

Then I felt a cold towel on my forehead and Yaneba's lovely voice saying, "Do you feel better? I am sorry about Sandra, but I hope you have learned a lesson. Alcohol is not a remedy for a broken heart or for any disease, as Marcos told you. It only extends our pain."

I looked at her with gratitude and smiled. "Oh, you are a philosopher, too? I think I am already a little in love with you. You have so many good qualities."

She returned my smile, touched my shoulder, and said, "Shut up. You're drunk. You don't know what you're saying. Do you think you can walk out of here? Do I need to call anybody for help?"

I looked at her in disbelief and said, "Of course I can get out of here myself!" I stood up and said, "Do you think I am going to give your ex-boyfriend the satisfaction of seeing me weak and unstable?" I steadied myself by holding on to the counter and said, "Besides, I am not drunk just because I smell a little bit like alcohol. Maybe I am a little tipsy, but I will wash my face and be just fine."

She said, "Good, I'm proud of you that you can walk out of here all by yourself. Go ahead, wash your face. By the way, Victor has never been my boyfriend. That was just a stupid mistake."

"I'm sorry."

"It's OK."

I took off my shirt and washed not only my face but my hair and my body. I gargled with cold water and rinsed my mouth. I dried myself and said, "Okay, let's go. I am ready to take the driving test."

She said, "I am happy that you can walk out of here by yourself. I am not so sure you are ready for the driving test!"

I grabbed my belly, looked at myself in the mirror, kissed her on her cheek and said, "Okay, honey. Let's go."

She shook her head, smiled and gave me a stick of gum to sweeten my breath. I walked out of the bathroom and she followed me closely. Marcos, Hernesto, Arturo, and Elizabeth were waiting outside for us. They were a bit worried, as Marcos had told them that I had had just a little bit too much to drink.

Marcos asked, "Are you okay?"

I answered, "Of course I am okay."

Marcos smiled with satisfaction and said, "I know. I told Yaneba that we did not drink that much. It is just that you are not used to drinking. I have gotten used to the luxury of having whatever I want to drink, outside of Cuba."

Elizabeth and Hernesto said goodbye affectionately and shook my hand. I told them I would see them soon. I said goodbye to everyone else, including Victor, who had stood up and walked to the door to be polite. I knew his resentment was still there when I looked into his eyes. I could tell his feelings went farther than his jealousy of me and Yaneba. I did not know what caused his resentment, but my gut instinct told me that I needed to be careful of this guy.

Yaneba and I went to her car and she drove towards the motor vehicle department, but my stomach started to betray me again. It was making funny noises. I put one hand on my stomach and the other over my mouth and asked her to please pull over. Without a word, she immediately pulled over and stopped. I ran into the grass to the closest tree and baptized it with the rest of the Bacardi that was left in my stomach.

Yaneba brought a napkin to me and said, "I think we should go back to the house and go to the DMV another day. You are in no condition right now. You might even get sick in there."

"Okay," I said with resignation. My head was spinning around, and I felt miserable. I hated to admit it, but she was right.

When we arrived at her house, I went immediately into the bathroom and took a cold shower. I was still feeling a bit shaky. I asked Yaneba if it would be okay if I went outside and lay in the hammock, as I was feeling warm. She said okay and brought a pillow and a blanket out into the patio for me. The patio was full of mango and coconut trees. It was beautiful, and the breeze from the ocean felt wonderful to me. I made myself comfortable in the hammock. Yaneba went back into the house and returned with a big cup of chicken soup and a couple of aspirins. I fell asleep and remained there for many hours.

By the time I woke up, it was late afternoon and the sun was beginning to set. I felt a cool mist on my face. When I opened my eyes completely, I saw Yaneba's smiling face and felt her long nails massaging my neck.

She said, "You have been sleeping all day!" She had a glass with ice and a yellow liquid in it. "Don't ask what this is. Just drink it."

I drank the whole glass full, and it was delicious. I said, "What is this? It really tastes good."

She responded, "*Un remedio para la borrachera*!" (a remedy for drunkards.)

"What drunkard?" I said.

She smiled and said, "Listen, sweetie, there is a first time for everyone. If you were not drunk today, you were on the borderline for sure!"

I smiled back at her and said, "Okay, mama, whatever you say. Whatever you want. You are always right, and I am wrong. You are like the Jalisco people. If they don't win, they pull out a gun and kill the opponent, so they win anyway!"

She said, "I am not! *Mentiroso, mentiroso, tu hueles como un oso* (Liar, liar, you smell like a bear.) And I am not from Jalisco! I was born in Cuba. And you are *boracho*" (drunk).

She leaned over the hammock and began to tickle me. I tried to grab her hands to stop her but because the hammock was moving, I had a hard time holding on to them. We struggled for a few minutes and then she fell completely into the hammock with me. As she fell the hammock rocked from side to side and somehow, she wound up underneath me. Her blouse opened up, revealing her bra and one of her breasts. I looked at her with sexual excitement and she stopped struggling. We looked into each other's eyes and I released her hands so she could free herself. She made no move to restore her breast to the bra and she began to caress my beard. We kissed passionately for a few minutes and I started to open her blouse exposing more and more of both of her breasts. I helped her to remove her blouse and bra. When her breasts were completely exposed, I began to kiss them slowly and gently and little by little. As we became more excited, the kisses became more passionate. I removed my pants and helped her to remove her clothing also. The clothes were falling to the ground from both sides of the hammock. She started to kiss my chest, and her nails continued to caress my neck and my sides. Slowly her kisses went down to my belly.

We held each other with great satisfaction. She raised herself up and looked into my eyes with lust. She smiled as we moved back and forth in the hammock for a while changing positions with a great thirst for each other which we could not seem to satisfy. It was a beautiful night, and although the sky was filled with stars, it suddenly began to sprinkle. We felt the drops of water running on our faces and on our naked bodies. She screamed even louder with passion and dug her nails into my back. I knew she was reaching her climax. She looked at me and told me she had never felt this way before. Her body was convulsing under mine in little spasms. I held her hard and I moaned and bit her lips gently as we reached our climax simultaneously. She moved convulsively while holding me tightly and we rolled out of the hammock onto the wet grass. We looked at each other and laughed and our naked bodies felt wonderful as we rolled back and forth on the wet grass.

She held my face and said, "This is beautiful. I don't want to scare you, but I think I am falling in love with you."

I held her face in my hands and said, "I think I am in trouble, too." And I kissed her tenderly.

Up until now we had not felt chilly but a cold breeze from the ocean enveloped us just then. She said quietly, "Maybe we should go inside. I didn't feel cold before but now I am starting to freeze. You don't feel cold?"

I replied, "A little. If you feel uncomfortable, we can go in."

She bent over and began to pick up our clothes from the ground. I helped her and then it began to rain harder and we ran into the house laughing like little kids. We were soaking wet. We went into the bathroom, dropped the clothes on the floor and jumped naked into a hot shower. Inside the shower we started kissing each other, and ultimately, we became aroused and started to have sex again. This time we made love more emotionally, and it lasted for a long time. When we finished, we went to bed exhausted, and we fell asleep looking at each other in love.

The next day, very early in the morning, the phone rang several times. It was the code O'Brien and I had established together. Yaneba was still sleeping, and I jumped out of the bed to answer it in order to let her sleep a little longer. I answered it as I walked out of the room.

"How are things going?" O'Brien asked.

"Not bad," I answered.

"I don't know if this is good or bad news, but your friend Steffan never made it to Washington, and we can't find him."

"Look for him in Cuba."

"Cuba," he said, "Why?"

"Because he is a Cuban spy. He probably went back for his paycheck."

"Are you sure about this?" O'Brien said.

"Actually, I am not sure about anything except that we will probably all be dead one hundred years from now. But I have some very reliable information that he is working for Castro."

O'Brien was silent for a moment. Then he said, "Oh my God, what about those names you gave him of the people who worked with you in Cuba!"

I smiled and said, "Well now, I thought you were not listening."

O'Brien answered, "Are you kidding? With you two yelling at each other, it wasn't difficult for me to hear what you were saying."

I replied, "Well, you don't have to worry about it because he doesn't like Cubans, and I didn't like him from the beginning. All the names I gave to him were of people who work in Castro's inner circle. The worst sons of bitches and the ones who are the most loyal to Castro. Those were the names of the assholes that came into my mind, and I gave them to him."

He laughed and said, "You have been well trained. I would love to shake the hand of your coach." Before he hung up, he said, "I want to meet your contact to verify this information. My boss is going to be extremely surprised."

I replied, "I am sorry, but my contact doesn't trust you. As a matter of fact, she does not trust anyone who works for the government. She feels anyone who gets paid for their work in the intelligence community is for sale and cannot be trusted. In other words, the only confirmation you will get is what I am telling you right now. Take it or leave it. Don't expect anything else."

We said goodbye, and I hung up the phone.

A few days later as I was riding in Yaneba's car, we decided to stop in El Pelicano restaurant to order some food to take home. We drove into the back side of the restaurant and as we passed the front, I noticed a man standing across the street wearing a white suit and dark glasses. He was with another man who was short and was wearing a Panama hat. The two were talking. As we crossed in front of them, I noticed the man in the white suit stared into our car with a little more interest than was usual. I asked Yaneba if she had ever seen those guys before.

She looked at them carefully and she said, "No, I haven't. Why?"

I replied, "Never mind. I just don't like the way they look. They seem to be staring at us in an unusual way."

We parked the car and went into the back entrance of the restaurant. Alfredo greeted us, and we told him we wanted some food to take out. He told us to wait in his office until it was ready, as we would be safer there. We waited for a while, and when we were ready to leave, we walked out the back entrance. Both men walked into the alley in our direction.

The man in the white suit, apparently the boss, told the other one, "I'll take care of him. You take care of her. Make sure you wound her, but don't kill her."

The little man with the hat replied, "Fine. Don't worry about it."

The guy with the white suit started to pull out his pistol and said, "Get ready. We cannot miss this time. We have to make sure we kill him."

As he approached us, Yaneba noticed that the guy was digging inside of his coat as if for a pistol. She told me, "Get into the car quickly! I think you are right about those guys."

When we got into the car, she reached for the glove compartment, took out a pistol, and put it on the seat in between us. I reached for my pistol and I prepared myself, too, expecting the worst.

Yaneba started the car and we began to move slowly into the driveway. The guy in the white suit was coming towards us, and at the same time, a police car with two police officers inside turned into the opposite side of the alley. When he saw the police car, the man in the white suit quickly hid his pistol and pulled out a piece of paper, showing it to the other man as if he were asking for directions. He changed his attitude and smiled at the second guy, putting on a show for the police.

Yaneba said, "Let's get out of here right away. I think you're right about those two guys. They don't have good intentions. They look like assassins."

As we were driving out of the driveway my eyes met those of the man in the white suit, and I burned his face into my memory. I wanted to recognize him in the future since I felt we would probably meet again. The two men started walking quickly towards their car in order to be able to follow us, but the police car stopped almost directly in front of them and blocked their exit from the alley. I told Yaneba to step on it to take advantage of our good luck. I knew they would not do anything stupid in front of the police.

"You should have stayed in the car like I told you," Yaneba said harshly.

I smiled and patted her on her shoulder and said, "That's okay honey. Don't worry about it. We are safe now. You can relax. Do you want to spank me? I am all yours."

She looked at me seriously for a few seconds and then she could no longer keep a straight face. "I'm sorry," she said. "I should not have talked to you that way."

I smiled. "That's okay. I know you love me!"

She replied, "How do you know that?"

We both smiled and continued driving while looking at the beautiful scenery until we arrived at her house in Golden Beach.

The next day in the morning I went to meet O'Brien. He picked me up at Miami Beach in front of the Hotel Carrillion, where Yaneba had dropped me off earlier. We drove towards downtown Miami. He pulled into the underground parking lot of the Federal Building. I asked, "What is so special about this meeting we are going to have with these guys?"

O'Brien replied, "You will see. You are going to meet my boss. This is the man who actually can walk on water!"

We walked down a hallway with many offices, but there were people inside. We then walked into a huge office where four men were waiting. The tallest, who was sitting behind the desk, stood up, greeted O'Brien, and took charge of the conversation. He extended his hand to me and said, "I'm Harry Addison." He was an Anglo in his mid-fifties, almost six feet tall, with brown hair. He was slightly rotund and had a very strong personality. After he offered us a drink and invited us to sit down, he asked O'Brien, "Did you brief him?"

O'Brien nodded.

Addison said to me, "O'Brien has told me great things about you. Are they all true, or did he exaggerate a little bit? He makes you sound like a hero!"

"I don't know what O'Brien told you," I replied seriously, "but I am not a hero."

He smiled and said, "How do you like Miami?"

"I am sorry. I don't want to be rude, but I don't think you brought me here to check on my happiness. What is this all about?"

Addison was taken aback by my boldness and he said, "Alright, how would you like to go back to Cuba?"

I looked at him and said, "Okay, if you send six thousand Marines behind me, I will go tonight!"

Addison stretched out and put his feet on the desk, laced his hands behind his head, and smiled. "Listen, we can't send any Marines with you right now, but you have unique and precious connections in Cuba inside Castro's inner circle. That puts you in an invaluable position for our operations in Cuba, and we're willing to pay a high price for this."

He stood up and looked at a Cuban map on the wall. He pointed to it and said, "In a few months there'll be a reunion of an international conference in Havana, which the communists call the 'Three Continental Reunion Meeting.' Have you ever heard about it?"

I smiled and said, "Yes, I know all about it. It is one of Castro's plans to control the world, including Asia, Africa, and the

Americas. They want to create distress and chaos for you guys all over the world."

Addison looked straight into my eyes and asked me, "Do you think there's any way you could infiltrate that meeting?"

I reclined in my chair and said, "You want me to be in that meeting? Don't you have enough agents who could do that? Why me?"

"Because your record is impeccable, and nobody else has survived for more than a decade passing through confidential information from Cuba. You know everybody there, and not one of our agents in Cuba will be able to penetrate that meeting. You have great contacts. You just came out of there and we need to know what that son of a bitch is going to do next. It's extremely important for our national security. It is vital for us to get this information."

I listened to him quietly. I turned around and looked at O'Brien, and he looked at me. He said, "You don't have to worry about anything. Our people will teach you what to look for and what to avoid. How to smell a trap and how to get out of a place before things get too hot. Basically, I need your help and no one but you can do this. Will you help us, please? We are willing to pay very highly for this."

I took a deep breath and slowly exhaled. My jaws tightened and I looked at O'Brien and said, "If you guys pay me, you cannot trust me. I will do it with no pay under one condition. If I find my girlfriend, Sandra, I want you to help me. When I bring her to Miami, I will need you to help me with the paperwork."

O'Brien and Addison looked at one another for a few seconds and Addison said, "Assuming she doesn't screw things up and you don't waste a second on anything including her until the meeting is over, I have no problem with that. I will take care of her when you guys arrive here. I will give her whatever you ask—even a citizenship—if you accomplish this with no problems."

"Fair enough," I replied and smiled.

Addison looked at me and said, "Let me tell you something just for your information. We received confidential reports after you left. She is working with the Castro intelligence."

I looked at him and nodded, but with assurance I said, "I can guarantee you she is pretending because in her heart she hates those people, and she would do anything to destroy them."

Addison extended his hand, smiled, and said, "I hope you're right."

I looked around and saw everybody was smiling. I said very soberly, "Don't smile. I haven't done anything yet. I might even get killed."

The smiles disappeared from the faces of all five men. Addison looked at me with appreciation and told O'Brien, "Get him trained and get him whatever he needs." Then he asked me, "How much money do you need?"

I replied, "You are going to pay for everything, so I don't need any money. For myself, personally, I will let you know later how you can compensate me. But not with money."

He looked at me in surprise and said, "No money?"

I said, "Not for me personally, but I need lots of money to fight Castro. To buy explosives, to buy weapons, to buy things for the people who are starving and powerless in Cuba. But we can talk about that later."

Addison looked at me and smiled again and said, "Okay partner. We can talk about that later. I can see nobody owns you."

I replied "No. Things work better that way, and you can trust me more because my motivation is not money."

With that, we shook hands and we said goodbye. O'Brien and I walked out. As we walked out of the Federal Building into the underground parking lot, O'Brien put his hand on my shoulder and said, "You can trust me. I'll get the best man to train you, even though I know you've been trained by the best in Cuba. Thank God for that. That is probably why you earned the name the Lightning. But we're going to give you training in new technology and make sure you learn to use it effectively. I say again, you can trust me. I will always be by your side—even though I do get paid for it!"

We smiled at each other, shook hands and drove out of the parking lot.

As we drove towards Miami, O'Brien asked me what kind of disguise I would feel more comfortable with. I replied I already had assumed a new look. My Arabian disguise suited me well.

O'Brien smiled and looked at me and said, "You! An Arabian! That's hard to believe. I'd like to see that!"

I replied, "You will...eventually."

Havana, Cuba
Havana Libre Hotel: a few months later

At the Havana Libre Hotel stood a man dressed in Royal Arabian garb with a tall gold turban, thick black beard, harem pants, and small gold pointed shoes. His turban had a very large purple jewel in front. Behind the jewel was a big purple peacock feather. He wore sunglasses and carried a leather bag. On his bag in a crest engraved in beautiful golden letters read, "King Kobe."

As I walked, disguised, through the main door with the other delegates from third world countries, I appeared very much in control and full of confidence. There were many signs in different languages indicating that no cameras or recording devices were allowed in the conference. Anyone found to have one of those devices would be considered in violation of the rules of the conference and would be expelled immediately.

The crowd was ushered in through the doors and diverted to large rooms for security checks by the Cuban G-2 agents, and without exception, all were subjected to a strip search. The security was very tight as Castro was going to be there and they wanted to make sure that there would be no leaks to their enemies.

Some people were not too happy with this search, as they were not used to this kind of treatment. But there were young beautiful Cuban women dressed in outfits designed like the different flags of the many countries which were represented. They were holding a little flag of that country in their hand and approached the delegates and spoke in their own language to them in a very cordial and very friendly manner, explaining to them the importance of the security measures both to the delegates and to the Prime Minister, Fidel Castro.

To my surprise, as I looked to my right, I saw Sandra dressed in an outfit that represented Puerto Rico. I stared at her in disbelief for a full minute. I could not believe my eyes. I had been afraid it might be difficult to find her, but here she was. Now I could see that she was definitely working for the government at the highest levels. She noticed me staring at her. She looked at me and smiled, but she did not recognize me.

There were many protests as the G-2 men made them all line up and checked out their clothes, pants, and shirts. One man was found to have a hidden camera and escorted away in an arm lock. Another man was found to have a recording device and he, too, was taken away.

I scanned the area to my right and to my left. A tall man in a parallel line looked at me and our eyes met. When it was my turn to be searched, I stepped up. They opened my bag and inside found a small sealed package. The G-2 man smiled as he thought he had found something illegal. He showed it to the other guard who at that moment was searching the tall man. In a loud voice, I exclaimed, "Please do not open that! There is nothing illegal in there."

I cringed with false embarrassment as the G-2 men ignored my plea and proceeded to open the little package. Meanwhile, the other guard passed the tall man through with only a perfunctory search and approached us, thinking they had found something incriminating in my bag.

As the tall man passed into the conference room, our eyes met again. The G-2 man and his partner who had crossed the line opened the package and to their surprise found it contained a string of condoms which fell to the floor like an accordion. The two G-2 men were ashamed and tried to fit the condoms back together and place them back into the box. They both apologized profusely. The G-2 men were mortified that they had caused this Arabian royal such embarrassment. I feigned indignation, took my box of condoms, wrapped it up, put it back in my bag, and strode away.

As "King Kobe," I was directed to a seat next to the podium, in that huge conference room with aisles of seats all around and a raised speaker's platform. As the meeting progressed, I sat and watched and took notes on a pad in plain sight of everyone.

After several speakers had concluded their speeches, Castro came to the podium. He proceeded to talk and talk redundantly for about three hours. The main theme was to create many Vietnams all over the world in order to strain the U.S. forces to the limit. He continued to rant and rave about the laziness of American society and the capitalist governments of the U.S., Israel, France, and England. He said the people were getting fatter every day and would not even walk to the store for cigarettes if they did not have a car. They would rather give up smoking! Everybody laughed and applauded his comments.

He said derisively that we are going to get all these fat asses because no one is going to raise a finger to defend their country or themselves. "Mark my words! You can count on that!" he said. "These people are so used to their ham sandwiches with mayonnaise, pickles, and mustard and Coca Cola that if only the mayonnaise is left out, they won't fight anymore! They are confused! They say, 'What is going on...there is no mayonnaise on my sandwich?'"

I yelled my approval and applauded his remarks, and looking across the room, my eyes met again with those of the tall Arabian man. We smiled at each other but continued to applaud Castro.

Finally, the conference ended, and everybody walked out of the doors. As the crowd approached the main exit in the lobby, taxis and limousines from diverse embassies entered the main driveway to the hotel to take people away. The tall Arabian man approached me as he was leaving the hotel lobby. We crossed close to each other, and he casually placed a small box in my hand. I slid it into the big pocket in my pants, and as I touched it, I smiled and walked away.

I slipped away from the main crowd and went around the hotel building into the underground parking area. I hid myself and waited. About fifteen minutes later, the women who had welcomed the delegates began to leave the hotel. They came out of the elevator into the underground parking area. When Sandra came out, I followed her to her car. I approached her as she opened the car door and put my hand on her shoulder. She turned around abruptly and said, "Oh my God! You scared me!" She recognized me as one of the delegates, and trying to be nice, she asked if there was anything she could do to help me.

I said in my normal voice, "Yes, you can do a lot for me."

When she heard my voice, she stepped back and looked at me carefully. I took off my sunglasses and smiled at her.

"Julio Antonio?" she whispered in disbelief.

"Yes, my love. It is me. I have always loved you, and when the G-2 men took you away from me at the train station, I thought I would never see you again."

She placed her right hand over her mouth and a very happy and surprised expression flooded her face. She could not believe what she was seeing. She looked me up and down again and said, "Julio Antonio...is it really you?"

I put my hands on her waist and said softly, "Yes, *amor mio*, it is really."

She touched my beard and tried to pull it to see if it would come off. Then the mustache. She touched my false nose and said, "What have you done to yourself, or what has been done to you?"

I smiled and said, "Everything is false. Don't worry. The real me is under all this and that real me is still in love with you."

At that, tears came to her eyes. She put her arms around me and began to kiss me all over my face. "I thought I would never see you again." Then she kissed me passionately.

She collapsed into my arms, sobbing. I held her close, letting her cry. Tears rolled down my own cheeks. I embraced her and we kissed again and again, not realizing that the other women who were coming out of the elevators were watching us.

She said, "Oh, my God. Those women will think I'm a slut and am sleeping with one of the delegates in order to get my ticket out of Cuba! This could be dangerous for both of us. They might report me. Let's get out of here quickly!"

She started up her Alpha Romeo, and we left immediately.

"I thought you were dead!" she said as she drove. "They told me they killed you. They said you stepped on a mine at Guantanamo and were blown to pieces."

She was holding my hand, and from time to time, she looked at me in disbelief, as if it was a dream and she wanted to make sure it was real.

I smiled at her and told her, "That was not me. The one who stepped on the mine was Cisneros. He was blown apart. It was awful. He was a great friend, and we are all devastated that he is dead."

"Dear God."

I said, "It took us nearly twelve hours swimming under the water to get to the North American base. And there is more bad news. Kinqui, Pablo, and Joaquin are all dead. They were killed in Miami by one of Castro's assassins. He placed a bomb under our table trying to kill all of us. I escaped by a fluke."

"Oh no!" said, shaking her head. "You have been through hell in such a short time, losing all your friends."

We were both silent for a while. Just thinking and remembering.

We arrived at a tall building and she drove into the underground garage. I said, "Why are we here? What is this place?"

She said ashamedly, "I live here. Life goes on. I obtained diplomatic credentials through my special friend in Cuban intelligence. He got me out of trouble when I was arrested. I am afforded special privileges."

As we walked from the car to the elevator, she held my hand and looked into my eyes. "Please, no questions," she said.

"Whatever has happened in your life or in mine since the last time we saw each other is in the past. Let's not talk about it."

The elevator arrived and we got in. She inserted a special key, and I observed that she pressed the penthouse button. She looked at me and smiled again.

As the elevator rose, I said, "I am sorry, but I would like to know what has been going on in your life. You may not be interested in my life, but I am interested in yours."

She tried to avoid answering my questions by grabbing my hand, pulling me close to her, and kissing me with passion. I asked her again, "Did they beat you up when they arrested you? Did they torture you?"

She put her fingers to my lips and smilingly said, "What difference does it make? You know who I am and how I feel—no matter what I pretend to be. And you know that I will love you forever. That is the only thing that is important now. I used my intelligence, and I survived. I did very well. Just as you probably did it, too, wherever you went. Maybe one day we can be together with no more political barriers. We can be together with our son."

"What? I have a son!"

"Yes, she replied, "and his name is the same as yours. Julio Antonio...Junior."

"This is wonderful!" I said. "I will take you and the baby with me to the USA when I leave."

We walked out of the elevator and into the penthouse. Sandra looked at me with remorse and said, "No. I cannot go. I am sorry. They will kill my parents and my brothers if I don't report to them. I can't go."

I sighed and leaned back against the wall. I said, "Now that I have found you, you're telling me that I have to leave you behind again?"

She smiled and said, "We will work it out. It will not be for too long. We will always be together."

As we walked into the living room of the penthouse, I realized that she was doing very well, as the furniture and everything in the place was of high quality. I asked her, "Where is my son?" as I did not see any sign of the baby.

She replied, "I am a working woman. He is with my parents. In Cuba, the communists say if you don't work, you don't eat. But sometimes even working twenty-four hours a day, you don't get enough to eat."

I said to her, "Yes, you are right. I would love to see my baby before I leave. Is there any way you can arrange it?"

She smiled and smacked me on my shoulder and said, "Of course you can see him! I can bring him here tonight. Oh, my wonderful Julio. I've missed you so much." Sandra then took off my turban and put her arms around my neck and kissed me passionately.

She said, "Hmmm, I like the beard. I thought you said everything was false."

I replied, "Well, everything except the beard and the mustache because that would be too obvious." As I said this, I removed my false nose and handed it to her. She looked at it for a few seconds and then began to laugh. She said, "My God. You really looked like somebody else."

I put my finger to my mouth and said, "Shhh. We don't have a lot of time."

She smiled and kissed me and said, "Do we at least have time for a glass of wine?"

I asked if it would be okay for me to take a shower, as the disguise I had been wearing caused me to sweat. When I got out of the shower, she was waiting with a glass of wine for me. She was wearing a negligee. She led me to the bedroom, and I was wearing only a towel around my waist. She unwrapped the towel which slid down to the floor. She said, "Oh, I have really missed you," and she kissed me passionately. I was overcome with love for her. I held her in my arms and slowly I removed her negligee and let it slide to the floor. I kissed her breasts, and she threw her head back with passion. As we kissed, we slid onto the bed and lost ourselves in each other. After a few hours when we had finished making love, she asked me, "How much time do you have?"

I looked at my watch and said, "Only a few more hours. I have to be safe."

She said, "Okay, you wait here. I don't want anyone to see you. I am going to get the baby. Go ahead and put your disguise back on again. It will take me at least an hour to go to my parents' house and come back."

She dressed quickly, kissed me, and left.

I began to get myself ready. About forty-five minutes later, Sandra returned with a beautiful baby in her arms. He had curly, light brown hair and eyes the color of honey. He looked a lot like Sandra. She handed him to me, and I held him in my arms. The baby looked at me like a toy and tried to grab my nose. He made a gurgling sound and smiled. I gave him my finger and he held on to it for dear life. He did not want to release it. As I gave him back to Sandry, she had tears in her eyes. She said it was as if he knew his daddy was leaving and he did not want him to go. I hugged her and the baby, kissed them both, and said, "I have to go. You sure you don't want to come with me?"

She shook her head and said, "I can't. I'm sorry." Then she asked me, "Are you sure you don't need me to take you someplace?"

"No," I said. "I have already made arrangements for someone to pick me up downstairs. Take care of yourself and the baby. I will see you soon."

We said goodbye at the elevator, and as the door closed, I released her hand and watched her and the baby disappear.

My contact, Erotido, a trustworthy old friend of mine, was waiting for me and gave me another set of clothes to replace my King Kobe outfit when we reached the city limits. The outfit he gave me was that of a typical peasant in Cuba. He also gave me another set of ID papers in case I was stopped by the authorities. He drove me to the dense growth at the coast and left me at the designated place which was out of view of the coastal patrols. Several men in Russian jeeps drove by, slowly scouting the area.

When the coast was clear, I came out of my hiding place and dug up the plastic bag which I had left in the ground previously when I came in. It contained my swimming gear—fins, a snorkel, and a mask. I made a dash to the ocean, dove in, and started swimming out to sea. After swimming for a while, I looked back towards the mainland and I saw one of the high-speed torpedo patrol boats crossing by checking the coast. I put my head under water and continued swimming to deep water. Once in a while when I raised my head out of the water, I could see a cruise ship which was anchored a few miles away. It was the same one that had dropped me off a few days ago when I came to Cuba. When I got close to the ship, they lowered a lifeboat down nearly to the water as they had been doing with all the lifeboats for almost an hour in order to make it look as if they were checking the equipment to make sure it was functioning properly. With the help of two sailors who gave me a hand, I was able to jump into the boat. They covered me with a blanket, signaled to the sailors above and the boat was raised immediately up to the deck. On the deck, three sailors helped us all out of the boat. I took off my mask and handed my fins to one of the sailors. Then they escorted me to the captain's cabin.

When I got to the cabin, the captain smiled with satisfaction to see me well and in apparently good shape. He shook my hand and asked, "Is everything okay? Did you get everything you needed?"

I laughed with satisfaction and replied, "Hell yes. I got more than I went for."

The captain smiled and said, "You look very happy. I am glad for you."

I replied, "Yes, I am very happy. I am a father. I did not even know it until today!"

He said, "Wonderful! Congratulations! I'll have to give you a Havana cigar and we can drink to that!"

He went to a cabinet and pulled out a bottle of Grand Marnier and two glasses and put them on his desk. He filled up the glasses, extended one to me, and said, "What is the boy's name?"

I replied proudly, "Julio Antonio del Marmol, Junior!"

He laughed and said, "Of course, this is your future heir."

We laughed together and drank. I said, "My thanks again, *Capitan*. Someday I'll be able to repay you for your kindness."

The captain replied, "Don't thank me. I owe your family plenty. Whenever I can help, I expect you to call on me. I am honored to help you."

I said, "Thank you very much, anyway. I know how much you are risking doing this for me."

He replied, "Anytime, anytime. It's a pleasure. I hate that son of a bitch Castro, anyway. I could put you in a private cabin, but I think it's better if you stay here in my cabin for your own security. My steward will bring you dinner and anything else you need shortly. We will dock tomorrow morning in the Cayman Islands. You can walk off the ship with the other passengers and no one will ever notice you."

Castro with some of his Tricontinental Union allies

CHAPTER XI: TWISTING ROADS TO FREEDOM

Federal Building, Miami
Addison's Office

Around 9:00 the morning after I returned to Miami, I was sitting on a comfortable sofa, observing Addison and O'Brien as they watched the film, listened to the recordings, and looked at the notes I had brought from the Three Continental Reunion Meeting in Cuba.

"I just want to know one thing," Addison said. "How the hell did you get these pictures and recordings?"

I replied "How I do things is my business. I got what you wanted. That's all that matters."

Addison responded, "Yes, indeed, that's all that matters. I can't believe how you nailed the entire meeting, their ideas, and plans."

I said, "Their plans are simple. Start twenty or thirty Vietnams all over the world. Stretch the United States so thin that it can't cover its obligations. Then Castro can spread his revolution anywhere he wants and nobody from the U.S. will do anything to stop him. Currently he has thousands of young men from Venezuela, Salvador, Nicaragua, Argentina, Honduras, and many other countries—even Puerto Rico—that are attending college in Cuba, supposedly 'for free,' that he is teaching how to be terrorists and political leaders in their own countries. That way no one can blame Castro and his regime for supporting their communist revolutions. They will make their own revolutions under the intellectual guidance of Fidel Castro. This is nothing new. This meeting was only a way to get new recruits.

I did not learn anything in this meeting that I did not know already from the previous meeting many years ago.

"There is an old saying in Cuba: kill the dog and you kill the rabies. Until you guys do something radical with Castro and his bandidos, you will be spending millions, if not billions, of dollars trying to stop these terrorist revolutions all over the world. The longer you prolong this, the longer the agony is going to last. We will lose millions of innocent lives everywhere. These people will at nothing to accomplish their purpose. He makes fun of our society, saying we are so hung up on material things, such as owning the latest model automobile or Cartier sunglasses, that we don't even care about voting in our elections. When we open our eyes one day, we will find ourselves with a person just like Castro in control of our destiny. What a catastrophe!"

"A catastrophe is right," O'Brien said. "But the son of a bitch isn't wrong to laugh about us. I don't know how it can be accomplished, but we need to get our people more involved in the political process and not let ourselves be charmed by the romantic ideas they preach. They say they're going to reform society and make things better for the poor and eliminate social injustice. This is just bullshit because it will never happen."

Addison said, "I still want to know how the hell you got all this information out of that meeting."

I just smiled and shook my head.

"You're not very old," he said, "but you act and sound as if you have been in this business for a hundred years!"

"When I was a child, my father called me the 'little old man,'" I said. "He said I was like the reincarnation of his grandfather. Maybe you are right, and I am more than a hundred years old. But the cruel reality of growing up in Cuba taught me to be extra careful; otherwise your life would end early."

Addison nodded in agreement. "Yeah, you are one hundred percent right. We never know what's going to happen next, do we?"

O'Brien smiled and said, "Well, this mission is accomplished, and very successfully." Then he turned to Addison and said, "Why don't we take Dr. del Marmol to the Pelicano restaurant and celebrate his success with a great Cuban meal and a good Spanish wine? Blanco Brillante from Riojas wine reserve." He looked at me. "I'll bet you would like that!"

I returned his smile and said, "You bet I'd like that. And I'll bet you would, too!"

"Addison probably wouldn't mind it, and since you're not being paid for your work, it's the least we can do for you. Let Uncle Sam pick up the bill!"

Addison agreed and said, "Okay! Let's go!"

After we finished our meal and said goodbye outside the restaurant, I called Yaneba to pick me up nearby. I turned to walk down the street, and about two blocks from the restaurant, I noticed many Cubans walking around. Some were playing guitars and singing on the sidewalks, some were playing cards, and some were playing dominos on small folding tables. A woman was selling flowers. Just then a car came screeching around the corner. I noticed the rear windows of the car were down. As the car approached, it swung across the dividing island and headed toward me. I saw a hand with a pistol coming out of the rear window. Looking for cover, I dove for a trash can near a vendor selling juices.

As the car approached me, shots were fired, and the bullets hit the bottles, spraying juice everywhere. Everyone started to scream, and they ran every which way. I pulled out my gun and hit one of the front tires, but the car continued toward me. The lady selling flowers dropped them and ran directly in front of the car. The driver swerved to avoid her and lost control of the car, running into the window of a pastry shop. Pastry went everywhere. The pistol flew out of the hand of the backseat passenger, and the driver hit his head on the windshield. The car came to a halt, and the driver tried to get out, but his door was jammed shut. His head was bleeding profusely, and it ran down the side of his face. The man with the gun was also trapped. The second passenger, who also carried a pistol, managed to escape. He walked towards me and began shooting. One of the bullets hit the window of the store behind me and glass flew everywhere. I was hit in the face and on the right side of my chest by the broken glass. The man was now only about forty or fifty feet from me and continued to walk towards me, shooting all the while. Broken glass was everywhere. People were screaming and running away. I raised my gun, aimed at the man, and pulled the trigger. I hit him in his left leg. He nearly lost his balance, but he held his leg with his left hand and continued towards me, still shooting. I fired again, and this time I hit him in the right shoulder. This time, he fell to the ground. I shot two more times towards the car as one of the passengers was trying to get out through the window. I managed to wound him, and he fell back into the car. I stood up and walked towards the man on the ground. As I approached him, I kicked his pistol away from him.

Pointing my pistol at his face I asked him, "Who sent you?"

He looked at me with hatred in his eyes and said, "Count your minutes because you are a dead man!"

"Not yet," I said. "But you are!" And I shot him point blank in the face. I continued walking towards the car, which was on fire from the impact, and shot two times into the gas tank. The car was immediately engulfed and exploded. One of the tires rolled down the street as I walked away. As I looked at the tire rolling down the street, I heard sirens of the police and fire department approaching.

A car pulled up behind me and stopped abruptly. I turned around and reaching for my pistol. I saw that it was Yaneba.

She yelled at me, "Get in! Let's get out of here fast!"

I looked at her and smiled and said, "God, am I ever glad to see you!"

After I got into her car, she reprimanded me as usual. "You should not walk around the streets of Miami if you want to reach old age!" she said. "You have to leave Miami as soon as possible. Castro is looking for you and eventually he is going to get to you."

"I know," I replied. "He nearly got me today but instead he lost three of his assassins."

Yaneba said, "I am going to get a ticket for you tonight. You will be leaving on the next plane headed for the West Coast. It will be almost impossible or at least very difficult for them to find you there. Don't worry. We'll arrange everything. We need you alive."

She took a handkerchief and cleaned the blood from my face. She said, "Let's go home right now to clean those wounds so they don't get infected. You can call your friend O'Brien from there and tell him you are leaving town. Don't tell him on the phone specifically where you are going. You can meet with him before you go and tell him in person...if you really trust him."

I nodded my head and said, "Yes, I really trust him."

She smiled and said, "Well, it looks like you have made a friend!"

I nodded approval, pursed my lips and said, "Maybe."

We arrived at her house and as she was cleaning the wound in my chest she remarked, "You might need a few stitches on that cut. It looks pretty deep."

I asked her if she had a surgical needle and thread and she said she did. She produced a medical supply case and a bottle of Grand Marnier. She offered to do the stitches for me as it would be very difficult for me to stitch myself with her holding a mirror in front of me. I agreed. She tried to do it but when she inserted the needle the first time, I cringed a little and she just could not stand it. She apologized profusely, said she could not do it and gave the surgical needle to me. She then proceeded to hold the mirror for me as I stitched the cut myself. She looked away with discomfort with every puncture and made a face as if she were the one who was being stitched.

It took a while to complete the stitches. When I finished, she applied an antiseptic and an antibiotic cream to the wound and covered it with a bandage. I finished half a bottle of Grand Marnier in the meantime, since we had no anesthetic. I had been perspiring profusely while stitching myself up, so when we finished, I asked if she would mind if I took a bath to wash up.

She said, "Of course not. I'll run the water for you. Then I'm going to call and make a reservation for you to leave. I want you out of Miami tonight."

I smiled and said, "Oh, so you want to get rid of me, huh?"

She replied, "Yes. I want you alive even though you cannot be mine. I am not a selfish woman."

I asked, "What do you mean, I cannot be yours? Even if we are not together, you will always have my love."

She looked at me with tears in her eyes and said, "Your friend O'Brien told me. You found your lost love again in Cuba."

I looked at her straight into her eyes and said, "I don't know if I found it or I finally lost it. I am not a genius, but I am not a fool either. Based on the luxurious life she is living now in Cuba, I feel that either she has found an extremely comfortable replacement for me or else she is in the process of securing herself for life."

Yaneba looked at me with surprise and discomfort for a second and said, "Really? It must be very painful to be replaced in such a short period of time. Are you sure she's not just playing their game?"

I looked at her and knotted my eyebrows together. I shook my head and said, "I don't know. This is what is so hard. I don't know. But I do know that when you are separated from someone you love and then able to connect with them again, you feel that something is missing. You know in your heart it is not the same. Something is lost. The thing that bothers me the most is that she has my baby there with her."

Yaneba put away the medical case and said, "There is something very important that I need to share with you. No matter what I say, you must leave tonight. You have to promise me that, or I am not going to tell you."

I asked her, "Wow, is it that important?"

She answered, "To me it is. I don't know how you feel about it. That is why you have to promise me. You must leave tonight, no matter what!"

I replied, "Okay sweetie, I promise."

She looked at me straight in the eye and said, "I am pregnant."

I was completely shocked. My mouth dropped open. I tried to pull myself together in order to say something appropriate to the circumstance and not hurt her feelings. I said, "You are sure about this?"

She said, "Yes. A doctor confirmed it." She looked at me expecting more of a reaction.

I said, "Well, I know you didn't plan this, and neither did I, but I think it is beautiful. A child can be so wonderful. Especially if it is brought into this world with love, and there is plenty of that between us. What do you plan to do?"

She said, "I don't know." She paused and then said, "The life we are living, and the way things are right now, I don't want to have a child with no father."

I said, "I will stay with you."

She replied firmly, "No! You promised. I want you out of here!"

I said, "But I can help you. I can be supportive of you...whatever decision you want to make."

She said firmly again, "No buts! You are out of here tonight!"

I asked her, "Are you sure that is the way you want it?"

She said, "Yes, it will make me very happy when you are not in Miami anymore!"

I stood up and hugged her. "If that is the way you want it, then that is the way it will be. Call and make the reservation."

We embraced emotionally. Yaneba had tears in her eyes and she whispered in my ear, "Thank you. I will always love you." She left the bathroom and went into another room to make the reservation. In a few minutes she returned and told me, "Your plane leaves tonight for California at eleven forty-five. Our people will be waiting for you when you arrive at LAX."

"You know, I haven't had time to talk with Arturo since I saw him again. Would it be all right if we had dinner together with him tonight?"

"As long as you save a few minutes after for me," she replied with a wink.

"Of course. You are for dessert. Speaking of dessert, have you ever had my special vanilla ice cream with tropical fruit, toasted almonds, and Grand Marnier?"

"No, but I would like that."

"Do you have Grand Marnier and the other ingredients?"

"No, I just have the ice cream."

"I'll go out and get some!" I got up excitedly.

"What? You can't go out by yourself! After what just happened, are you crazy?" She stood up protectively.

"It's just to the store on the corner. I'll be fine." I pushed her gently back into her seat. "We are in Golden Beach. Nobody even knows I'm here. We are far away from all the craziness."

"All right, I'll call Arturo. Go on." She waved me away with a smile.

I left the house, walking toward the small corner market. Immediately, around the corner came a couple in jogging suits, running right for me. It made me nervous and I put my hand on my gun hidden under my pants. They smiled at me and jogged by and I wondered if I was becoming too paranoid. Seeing Yaneba and Arturo again brought me back to thoughts of my childhood and I daydreamed all the way to the store.

The jingle of the bell on the glass door as I opened it brought me back to reality as I saw a cute young lady behind the cash register. She greeted me, looking up from her magazine saying, "You look like a movie actor. Or, no, a detective? Both? Which are you?"

I smiled and replied, "I'm not an actor. Maybe something like a detective." I was wearing my black London Fog raincoat and my black suit, so I realized I looked the part. I found the Grand Marnier and the other ingredients in the aisles. As I did so, two more people entered the store. I was in shock as I saw they were bearded men with weapons and had them pointed at the lady at the register.

"Give me the money or I'll kill you!" one exclaimed. The cashier was frozen in terror. I ducked behind some paper towels and took out my gun, peering between the rolls to watch.

"No, not the register! The real money! The safe, now!" The other man jumped behind the counter and pulled out a carpet hiding a floor safe. These men knew what they were after. "Give us the combination or I will shoot you in the head."

The poor lady began to cry, "I swear! I don't know it! The manager comes in to open that. He's the only one!"

The man became angry. "We will kill you, bitch!"

His partner spoke up, "Maybe she doesn't know. Shit. When does the manager come to open it?"

"Tomorrow morning. That's when he is supposed to come next."

"Tomorrow? We can't wait for that!" He shoved the girl against the counter as his partner got out a crowbar. He tried to pry and bash the safe out of the floor, but to no avail. Meanwhile, the first man took all the money in the register, keeping the gun on the cashier.

Outside, two giggling teens, totally unaware of the situation, walked through the doors. The bell rang and the leader said, "On the ground! Now!"

The two kids put up their hands instead, saying, "Please! Don't shoot us!"

The other teen said, "We don't care! We didn't see anything!"

"Are you deaf? On the floor or you die!" He gestured with his gun at them.

"Don't worry. Don't worry. We won't give you any trouble."

"Shut up, stupid! Put your head down. On the floor!"

The doorbell jingled again, as two blonde teenage girls came in looking for their friends. "What is taking so—Oh, my God!"

"Everyone, on the floor! Now!"

One girl dropped to the floor, but the other panicked and ran. The gunman fired, twice, one hitting the door, shattering it, and the second going into the young girls' back. She fell to the ground in a growing pool of blood.

Her friend started screaming at the men, "Why did you do that? You son of a bitch! What is wrong with you?"

The man, now angry, shot her in the chest, with no remorse. All of this before I could even react. The man banging on the safe interjected, "We can't stay here any longer now; this is getting too complicated."

"What do we do with the rest of them?"

"Kill them, of course."

I steadied my pistol on top of the aisle, taking aim at the man behind the counter first. His partner was looking at him as a small, neat hole appeared in his head, and he collapsed. I took advantage of his confusion and stepped out into the clear, gun pointed at the remaining man.

"Put the gun down! I do not want to kill you, but I will. Do it now."

At that moment, the cashier rose from behind the counter, smashing the man on the head with a vase of flowers. He fired randomly in surprise three times. I had to take him down. Two shots in the chest, and he lay bleeding on the floor.

I scouted around to see if there were any more hostiles, inside and outside the store. At some point the alarm was set off, and it rang in my ears. The clerk was calling 911. I went to the doorway and knelt by the girl who had been shot in the back. She was still breathing. She looked up into my eyes as I took her hand. She tried to speak, squeezed my hand, and died.

"She is gone," I said to the rest. The door jangled and the jogging couple from before entered. I lowered my gun, realizing I had almost shot them. I stood up, starting to feel shock take over me.

I never would have expected that the woman was about to inject me with a powerful sedative.

In a slow-motion drugged haze, I watched as the man in the jogging suit shot everyone else in the store. I fell to the ground, helpless.

I realized that I was in a vehicle, perhaps a van. I heard voices. "Did you get paid for this already?"

"No, not yet. Once we drop off our package at the funeral home, we'll get our money."

I realized the package was me, and that a funeral home was not a great place to be dropped off at. The sedative took hold again and I passed out.

I awoke in total darkness, unable to move. I had a vague memory of being placed inside a coffin. I could open my eyes, but whatever they gave me still paralyzed the rest of my body.

I wondered if I was to be buried or incinerated. Neither one of those sounded pleasant. If only I had listened to Yaneba.

"Don't worry, we'll do just as you have instructed." I heard from outside the coffin. Another voice answered,

"You'd better. We're taking a big risk. The drug should last eight to ten hours."

"What if he wakes up before that?"

"He won't. Even if he does, he'll still be paralyzed for a while, barely able to move his extremities."

"That sounds spooky." The voice got louder, "Can you hear me? Are you in there? Or are you gone?"

"I think he is gone. Far gone. Maybe Disneyland." They laughed. One of the voices sounded familiar, but I couldn't place it.

"Just make sure he makes it back to Cuba alive."

Oh, my God. They were taking me back to Cuba! That would be the end for me. I was frightened, but the drug still made me sleep once more. I woke up with a terrible urge to urinate, and, unable to take any other action, I let it go into the soft, silk padding of the coffin.

I felt the rolling of the sea then, and I realized I was on some kind of ship, probably bound for Cuba. Not long afterward, the waves got stronger and stronger, and I realized that we were in the midst of a storm. I might not even make it to Cuba but instead drown in the ocean, lost with the rest of the cargo.

A huge wave threw my coffin through the air and it smashed open on the hard metal floor of a storage hold. Barely able to move, I wormed my way out on to the floor. My eyes that were in total darkness before could make out some details in the dim light. There were boxes and packages everywhere, thrown by the storm, many of the securing lines broken.

My legs were numb, and it was hard to stand. I noticed for the first time that my feet were swollen and in pain. I heard someone coming and hid behind some boxes. The ship was still lurching, and I grabbed a metal shelf for support. A flashlight shone in the room. It looked around frantically until it stopped on the overturned coffin. The man walked right up to it carefully, fighting the lurching of the ship, and realized it was empty.

"Oh, no."

CHAPTER XII: DEADLY DEAL

He bent to turn the coffin over when another huge wave rocked the ship and threw the heavy metal coffin onto his legs. I heard a sickening sound as they bent in a way they were not supposed to bend. The flashlight rolled across the floor, and after a moment I heard a pathetic, "Help. Please. Help me."

I managed to get the flashlight and stumbled over to the helpless man. I shone the flashlight into his face. It was Roberto, the quiet man had I met at Marcos' office. A traitor, I now realized. He couldn't tell who I was with the light in his face.

"Help me. My legs..."

I shined the light back onto my own face. He gasped in surprise.

"Why should I help you, traitor? How could you do this?"

"Money. They offered eight hundred thousand. Too much... to turn down." He was still gasping in pain.

"You made a deadly deal with our enemies. You are a royal idiot. And you believed them? The people who lie to their own countrymen on a daily basis?"

He shook his head. I pointed the flashlight away from myself and saw a small case lying on the floor next to Roberto. It was moving side to side with the ship's rocking. I put the flashlight right on it.

"What is this?"

I picked it up and saw a syringe and more of the drug inside it.

"This is what you put in me, isn't it? You son of a bitch. Do you realize what they would do to me in Cuba? What torture? And what about those innocent people in the convenience store? All dead... and me, lying in the coffin, waiting for a horrible death by cremation or worse! You bastard! I'm not going to kill you, though."

He looked up at me with a little hope in his eyes.

"No, I'm going to let you experience the same thing that I did."

I drew a full dose of the drug into the syringe as he watched in terror.

"Don't worry, you'll get to lie in the coffin just like I did, nice and safe. That is, until Castro's men open it and find you there instead of me. I don't think they will be as kind to you as I am."

The drug sent him to sleep—actually, a mercy considering the pain he must have been in. I placed him back in the coffin and began to examine the contents of the room.

I found diving equipment and even shark guns and spear rifles. There were also boxes and boxes of guns and ammunition for Castro's infiltrators in different countries. Guns made in the United States. I took the diving gear and some equipment, including a CO_2 gun, and returned the boxes to their original condition, replacing the nails in the crates.

I made my way to the deck that night and hid near the lifeboats. I had to wait a few hours for the rain to subside and the storm to lessen. I finally saw some lights in the distance. We were near a harbor. I prepared myself to jump over the rail.

"Stop. Turn around slowly. Any quick movements and I will shoot."

I turned around to see a man in a raincoat pointing a gun at me. "What did you do to Roberto?"

"Nothing that you haven't done to me already."

"Put your rifle down and hands up."

As I released the rifle, I pulled out a small gun I had strapped to my ankle and fired quickly at the man. It hit him in the stomach, and he dropped slowly and painfully. The CO_2 cartridge then expanded and exploded his torso, flinging his insides everywhere.

I didn't wait to see what happened next. I was in the water and diving deep, swimming toward the lights in the distance.

After an hour I made it to a beach. I squinted and made out a sign: "Welcome to Nassau." Unfortunately, the beach I arrived on was not comprised of sand, but of sharp rocks. By the time I had gotten away from the shore, my feet were badly cut.

I hobbled barefoot through the quiet streets. It was about four in the morning, and it was still sprinkling. A police car turned down the alley I was in and I scrambled over the nearest wall. It seemed they didn't see me. I had entered a yard and saw a gazebo with two hammocks. There was a clothesline with what appeared to be monk robes on them. I grabbed one as a blanket and fell asleep in the hammock, exhausted.

"Good morning, my son. I am Father Lara." I looked up into the sunlight to see a smiling priest above me. "You must have had a rough night," he continued.

"You have no idea. I'm sorry to intrude. I can explain—"

"You can explain later. First, we will help you with clothes, a bath, and some food."

I looked into his eyes with gratitude, "God bless you, Father."

I climbed out of the hammock and almost fell to the ground in pain at the touch of the ground on my cut-up and badly infected feet. Father Lara gently grabbed my arm and supported my weight. "You are injured, my son. Here—" he removed his own sandals. "Take these. If nothing else, they will be less painful to walk in than your bare feet."

I slipped on the sandals gratefully. "Thank you." I took a tentative step. "These are very comfortable." As we walked to the main building of the mission, I spoke of my kidnapping, my escape from Cuba, and the illegal arms aboard the ship. "There is no doubt in my mind that God guided my steps here to you."

"Indeed. You are in good hands now, my son."

It took me a while to thoroughly wash myself, which unfortunately included removing the urine as well as blood and guts from my body. They gave me a jogging suit to wear, and a nun, Mother Ella, brought me food.

"Thank you, Mother Ella."

"Of course. Father Lara would like to see you as soon as you are done in his office."

I knocked on the office door, which was slightly open. Father Lara waved me in while he spoke on the phone.

"Yes, Lieutenant Phillip." He motioned for me to sit down and continued his conversation. "Of course. We are glad to have provided the floral arrangements for you. Mother April and the others worked very hard on that particular one. Yes. I wanted to ask you a question..."

He picked up a newspaper, which had a picture of me on the front cover with the title, "Dangerous Fugitive." I saw it and restrained a gasp.

"About this fugitive. I read that he killed someone on the ship, La Esperanza? And left another man unconscious? Yes. I was thinking that this man looks... familiar." His eyes met mine as he spoke.

"Father? Have you seen this man?" the voice on the phone inquired.

"No, my son," he crossed himself and looked skyward for forgiveness. "I only asked because I don't believe everything I read in the papers." Again he looked at me meaningfully.

The voice on the other end continued. "Apparently the FBI is looking for this man, a criminal to be extradited to another country."

"I see," the priest replied, "It does sound serious. Thank you for your time, Lieutenant. Give your wife and daughter my blessings." He hung up then looked up at me.

"How was your breakfast?"

"Very good, thank you."

"Have you told me the whole truth? You can lie to me, but not to God, my son."

"Yes, I have, Father."

"Here," he said, and tossed me the newspaper. "Read what this says."

The article included details of how I was wanted in many countries in Europe and Asia, dead or alive, for terrorism. A reward was offered: $100,000.

"Father," I said, "I give you my word that none of this is true. I have no idea how they convinced the paper to print this."

"Money, no doubt."

For the next half hour, I explained in more detail my situation, including the people who had kidnapped me and what they were up to.

A knock came at the door and Mother Ella called, "Lieutenant Phillip just arrived with a few policemen."

Father Lara and I looked at each other gravely. Something happened then that I did not expect. He moved his bookshelf to reveal a hidden door behind, and Mother Ella ushered me into it.

"Stay here and remain quiet!" she warned before closing the door.

Father Lara was walking with the policemen and Lieutenant Philip on the mission grounds. "I will tell you, I had a vision. It included this man you speak of. But also, that there are weapons, illegal contraband, on this ship that is in port right now."

"You... did?" Phillip replied.

"Not only that, I saw that you were the one responsible for finding them and received much credit."

"I... did you see where they were?"

"Yes, my son. In the cargo hold. In unmarked crates. You will find them there."

"Father, this is amazing! Thank you!"

"Don't thank me, Lieutenant, thank the Lord." He crossed himself solemnly.

Later, I sat in Father Lara's office with him, drinking tea.

"He really believed you?" I exclaimed.

"I think so, my son. At least, he believed me about the ship, but maybe not where the information came from."

"He may come to you to help him with every difficult case he has now!" I laughed.

"And I pray that God will help me to assist him."

"Father, why did you believe in me?"

"The answer is simple my son. God told me to."

"Thank you very much for your help."

"As I told Lieutenant Phillip, thank the Lord, not me. The next time someone crosses your path who needs help, you help them. That will be thanks enough."

"I will, I promise. Father, I hate to ask, but can you help me to escape this island?"

"Indeed. Twice a month our mission sends a delegation to Tampa. Monks and nuns travel there; they leave in a few days."

I thanked him again and asked if I might use his telephone. I dialed the number and a welcomed voice answered.

"Yaneba," I said, longingly.

"Julio Antonio?"

"Yes, it's me." The phone was quiet for a few moments. "Hello? Are you there?"

"Yes!" she said. "I was so worried. Where have you been? What happened to you? Are you all right?"

"Yes, yes! A kiss for you and a hug for Arturo. I'm safe. I'll be in Miami in a few days."

"Oh, I am so happy. We have been doing everything to find you."

"I have to tell you this – Roberto, the man we met at Marcos' office, is a traitor. He is the one who kidnapped me."

"That son of a bitch."

"Call O'Brien and tell him I'm alive and that when I arrive in Miami, I will need new papers. They took everything that was on me."

"Yes, yes. Please, be careful."

"I will. I will see you soon. You be careful too, Yaneba."

Later that day Father Lara told me about the history of his mission, which had been built in the 18th century by Spanish conquistadors. He also introduced me to another priest, Father Salomon. He was older, short, half bald, and wore thick glasses. He was pleasant and had a big smile.

"Father Salomon, this is Dr. del Marmol. But to the rest of the world, he is a ghost – he does not exist."

"I see. Good to meet you."

Over the next few days, I spent some of my time with Father Salomon. He had a large work area with cameras and lighting and a printing press. They printed many religious guides and programs, many which were given free to tourists. He showed me some of his work, including a replica of the Mona Lisa.

"This is amazing!"

"That is nothing, my son. Look here." He started rummaging through boxes, trying to find something. He knocked over a box and its contents spilled out, including some metal plates. I saw that they were engraved plates for fifty- and hundred-dollar bills. I helped him pick them up, and he became very nervous, his hands shaking.

"Father Salomon, do not worry. I did not see anything. I can even leave until you put everything away."

"Thank you, my son. Father Lara would be very upset if he knew about this little accident." He finished putting the box on the shelf. "You see, some days the money gets very tight, and we need medicine for the poor and the sick. Sometimes there are children with no food. In these times...I create my own miracle."

"I understand Father. What you do results in good. I will not mention it to anyone."

"Thank you. I think we are going to be very good friends."

The days went by quickly. On the day before I was to leave, I was used to wearing a monk's robe and had grown a decent beard. Inspector Phillip came to the mission again to talk to Father Lara about the investigation. He did not even spare me a second glance. I supposed my own mother might not recognize me the way I looked.

On the deck of *La Esperanza*, an angry man in a wheelchair was meeting with a local police officer. The man, Sergeant Garre, was counting the money from an envelope. Roberto looked up at him from the wheelchair.

"Well?" he sneered.

"I think I know where he is," the sergeant replied.

"Find him! We have to leave port soon, before that Lieutenant can get permission to search us!"

The sergeant put the money away and smiled. "I will."

That night, I was saying goodbye to my friends at the mission. I entered the printing room, looking for Father Salomon. Instead I found two of the sisters sitting at the table, looking nervous. I could feel something was wrong. A man with a mask jumped out from behind a door and tried to grab me. I dropped and hit the man in the crotch, but there were others. I punched another in the face, feeling some of his teeth come out, and found myself with a gun pointed at me.

"Okay, that's enough."

I put my hands up, feeling on the wall behind me a family crest with shield and swords, a relic of the conquistadors, no doubt. I grabbed the sword and flung it at the gunman. He flinched and by sheer luck, it pierced his chest. He fell to the ground, and I made sure the other two men were disabled.

Salomon rose up from behind his desk. "I'm sorry, I think there are more," he said.

I ran through the mission with Salomon at my side. I heard yelling and running from time to time. Two men turned a corner with guns; I threw the sword I was carrying at them to delay them and ducked with Father Salomon into Lara's office, where I locked the door.

Salomon grabbed my shoulders. "The window."

He opened the window and gestured me out. We ran outside, stopping by the gazebo I had slept in when I arrived. A storm drain was next to it.

"Bless you, my son." Salomon gestured the sign of the cross over me.

I climbed down the grating and into the water. The current pulled me out toward the ocean.

I wandered on the beach, near a resort, wondering what to do next. As I pondered, two lights approached me. I realized that there were two motorcycles and they had probably seen me. Before I could get far, they were on me. One of the riders threw a fishing net on me as he passed, and I tumbled to the sand. The bikes turned around and stopped. The riders walked toward me.

One took out a radio and spoke, "We got him." A voice on the other end said they were sending a car. The other man trained a gun on me.

"You're not going to escape this time."

At that moment, another motorcycle came towards us on the beach. The man with the radio said, "They are supposed to send a car. What the hell?"

That was the last thing he said, as two bullets sent him to the ground. His partner turned and fired at the other rider, but he never had a chance. He also fell with barely any sound. I surmised that the rider was using a silencer.

Still tangled in the net, I stood as the rider stopped. She took off her helmet, and long cascades of silky black hair fell out. It seemed my old friend had escaped from Cuba as well.

"Chandee? How?"

She smiled as she began to untangle me. "It seems we have a mutual friend. Grab that motorcycle and let's go!"

I climbed on the motorcycle quickly and we sped off into the night. Two police cruisers passed by, not quite a hundred yards from us, and slammed on their brakes. We both scarcely took time to look at them. We gunned it. The tires squealed in protest as we opened up our throttles, the police cars blazing behind us with lights flaring and sirens blasting. Our more maneuverable bikes were able to maintain speed better on the twisting road, and so we were beginning to outpace our followers. Once we had gained enough distance on the cruisers, Chandee signaled for me to pull over.

Even as I slid to a halt, she slammed on her brakes and left her motorcycle lying in the middle of the road lengthwise. She ran over to me and jumped on the back of my bike.

"Go!"

The tires spun again as we took off. We flew around the corner and could hear the tremendous shriek of metal as the first police car slammed into the bike, followed shortly by a series of crashing noises as the second car collided with the first.

Not long after, we arrived at the dark airport parking lot. When Chandee got off the bike, I noticed she was limping. One of the bullets had grazed her leg.

"I should really take a look at that leg."

"We have a few minutes," she replied, and proceeded to pull her tight racing pants down, revealing lacy underwear. I looked at her beautiful thigh for a moment, then, noticing she was embarrassed, I inspected the wound.

"It's not serious."

She pulled her pants up giving me a shy look, and then unlocked a car in the parking lot, throwing me a case.

"Here. You are Mr. Qasim, from Dubai. Your ticket and passport are in there. You have thirty minutes."

"Chandee," I said in surprise. "Thank you. I didn't... I wish we had more time."

She embraced me and kissed both my cheeks.

"Go! Interpol is coming, and Roberto will be captured tomorrow before his ship leaves."

I embraced her again and turned to go.

The police who had been chasing us must have radioed in because by the time we got to the airport, an officer was already there: Roberto's friend, Sergeant Garre. He was by the boarding gate, checking the passports of everyone who could possibly be me. Women, old men, and very young men he quickly allowed through. He stopped to check the passport of a man close to my age and height. He examined the passport and the man's face very carefully and then moved on. He turned to the police officer next to him.

"These are the only flights leaving now? Tampa and Dubai?"

"Yes, Sergeant," the officer acknowledged.

"Damn," Garre exclaimed. He pulled out his radio and spoke into it. "Search everywhere. Keep the exits blocked. Everywhere, you hear me?"

One of the airport employees looked up from his desk at Garre. "Sergeant, may we board our flight now?"

"Yes," he said as he looked at those of us lining up for the flight to Tampa. "Yes, go ahead."

The employee picked up the microphone for the loudspeaker. "Flight 4080 for Tampa, Florida, now boarding. Flight 1688 for Dubai is also boarding at Gate 6, first class."

Garre started at the front of the line once more, examining only the males between the ages of twenty and thirty. He paused in front of me. "Passport?" he demanded.

I handed him my Qasim passport, which he examined briefly. He then looked closely at my face, minutely scrutinizing my long beard. He took the beard between two of his fingers and gently pulled, and it started to come free, revealing a shorter growth beneath the fake one. He then looked down and noticed my sandals. His eyes lit up.

"You're under arrest," he said smugly. "Put your hands behind your head and turn around slowly." I thought my game was up. I slowly raised my hands to put them behind my head as Garre smiled cruelly.

"That's enough, Garre," said Phillip, who had just arrived. "Stand down." He had several of his own team with him, and all had weapons out covering Garre and his men. Garre reached for his gun. "Drop it, Garre, or I'll damn well shoot you myself!"

His men rounded up the others and took the passport Garre was holding. He looked at it for a moment and then handed it back to me. "I believe this belongs to you, sir." He looked down and noticed my sandals. "Nice sandals," he commented. "I have a pair just like them. Where did you buy them? They're very comfortable. Only one place I know of that makes them."

"I didn't buy them," I answered. "They were a gift from a friend."

"What a coincidence. Mine are a gift from a very good friend, too. Have a good trip, Mr. Qasim." He looked at me again and smiled.

The bewildered employee came up to Phillip. "Uh, sir, may we go ahead and board?"

"Yes," Phillip answered, "please, go ahead."

I walked down the aisle of the airplane with my small case and located my seat. Next to it was sitting one Mr. O'Brien, with a pleased look on his face.

"Nice to see you, Mr. Qasim."

After we were in the air a while, I spoke to him in a quiet voice. "My friends are very concerned. They want me out of Miami. I agree with them. I will probably go to the West Coast."

O'Brien nodded. "We will talk more about that soon, after we land."

Not long after I arrived in Miami, Yaneba once again put me under her protective and loving guard. She fed me and sent me to take a bath while she arranged another flight for me.

As I came out of the bathroom and started to dress, Yaneba came into the bedroom and said, "Don't worry. I have already put your luggage in the car. When you open your bag, you will find a little surprise. A week ago, I bought some clothes for you because it is cold in California this time of the year. You'll have to call me and let me know whether you like them or not."

I said, "Thank you very much. You did not have to do that. It was very sweet of you."

She asked me to not take too much time with O'Brien because she would like to have dinner with me before I left. She said, "There is excellent food at a little hole-in-the-wall restaurant called Yoyito where I want to take you. They make the best arroz con pollo in Miami."

"That sounds great. I like that.'

It was about 7:30 when we got into the car and headed for Miami Beach, which was very close. We arrived in ten minutes and were early. We parked the car in the street where we could see the people coming and going. O'Brien was not there yet. We sat in the car for a little while just talking and waiting until I saw O'Brien arrive and sit at a street-side table under one of the patio umbrellas.

Yaneba reminded me, "Remember, don't take too long. I will be waiting for you."

I smiled. "Okay, Mama. I won't forget."

I got out of the car, crossed the street and went to meet him. He had already ordered two big glasses of iced *guarapo*—cold sugar cane juice, a very typical Cuban drink. As the waitress put the drinks on the table, I said, "Oh, my God. You ordered this?

Cuba: Russian Roulette of the World

You will get fat like a pig with this! This is like a pure sugar injection!"

The waitress smiled and nodded agreement.

O'Brien laughed and said, "But it's so good! Besides, you don't need to worry about your weight. You could use a few extra pounds!"

"You are going to kill yourself with all this Cuban food. Don't kill me in the process!"

The waitress left and I said to O'Brien, "Well I've come to tell you goodbye and to thank you for everything."

"Why the West Coast?" he asked.

"Because my friends here suggested it," I said. "And I too think it is the best spot because I can cross the border to Mexico and go anywhere in the world from there. I can come back to the USA a couple of weeks later, and no one can track me down."

O'Brien stretched himself out in his chair and said, "Hmm, very smart. I don't think that even we could track where you had been."

I replied, "You have to understand I came to the United States not to sit on my fat ass. I need lots of money to fight Castro. I need heavy duty money!"

O'Brien looked at me and said, "Maybe you don't have to go that far. Maybe we can help you. You can't do that alone. What part of California are you going to? I hope it's not San Francisco because my ex lives there, and if she finds out I'm back in San Francisco, there will be hell to pay."

I replied, "What does this have to do with you?"

He said, "I told you, we're a team. The agency wants it that way. If you go out to the West Coast, then I have to go out there, too."

I said, "No, you don't. I don't work for your government. You don't have to go where I go."

He looked at me solemnly. "But I do work for the government. You and I don't have to live together, but we do have to work together. Believe me, that'll make your life a lot easier and save you a lot of hassles. If you get in trouble one day, when you try to ship weapons or anything to your people in Cuba—I mean, just so you know, you can't do these things yourself. It's illegal to export weapons unless you're a licensed gun dealer and are authorized by my government. Otherwise, you could wind up in a federal prison . . . unless you have my people in the intelligence community behind you. Remember, we can sometimes walk on water and get away with it!"

I looked at him seriously as I didn't like to be pressured to do what I did not feel comfortable with. Evidently, he realized that, and he smiled. "Remember, I told you before: I am your friend. Who better to work with than a friend?"

I said, "Okay, you and Addison. I don't want anyone else to know what I am doing. I don't want any involvement with anyone else. I don't want to cross with another Steffan."

He looked at me and smiled and said, "Okay. If that is how you want it, I don't think Addison will have any problem with that." Then he asked me, "Are you going to north or south California?"

I replied, "South. Los Angeles."

He said, "Good, good, very good. I can live with that. When are you leaving?"

I said, "Tonight. Eleven-forty-five".

He said, "Tonight? My God! You give me short notice. What airline?"

I pulled a piece of paper with the flight information out of my coat pocket and handed it to him.

He said, "Okay, I'll have to call and use my influence to get a seat on the same plane. I have to leave with you. Do you want to go with me to the airport, or do you already have a ride?"

I said, "Yes, I am going to have dinner with Yaneba. I will see you at eleven at the airport." I stood up from the table and said, "I want to ask a little favor of you. Is that okay?"

He said, "Of course. What do you need?"

"In the future, our conversations, even private ones, must be confidential. Please do not repeat anything we talk about to anyone else unless you consult with me before," I said.

He looked at me in surprise and asked, "What did I say?"

I said, "Well, you know the little conversation you had with Yaneba about me finding Sandra in Cuba...I was going to tell her anyway, but I didn't want someone else telling her first!"

He turned very serious. "I'm really sorry. She called me, and she was very worried about you. I didn't mean any harm." Then with a hint of sarcasm he said, "I didn't know you and she were involved. No, you are right. I should not talk about your business with anybody...especially a woman!" He stood up, put his hand on my shoulder and said, "I'm sorry. I'm really sorry."

I said, "That's okay. It's water under the bridge now. Don't worry about it. I have to go now. She is waiting for me in the car. I will see you at the airport."

He said, "Okay. See you later."

I walked away and headed for the car. Yaneba was happy to see I had done the meeting quickly. She thanked me and we headed for the restaurant. Half an hour later, we were sitting in Yoyito restaurant and enjoying a good *arroz con pollo* (yellow rice with chicken). After we had enjoyed a great dinner and conversation, it was time to go, and she drove me to the airport.

When we arrived, O'Brien was already waiting for me with two men who helped me carry in and check my luggage. Yaneba gave me a big hug and a big kiss, and with tears in her eyes she whispered to me, "Take care of yourself. I will let you know later what I decide to do with our secret package."

We boarded the plane, and I don't know how he managed it, but O'Brien not only managed to get a seat right next to me, but he also got seats in the same row for the other two men. I began to realize this guy apparently has some influence to make things happen with such short notice.

Of course, on the plane he asked me, "What is this secret package Yaneba referred to?"

"Jesus, you must have supersonic hearing!"

He smiled and said, "You don't have to answer me if you don't want to. I don't mean to pry."

I said with a smile, "Damn right! It's none of your business. I am not going to answer that!"

O'Brien was a little bit embarrassed and maintained silence for the rest of the trip. He pretended to be sleeping but I knew he was not. When they announced we were approaching LA and would soon be landing, I felt bad and decided to break the ice. I said, "Remember what I told you before...do not repeat what I say to anyone. Anyone! No exceptions!"

He nodded his head and said, "I know. You only have to tell me things once."

"She is pregnant. That is the secret package."

He smiled and said, "Oh, my God! What are you guys going to do? Do you want to have the baby?"

"I don't know," I replied.

He said, "'That must be great. If you guys love each other...maybe God arranged this in order to compensate for your child in Cuba that you may never see again."

I smiled and said jokingly to him, "God had very little to do with this. I think it has more to do with a moment of extreme passion and a shortage of condoms!"

He laughed and then asked me, "But do you love her?"

I nodded and said with my finger on my cheek, "I like her very much. She is an extraordinary woman and I can see that it might be easy to fall in love with her."

O'Brien shook his head and said, "Oh my friend, I think you are in deep trouble. I have enough with one woman in my life, and you already have two!"

The plane landed, we deplaned, and went down to pick up our luggage. I was approached by a tall and very well-groomed gentleman carrying a sign with my name on it. He was accompanied by three more well-dressed men and when he saw me, he asked, "Are you Dr. del Marmol?"

I replied, "Yes, who wants to know?"

He extended his hand and said, "I am Dr. Martin Perez. These are my colleagues. We are friends of Yaneba. We are freedom fighters. We are here to welcome you to Los Angeles, and we are in charge of your relocation and of making sure you are comfortable here in your new city. Whatever you need, we are at your service." With that, he indicated the limousine waiting for us. The driver waved at us cordially.

Julio Antonio with his Lancia in Marina Del Rey, Los Angeles

O'Brien and the other two men who had accompanied us looked at each other in dismay and O'Brien said, "Wow! You must have really great influence in my country! Even I've never had such a welcome. The only thing missing is the marching band."

We laughed at O'Brien's comments, and we went through the door towards the baggage claim area.

While we were walking, I said, "My dream is to get all the evil communists of the world, and put them in a big bag, close it, put a lock on them, and cripple them once and for all. My heart is praying to God for the best for my people, and my mind is full of plans for the future. I will carry this wonderful freedom that exists in this country, that some do not appreciate, with my heart full of sadness for my beloved one that I have left behind.

I promise to myself that never, ever will I abandon the fight for the freedom of my country of Cuba."

The passengers leisurely sat down in the baggage return area, while the ones with less time haunted the return carrel, anxious to retrieve their luggage and get out of the terminal. The area was so crowded on the way out that we had to walk very close to the patient people sitting in the chairs; our clothes brushed against their knees.

We were so into our conversation that I only saw the profile of a man sitting there with a newspaper in front of his face. He wore a black beret, had a tobacco pipe in his mouth, and sported a cartoonishly large, cowboy-style moustache. He seemed to be concentrating very hard on reading the newspaper. He was looking at the door more than anything, but through a tiny hole in the newspaper was photographing us as we crossed in front of him.

Our limo driver opened the door with a big smile. We said our goodbyes. The man with the newspaper stood up, rolled up his newspaper, making sure the camera was still in it, and crossed over to a public pay phone. To the extreme right of the four pay phones, a priest was making a call, keeping his back to the public as he tried to avoid the noise, and with his left hand covered his exposed ear so that he could hear better. The man hesitated before going over to the phones, as the furthest phone would be too close to the priest. There were not other phones, so he went to the one to the extreme left to make his call. He deposited some coins and dialed a long-distance number. The finger he dialed with wore a Masonic ring.

Not too far away from there, at a small book vendor's booth, a nun with a very thick Bible in her hand was seated in a nearby seating area, concealed by the wire mesh. She had the Bible open in front of her face, as though she were reading it. The "nun" was Elizabeth, and in her Bible was another concealed camera, which she was using to take pictures of the mustachioed man making his phone call next to the priest. The priest by the man with the moustache continued to hold his finger in his ear as he tried to isolate the noise around him.

The man with the phone said in a very low voice, "Yes, it's me." Apparently, his voice was too soft for the other party, so he repeated, "Yes, it's me. Victor. He just arrived in Los Angeles."

The priest on the other side was not actually talking but was listening to Victor. In fact, he had a small audio receiver in his ear. The voice on the other end of the line told Victor, "Be sure you find where they relocate him. We will take care of the rest."

"Yes, I will do that," Victor replied. "I will call you later."

Before he hung up, Victor looked at the priest by his side, but saw nothing suspicious.

"Yes, yes...fine," the priest was saying into the phone. "I understand."

Victor scanned his surroundings to make sure no one was watching him. He held his newspaper to make sure that the camera didn't fall out, turned around, and headed towards the main exit door. The nun on the other side of the room continued to take his picture as Victor walked out the door for as long as she had him in view. The priest hung up his phone and turned around, revealing himself to be Hernesto with a long, very thick beard. Out of his pocket he brought out what looked like a box of matches. He removed the small receiver from his ear and put it into the box. He nonchalantly looked around, saw that Victor had exited the door, and walked to the phones. He took a small metal disk, smaller than the size of a penny, from each phone and replaced them in the small box. They were so well-matched in color and size that they were indistinguishable. Hernesto put the box in his pocket and walked over to Elizabeth, who now stood up and waited for him.

Outside the terminal, we were still talking before we departed with Dr. Perez. Dr. Perez said to O'Brien, "3747 Sepulveda Boulevard, Apartment A-31."

O'Brien replied, "Very well. We'll follow you guys over there."

Dr. Perez got into the limo where his three friends were already waiting for us. O'Brien walked with his two bodyguards over to a black Ford sedan. I was the last one to get into the limo. I was surprised when I saw Yaneba, with a big smile of satisfaction, sitting there waiting for me.

"How the hell did you manage to get here before us?" I asked, a perplexed look on my face. "I left you in the Miami airport!"

She replied, still smiling, "I've got my ways. Super-sonic travel has tremendous advantages. Let's just say I have connections in the right places. I wanted to make sure you made it to Los Angeles in one piece and with no problems. I'll pay any price for that, even not telling you that I'm coming to meet you here." She added mischievously, "The only thing that has no price was the joy of seeing your face when you got into the limo. That was worth every penny I paid, and more!"

As I sat by her side, I said, "What a beautiful surprise!"

She smiled and said, "Really?" She discretely touched her belly, and with an even bigger smile, she added, "Even with the package?"

I nodded. "Yes. Even with the package."

She replied, "Well, now knowing that you're in good hands, I will go back tomorrow early in the morning to Miami."

I grabbed her hand, and with a big smile, I asked, "What is the rush, sweetie? I will feel a lot better and more secure if you stay here for a few days until I readjust in the big city of Los Angeles."

She smiled mischievously again, reclined over me in the seat, and kissed me lingeringly. It surprised me as she did this in front of the other people, but I returned the kiss. The others smiled and looked at each other understandingly, as they realized we had more than just a work relationship, but something deeper and more profound—something beautiful.

Dr. Martin Perez wrote a note for the limo driver and gave him the directions to our destination address. We were still parked in front of the terminal with the limo's hazard lights blinking. The chauffer looked at the note, and then looked into the mirror to wait for some cars to let him into the flow so that he could drive away. By this time, Victor had found a taxi and gotten in.

Elizabeth held out the Bible to Hernesto. They remained there for a second, until through the glass doors they saw Victor get into a taxi. They both rushed out the door, hailed another taxi, and requested the driver to follow.

The limousine had now moved into traffic, followed by the Ford sedan with O'Brien and his men. "Follow that limo closely," O'Brien said to his chauffer.

In the taxi, Victor instructed the driver, "Don't lose that limo."

And in the final taxi, Hernesto said to his driver, "Follow that taxi!"

Elizabeth said to Hernesto, "Now we know for sure who's been betraying our group's movements to our enemies for so many years."

Hernesto's face was disgusted as he nodded. "It's unbelievable how Dr. del Marmol in such a short time figured out that Victor is a traitor. He's been around us for so long. How could we even imagine that Victor was our enemy?"

Elizabeth said, "Do you have a range?"

He smiled, "Yeah, it's not going to go too far."

They sat back in anticipation while their taxi followed Victor's taxi as both cars threaded their way through the afternoon traffic. After a few blocks, Hernesto requested of the driver, "Could you please not follow so closely? Stay back a little."

The driver turned around. It was Chopin. "I got it, brother." He slowed down, allowing Victor's cab to pull ahead. "Be ready for the next intersection." He smiled as he changed lanes.

A garbage truck approached with a greater than normal speed. It cut in front of Victor's cab and slammed on its brakes. The driver tried to stop, but slid right into the back of the truck, and the filthiest garbage spilled all over the taxi's windshield and hood. Chopin continued on by. Hernesto and Elizabeth looked out the back window as they drove past and saw that the driver of the garbage truck was Arturo. They looked at each other, winked, and nodded.

Arturo watched the cars with his friends pass the accident as he slowly walked over to check on Victor. The cab driver was alive with some scratches; Victor's hand hung bloody out the window, the Masonic ring on his finger. Arturo checked his pulse and shrugged, as the blood from the hand loosened the ring which fell to the ground. Arturo looked at it for a moment, then picked it up. "You're not a Mason; just a thief."

Later, as we all gathered at the place on Venice Boulevard, Arturo handed me Victor's ring. I looked at it and saw the inscription inside; it was Dr. Noriega's. That night, I sat at my desk, penning a letter to Dr. Noriega: "I have found something that you've lost. No; something that was taken from you improperly. Don't ask how it came into my hands. Perhaps, if we are lucky, I will find your wife's wedding ring next. Sincerely, Dr. Julio Antonio del Marmol."

After my journey around the world, I will return to my land with no hate or revenge in my heart, but with love and happiness in my soul, bringing back with me the divine joy of my wonderful God. I will bring back all of that has been taken from my people by the bloody tyrant in control.

The tyrant steals joy through the horrendous persecution of spiritual souls, only to leave my beautiful Cuba in perpetual sorrow, suffering and tears, and in complete absence of our wonderful God's great love.

— Dr. Julio Antonio del Marmol

MY CREED
If only one person in a thousand could see life clear and beautiful as the pure waters of a crystalline brook.

If just one person were capable of living with a pure and clean mind happy to see sky and sun breathing a sweet breeze life could never be empty.

Honor and dignity are cloudy notions in declining minds. When they cease to have meant the sky will darken and life will conclude.

-Dr. J. Anthony D'Marmol

Dr. Julio Antonio del Marmol

Acknowledgements

I would like to give a special thanks to a group of friends that have helped me to put this book together, starting with my dear friend, Dorothy Biely (may her soul rest in peace and be in Heaven with God); to Jose F. Mota (Carlos) for the financial help that made this book come alive; Gervasio Neto for his protection and great effort in bringing life to the project; to those great friends, whose names I cannot mention, thanks for watching my back from the shadows for all these years; to Tad Atkinson for his time and effort in editing the text; to Mimi, my honey, for being a great trooper in her support in all my ordeals; to Mimi Atkinson for her offered support when we needed it; to Reggie Comunique for his contribution and for the beautiful artwork for the front cover and back cover design; and thanks to Stephen Weese for his splendid work in redesigning the front cover as well as his contributions in editing the text. And my most special thanks to Jesus Christ, my guide and protector, for keeping me alive through fifty-six attempts on my life, frustrating my enemies in their efforts to bring me down.

Dr. Julio Antonio del Marmol
January 26, 2013

Cuba: Russian Roulette of the World

ABOUT THE AUTHOR

Julio Antonio del Marmol is a Cuban who began to write during the hours of his embittered childhood, harsh adolescence, and tormented youth. He lived through the darkest moments of his country when the forces of the Cuban "Revolution" promised the false dawn of peace. In broad daylight, its reality meant tears and blood for most Cubans.

In *Cuba, Russian Roulette of the World*, the reader will find realism, emotion, tenderness, and bitterness. Adolescent disappointments are the most painful, and Julio Antonio del Marmol knew them all. In his case, fortunately, he was not dazzled by the revolution's petty tyrants with whom he became acquainted in extraordinary circumstances. Incredibly mature for his years, he extricated himself from demagogy and found the right way.

This book describes the drama of an eager young man, determined in the end to risk his life for a noble ideal. His selfless motives have been unmistakably proven. The success of his venture, his solid preparation, and his opportunities in the United States, where he now lives, have not made him forget the Cuban tragedy.

Learning from experience, the author looks ahead to free horizons beyond the bloody boundaries of his homeland. *Cuba, Russian Roulette of the World*, is a truly human document, its account vital for history and future generations.

We follow him and his companions in their thrilling escape and rejoice at its lucky completion, having first learned of the contradictions resulting from changed guidelines and the serious consequences of rejecting the "truths" formulated by the Cuban communists.

Julio Antonio del Marmol, born in 1947 in Pinar del Rio, Cuba, had all the necessary endowments to be a man of his time. In the pursuit of his first inclination, music, he already had composed various songs when, between wobbly steps initiated by the Revolution and his own opinions, he studied composition in the Havana Conservatory of Music before turning to a more practical career. In 1970 he graduated from the School of Veterinary in the University of Havana, obtaining a PhD in Animal Genetics.

Many events in his young life happened in quick succession, as it is with war and revolution. At an early age he was made a military leader by a seemingly ridiculous incident that nevertheless shows the mental "depth" of the revolutionaries. Luckily for him, Julio Antonio soon realized that arms can be enslaving and murderous in the hands of tyrants.

He decided to abandon his own privileged lifestyle as part of Castro's elite because his integrity and moral values passed on by his father and his ancestors did not allow him to watch the suffering of his people in silence. He then formed a group of brave men who were also dedicated to stopping the socialist regime as his uncle offered to him the opportunity to work in this resistance movement. At the tender age of thirteen, he was trained and prepared for the fight, and a most persecuted and feared spy was born, earning from his enemies his codename, "the Lightning."

Cuba, Russian Roulette of the World also could bear the title, "Destination: Freedom." This was the goal pursued by the small group making their getaway with Julio Antonio—freedom and dignity. Their destination was the United States and some of them, including the author, made it.

Included in this book is the score of a piano composition by Julio Antonio and various documents attesting to the truth of his narration. In addition to the "Julio Antonio's Ave Maria," he is the composer of "Pobre Bambino," "Lejos de Mi," "Cuba

Linda," "En tu Cumpleanos," "En un Jardin Encantado," "One More Attempt," and about forty-five other pieces.

Now living in a free land, Julio Antonio wants to show to the youth of the world, the present and future generations, that all are born to be free.

Full of political, historic, and social significance, *Cuba, Russian Roulette of the World* is a realistic and conclusive document that reveals the extreme cruelty used by the communists with those who do not accept their oppressive blood thirsty system.

You can read more about Dr. del Marmol and his adventures at www.spymasterspy.com.

www.ingramcontent.com/pod-product-compliance
Lightning Source LLC
Chambersburg PA
CBHW021800220426
43662CB00006B/136